ENDORSEMENTS

Jeff Oliver is an incredible historian and minister. His books portray the true history of the acts of the Holy Spirit in modern times. Much more than a history lesson, this is a must-read to understand our spiritual DNA as Spirit-filled believers. I strongly encourage everyone to read this book as a blueprint for the last-day outpouring that is surely coming.

Chris Reed
President & CEO, MorningStar Ministries

Once again, Jeff Oliver exceeds our expectations with his new book, *Keys to Experiencing Azuza Fire*. In the past, I have only found bits and pieces of the history and side stories surrounding this event, but Jeff masterfully brings them together, including many nuanced aspects. Jeff is a well-spoken, humble servant of God who seeks to bring special insight to the body of Christ about the continued move of the Holy Spirit in the church.

Dave Yarnes
Vice President Operations, MorningStar Ministries

While many Christians have heard of the great move of God that began on Azusa Street under William Seymour, Jeff Oliver's fabulous book tells us the rest of the story. As we stand on the verge of even greater signs, wonders, and miracles unfolding in the church, this book serves as an inspiration to those who hunger for God's glory as well as a sobering reminder of what to avoid when God moves powerfully. My exhortation is to read *and* study *Keys to Experiencing Azusa Fire*.

Tom Hardiman
VP of Spiritual Services, MorningStar Ministries

KEYS TO EXPERIENCING
AZUSA FIRE

LESSONS FROM THE REVIVAL THAT CHANGED
THE LANDSCAPE OF GLOBAL CHRISTIANITY

KEYS TO EXPERIENCING

AZUSA FIRE

JEFF OLIVER AND RICK JOYNER

DESTINY IMAGE® PUBLISHERS, INC.
P.O. Box 310, Shippensburg, PA 17257-0310

*"Publishing cutting-edge prophetic resources
to supernaturally empower the body of Christ"*

This book and all other Destiny Image and Destiny Image Fiction books are available at Christian bookstores and distributors worldwide.

For more information on foreign distributors, call 717-532-3040.

Reach us on the Internet: www.destinyimage.com.

ISBN 13 TP: 978-0-7684-7736-8

ISBN 13 eBook: 978-0-7684-7737-5

For Worldwide Distribution, Printed in the U.S.A.

1 2 3 4 5 6 7 8 / 28 27 26 25 24

CONTENTS

CHAPTER 1

"BECAUSE THEY WERE THE HUMBLEST"

After the *Pentecost to the Present* trilogy was published in 2017, Rick Joyner said to me, "These were the best books on church history I've ever read." I later learned this was no small compliment coming from such an avid reader of church history. Then he said, "You need to write another book." I chuckled a bit, but he was serious, adding, "You need to take one chapter from one of your books and expound on it." He said, "People are intimidated by big books until they know what's in them but enjoy reading smaller books." Coming from a marketing guru and author of more than seventy-five books, I immediately took his advice to heart. In fact, the moment he said that, I immediately knew which book and which chapter I would expound on—the Azusa Street story.

Everyone loves a good story. That's why Jesus spoke in parables and why I wrote *Pentecost to the Present* in story form. Instead of disseminating a bunch of history—names, places, and dates—I connected the dots through history to tell the story of the Holy Spirit's enduring work in the church. *Pentecost to the Present* truly is a continuation of the biblical narrative that includes the miraculous. While most authors write only bits and pieces of history, I put the pieces of the puzzle together both in *Pentecost to the Present* and in *Keys to Experiencing Azusa Fire*.

By extracting the testimonies from the people who were actually there and participated in the revival, I was able to weave together a beautiful tapestry of one of the greatest revivals ever. Best of all, this revival happened in America, in Los Angeles, in the twentieth century. So, while some language may sound racially charged or even offensive to today's ears, I felt it more important to preserve the original testimonies, so you would understand exactly what happened, both good and bad, and know the miracle that was Azusa Street. Such a revival can happen in any place and in any age where and when God's people come together.

The first time I studied the Azusa Street Revival, it was for the *Pentecost to the Present* series, so I studied it strictly from a linear viewpoint within the context of the historical events leading up to and following it. However, this time, by focusing on the testimonies of the people who were actually there, I was able to gain a more lateral, panoramic view of Los Angeles in 1906. In doing so, I discovered the Azusa Street gang was not the only group in Los Angeles at that time that was ripe and ready for revival.

THE PISGAH HOME MOVEMENT

Dr. Finis Yoakum, founder of the Pisgah Home movement, was also ministering in Los Angeles at that time. Dr. Yoakum was a medical doctor and businessman who, after receiving a debilitating blow from a drunken buggy driver in Denver, moved to Los Angeles, hoping the warmer climate might help him recuperate. Instead, after arriving in Los Angeles and receiving prayer for healing from a Christian and Missionary Alliance pastor, Dr. Yoakum was miraculously healed and began traveling throughout the U.S. and Britain, testifying of God's healing power. Also, during this time, Dr. Yoakum received a vision to reach the poor and downcast of Los Angeles. After founding several Pisgah Faith Homes and cottages in the Los Angeles area, the Pisgah Home movement spread both nationally and internationally.

Dr. Finis Yoakum opened a home for "wayward girls" in 1900 and a home to pray and care for the sick in 1901. By 1906 he quit practicing medicine to build Pisgah "Faith" Home on Echo Street with cottages for those dying of tuberculosis, called Pisgah Gardens. Early healings were reported regularly in Carrie Judd Montgomery's *Triumphs of Healing* magazine, including reports of two people being raised from the dead.

Photo: J.D. King of Christos Publishing (www.jdking.net).

But then, after a Brother Lankford received the baptism in the Holy Spirit and spoke in tongues at Charles Parham's Bible school in Topeka, Kansas and returned to Los Angeles in 1904, he shared his experience with Dr. Yoakum, who immediately embraced it and shared the experience with his church. Yoakum himself received the baptism in the Holy Spirit and reported speaking in tongues, for the very first time, while on a mining mission in Mexico. There, he spoke to a large church of Mexicans and Indians, through an interpreter, when a distinct rush of mighty wind suddenly came upon him. Then, he spoke beautifully in Spanish for the next 20 to 30 minutes, as everyone listened intently.

Much like the pioneer healing evangelist John Alexander Dowie, Dr. Yoakum reported hundreds of miraculous healings, including two who were raised from the dead. Many of the lame and blind who came to the Pisgah Homes left with their wheelchairs, crutches, braces, and canes as testimonies. Dr. Yoakum also founded Pisgah Ark women's shelter for prostitutes, Pisgah Store for donating food and goods to the poor in the Arroyo Seco area, and Pisgah Gardens in North Hollywood where 100 beds were maintained for patients with tuberculosis, cancer, and

The Pisgah Home at 6026 Echo Street in the Historic Highland Park District of Northeast Los Angeles. Originally owned by Dr. Finis Yoakum, it is now listed in the National Register of Historic Places.

Photo: Wikimedia/Ilmari Karonen.

mental disorders. He even held church services in his barn, which was also lined with beds to house the sick.

Though Dr. Yoakum never officially joined the Pentecostal movement, he visited Azusa Street, offered a place to stay for many who attended the revival, and after Yoakum's death, the "Old Pisgah Home" became a refuge for many of the Azusa Street faithful. You can read their amazing stories in *They Told Me Their Stories*, narrated by Tommy Welchel.

THE FIRST BAPTIST CHURCH

The First Baptist Church of Los Angeles was also experiencing a revival during that time when British-born, Spurgeon College-educated Pastor Joseph Smale returned from sabbatical. His trip included a visit to Wales where he developed a relationship with Evan Roberts, the leader of the great 1904-05 Welsh Revival. Smale brought the fresh fire from the Welsh Revival back to Los Angeles and immediately began holding similar protracted day and night meetings at the First Baptist Church of Los Angeles.

Postcard of the exterior view of the First Baptist Church of Los Angeles, California, c. 1900, Tichnor Bros. Inc., Los Angeles, CA.

Photo: Flower Pentecostal Heritage Center.

13

The meetings' slogan was, "Pentecost has not yet come, but it is coming."[1] For fifteen weeks the revival meetings continued—that is, until the deacon board had finally had enough. For them, this new emphasis on revival was bringing too much noise and confusion. Financial pledges had been replaced with free-will offerings, causing a decline in the church's finances and the choir director to be let go. Some wanted the "old, cold ecclesiastical order" back, so they shut down the meetings.[2] Smale promptly resigned, and the board accepted his resignation.

THE NEW TESTAMENT CHURCH

Undeterred, Joseph Smale established The New Testament Church of Los Angeles at Burbank Hall. Some two hundred members followed him. Smale self-described the new church as a "fellowship for evangelical preaching and teaching and Pentecostal life and service."[3] Now completely free to have Spirit-led meetings, they did.

Joseph Smale, a British Baptist pastor trained at Spurgeon's College in London, was an important catalyst behind the Azusa Street Revival.

Photo: 312azusa.com/adinapoli.it.

Frank Bartleman, who became a charter member of The New Testament Church, and who would later chronicle the Azusa Street Revival, wrote: "A wonderful work of the Spirit has broken out here in Los Angeles, California, preceded by a deep preparatory work of prayer and expectation. Conviction is rapidly spreading among the people, and they are rallying from all over the city to the meetings at Pastor Smale's church. Already these meetings are beginning to 'run themselves.' Souls are being saved all over the house, while the meeting sweeps on unguided by human hands.... Pastor Smale is prophesying of wonderful things to come. He prophesies the speedy return of the apostolic gifts to the church. Los Angeles is a veritable Jerusalem. Just the place for a mighty work of God to begin. I have been expecting just such a display of divine power for some time. Have felt it might break out at any hour. Also that it was liable to come where least expected, that God might get the glory. Pray for Pentecost."[4]

In one such meeting, they experienced the manifest presence of God: "One night at the New Testament Church, during a deep spirit of prayer on the congregation, the Lord came suddenly so near that we could feel His presence as though He were closing in on us around the edges of the meeting. Two-thirds of the people sprang to their feet in alarm, and some ran hurriedly out of the meeting, even leaving their hats behind them, almost scared out of their senses.... It was a supernatural manifestation of His nearness."[5]

THE METHODIST CHURCHES

Meanwhile, the Methodist churches in Los Angeles were eager for a spiritual awakening. From March 11-21, 1906, a ten-day "Pentecostal Convention" was held at the First Methodist Church at Sixth and Hill Streets. This convention was sponsored by the Pacific Pentecostal Association and featured Methodist and Presbyterian speakers. Florence Crawford, who attended the church before coming on staff at the Azusa Street Mission, said that the young men of that church especially began praying for revival in those days and became absolutely convinced that a revival would soon break out among them. She said,

"The young men in the First Methodist Church were holding all night prayer meetings, which were unprecedented and demonstrated how deeply the city's people sensed a need for revival."[6]

Frank Bartleman wrote about a similar revival that broke out at the Lake Avenue Methodist Episcopal Church in Pasadena in May 1905. In this revival, he said that many young men from that church, who also attended the Peniel Mission, were praying for a sweeping revival in Pasadena. The Methodist altar was full of seeking souls, and within two weeks, 200 souls had come to Christ. He wrote, "We then began to pray for an outpouring of the Spirit for Los Angeles and the whole of southern California." In his diary he wrote, "The Spirit is breathing prayer through us for a mighty, general outpouring. Great things are coming. We are asking largely, that our joy may be full. God is moving. We are praying for the churches and their pastors. The Lord will visit those willing to yield to Him."[7]

THE FREE METHODIST MOVEMENT

There was even a Free Methodist community founded in nearby Hermon on the Arroyo Seco in 1903. These Free Methodists had broken off from the Methodist Church to retain Wesley's original teachings on the Holy Spirit and sanctification and had recently experienced a bit of revival themselves.

THE PILLAR OF FIRE AND PENIEL MISSIONS

Frank Bartleman, who was also ministering in Los Angeles at that time, had been educated at Temple University and Moody Bible Institute before becoming an evangelist and missionary with the Salvation

Army, the Wesleyan Methodists, and various Holiness groups including the Pillar of Fire and Peniel Missions. After working with several churches and missions throughout Los Angeles, Bartleman heard about the Welsh Revival. British evangelist F.B. Meyer had just come and preached in Los Angeles in the Spring of 1906. Meyer was part of a British Holiness movement, known as the Keswick Convention or Higher Life Movement, and had been instrumental in the Welsh Revival as well. Bartleman said, "My soul was stirred to its depths."[8] Then Bartleman read S.B. Shaw's *The Great Revival in Wales*, and his heart was set on fire. He began distributing pamphlets on the Welsh Revival and corresponding with its leader, Evan Roberts, in hopes of sparking a similar revival in Los Angeles.

Evan Roberts replied to one of his letters stating, "I pray God to hear your prayer, to keep your faith strong, and to save California."[9] He even provided Bartleman with instructions on how to instigate a revival in Los Angeles saying, "My dear brother in the faith: Many thanks for your kind letter. I am impressed by your sincerity and honesty of purpose. Congregate the people together who are willing to make a total surrender. Pray and wait. Believe God's promises. Holy daily meetings. May God bless you, is my earnest prayer. Yours in Christ—Evan Roberts."[10]

Photo of Frank Bartleman in 1906. Best known for his chronicles of the Azusa Street Revival, Bartleman authored six books, four pamphlets, 500 published articles, and over 100 tracts, many covering the events leading up to and surrounding the revival and the subsequent worldwide Pentecostal movement.

Photo: Flower Pentecostal Heritage Center.

Convinced now more than ever that a Los Angeles revival was imminent, Bartleman wrote in *Way of Faith* magazine, "Los Angeles seems to be the place and this the time, in the mind of God, for the restoration of the Church."[11]

Bartleman supported Joseph Smale at The New Testament Church for a time before attending the Azusa Street Revival, even from its early days on Bonnie Brae Street until 1908. Bartleman also established his own mission at Eighth and Maple in Los Angeles. The Pillar of Fire had previously met there. Bartleman later turned over the mission to W.H. Pendleton, another pastor and Azusa Street missionary who joined the Eighth and Maple mission, after he and 90 percent of his congregation were expelled from the Los Angeles Holiness Church for being baptized in the Spirit and speaking in tongues. Though Bartleman attended, participated in, and even chronicled the Azusa Street Revival, in his missionary zeal, he rarely remained at one church or address for very long.

THE BURNING BUSH MOVEMENT

Meanwhile, Glenn Cook, who belonged to the radical Wesleyan-Holiness Burning Bush movement officially known as the Metropolitan Church Association and known for its demonstrative worship, was holding tent meetings on the corner of East Seventh and Spring Streets in Los Angeles at the time.

VARIOUS OTHER HOLINESS MISSIONS

Various other Holiness missions planted throughout Los Angeles were having "tarrying meetings" to invite the Holy Spirit to come at that time, and the Holy Spirit showed up in many of those meetings. For example,

Louis and Cena Osterberg and their son Arthur "A.G." Osterberg, the young pastor of the Full Gospel Assembly at 68th and Denver, had recently come to Los Angeles from William Durham's North Avenue Mission in Chicago and were expecting revival. Then there was A.G. Garr at the Burning Bush Mission, Thomas Atteberry, pastor of the People's Church, William Pendleton, another Holiness preacher, and A.H. Post, another Baptist minister—all were crying out for revival.

Yet another Holiness sect with dozens of churches, mostly in the Los Angeles area, held a camp meeting in nearby Downey, California, in 1905. The theme of the camp meeting? God's desire to send an outpouring of His Holy Spirit. They believed and feared, if the Holiness people did not dig in and get the blessing, God would pass them by and raise up another people who would.[12]

JULIA HUTCHINS' GROUP

Then there was Sister Julia Hutchins' group at the Second Baptist Church of Los Angeles, which was also the first black Baptist church and the second black congregation in Los Angeles. Since they were also seeking a deeper experience with God, Sister Hutchins began teaching sanctification and baptism in the Holy Spirit as a second work of grace. After the Baptists expelled her and eight other families for teaching against traditional Baptist doctrine, they joined William Manley, a white pastor, whose Household of Faith mission met in a tent near First and Bonnie Brae Streets. Then, when this group split along color lines, Hutchins' group moved to another tent near Seventh and Broadway.

However, as winter approached, they started meeting in church members Richard and Ruth Asberry's home on Bonnie Brae Street. On Monday nights, they would hold a gospel concert in front of the house to attract friends and neighbors. Neighbors would sit on their front porches and listen, then they would invite them in for an evangelistic service. Mr. Edward Lee, another member of that group, was also a member of the Peniel Mission where he had met Charles Parham two years prior. There, he had learned about the baptism in the Holy Spirit and had been seeking the experience ever since. The group again relocated to a building on the corner of Ninth and Santa Fe Street, before inviting William Seymour from Texas to come and lead them. Sadly, this group promptly rejected Seymour over doctrinal differences regarding the baptism in the Holy Spirit.

SPIRIT-FILLED ARMENIANS

Meanwhile, at 919 Boston Street, a group of Spirit-filled Armenian families were meeting and conducting a church in the home of Demos and Goolisar Shakarian. They were the grandparents of the Demos Shakarian who would later found the Full Gospel Business Men's Fellowship in the 1950s, which would help spawn the modern Charismatic movement. Six years prior, Demos Shakarian, the grandfather, and other family members had spoken in tongues after receiving prayer from some Russian missionaries. Shortly after that, they moved to America to escape persecution and were seeking a similar experience in Los Angeles.

Others in Los Angeles had also reportedly spoken in tongues before the Azusa Street Revival, including Mrs. Elmer Fisher, whose husband pastored the First Baptist Church in Glendale and later became Pastor Smale's associate at The New Testament Church, before establishing the Upper Room Mission in Los Angeles. Another was Sister Julia Carney who received the baptism experience and spoke in tongues after attending Dr. Finis Yoakum's Pisgah Home rescue mission. Sister Carney and a group from the First Baptist Church met at a home in

Home of Demos and Goolisar Shakarian at 919 Boston Street, Los Angeles, California. Demos was the grandfather of Demos Shakarian, founder of the Full Gospel Business Men's Fellowship International.

Photo: Flower Pentecostal Heritage Center.

Pasadena where they were praying weekly for revival and for the baptism in the Holy Spirit.

BECAUSE THEY WERE THE HUMBLEST

Among these many fires that were either already lighted or being lit all over the Los Angeles area, God chose yet another group that first met in the Asberry's home on Bonnie Brae Street and then rented an old building down on Azusa Street in the old industrial district of Los Angeles. Knowing this, I asked the Lord, "Of all these groups that were ripe for revival in Los Angeles at that time, why did You choose this

Azusa Street gang to bring worldwide revival?" He simply said, "Because they were the humblest."

It was the Christmas story of Mary and Joseph all over again. It seems God chooses the least likely people in the least likely places to give birth to the greatest movements on earth. In fact, guess what that old "barn-like" structure on Azusa Street had been used for just before William Seymour and his gang rented it for prayer meetings? Yep, the first floor, where revival services would be held for the next three years, sparking a worldwide revival, had most recently been used as a stable. Sister Carney even shared how she and others helped Brother Seymour clean up after the animals to get the building ready for services.

THE LORD IS NEAREST TO THE HUMBLE

"The Lord is near to those who have a broken heart, and saves such as have a contrite spirit."[13] The word *near* here is elsewhere translated "nearest" or "kinsmen." "[God] gives grace to the humble" (Proverbs 3:34). This means God gives gifts and charismatic graces to the humble (see James 4:6; 1 Peter 5:5). God also exalts the humble. "Humble yourselves in the sight of the Lord, and He will lift you up" (James 4:10). The only element of revival that precedes prayer in order and importance is humility: "If My people who are called by My name will humble themselves, and pray and seek My face, and turn from their wicked ways, then I will hear from heaven, and will forgive their sin and heal their land" (2 Chronicles 7:14).

There are many great churches, ministries, denominations, and movements, yet God will always look for the humblest to begin the next great revival, or as one Azusa Street Revival participant testified: "A band of humble people in Los Angeles had been praying for a year or more for more power with God for the salvation of the lost and suffering humanity.... They continued to hold cottage prayer meetings for several months.... There is no pope, Dowieism, or Sanfordism, but we are all little children knowing only Jesus and Him crucified.... Brother Seymour is simply a humble pastor of the flock."[14]

When *Life*, a secular magazine, published its list of "100 Most Important Events of the Millennium" (AD 1001–2000), they looked for the events with the greatest worldwide impact. The top three (all related to Christianity) were Gutenberg's press, Columbus' discovery of America, and Martin Luther's Reformation. Number forty-six on that list was this tiny stable on Azusa Street. *USA Today* published a similar list and the Azusa Street Revival made their list as well. If secular media outlets recognize "the humblest" among those making the greatest worldwide impact of the entire millennium, shouldn't we? They put the Azusa Street Revival right up there with man's first walk on the moon. Yet in God's kingdom, this revival had even greater importance. Read these firsthand witnesses for yourself.

AZUSA STREET TESTIMONIES

"Heroes will arise from the dust of obscure and despised circumstances, whose names will be emblazoned on heaven's eternal page of fame."

—Frank Bartleman, *Way of Faith*, November 16, 1905

"On March 26, I went to a cottage meeting on Bonnie Brae Street. Both white and black believers were meeting there for prayer. I had attended another cottage meeting shortly before this, where I first met a Brother Seymour. He had just come from Texas. He was a black man, blind in one eye, very plain, spiritual, and humble. He attended the meetings at Bonnie Brae Street."[15]

—Frank Bartleman, *Azusa Street*

"Many churches have been praying for Pentecost and Pentecost has come. The question is, will they accept it? God has answered in a way they did not look for. He came in a humble way as of old, born in a manger. The secular papers have been stirred and published reports against the movement, but it has only resulted in drawing hungry souls who understand that the devil would not fight a thing unless God was in it. They have come and found it was indeed the power of God. Jesus was too large for the synagogue. He preached outside because there was not room for Him inside. The Pentecostal movement is too large to be confined in any denomination or sect. It works outside, drawing all together in one bond of love, one church, and one body of Christ."

—*The Apostolic Faith* Vol. 1 No. 1., September 1906

"A message that was given in tongues for God's people was this, 'Humble yourselves under the mighty hand of God.' He is now about to move on the world in a mighty wave of Pentecostal power and salvation. A sister had a vision of God's people as vessels that were full, and the Lord said, 'The vessels must be emptied and I will fill them.'"

—*The Apostolic Faith* Vol. 1 No. 1., September 1906

"It was such an humble place with its low ceilings and rough floor. Cob webs were hanging in the windows and joist. As I looked around I thought of Jesus when He came to earth and was born in a manger. There was no place for Him in the inn. I thought of the fine church houses in Los Angeles, but the Lord had chosen this humble spot to gather all nationalities, to baptize them with the Holy Ghost."[16]

—Rachel Sizelove

"Very many of this company were Negroes, poor, lowly, ignorant, and despised. Less than 50 years ago Negroes were owned by white people in the United States as slaves. No one but an American can rightly understand how despised the Negro is. The twentieth century Pentecostal movement had its birth in a despised place amongst a despised people; because there was no room for it in the modern church."[17]

—Max Wood Morehead

"We keep building great temples and cathedrals with lavish decorations and furnishings, and He keeps showing up in the most humble of dwellings. Perhaps there is a lesson here as we watch for the outpouring of His Spirit and the return of His Shekinah Glory to fall upon us once again."[18]

—Sister Dundee

"This work began with some poor ignorant, colored people (what more appropriate instruments could God choose?)."[19]

—Etta Auringer Huff

"We went down to old Azusa Street. But why should I go down there? Was not my grandfather a Virginian and my grandmother from Kentucky and my very own mother raised with black slaves? Why should I go down to the black folks to get the Baptism of the Holy Ghost? But they had it and I wanted it. I went."[20]

—Kelso R. Grover

"I am so glad the Lord God has raised up a people right in Los Angeles, and San Francisco, they seem like Sodom and Gomorrah, but out of these cities the Lord God has raised up a people for His holy name. He has cleansed them from sin, He has sanctified them, and has baptized them with the Holy Ghost and sealed them unto the day of Redemption. Glory to His holy name!"[21]

—William J. Seymour

"Though there be counterfeits…. Let us all bow down before God, and be as humble and simple as little children, that we may miss nothing of the blessing God wants to pour upon His children in these last days."[22]

—Carrie Judd Montgomery

"Can any unbiased man doubt as to the source of this strange power, when these humble children of God were waiting only upon Him, seeking for Himself."[23]

—A.H. Post

"He was searching for a people sufficiently humble, sufficiently consecrated and of 'one accord' as were the hundred and twenty at the first Pentecostal outpouring."[24]

—A.G. Osterberg

"God has always sought a humble people.... The depth of any revival will be determined exactly by the spirit of repentance that is obtained. In fact, this is the key to every true revival born of God."[25]

—Frank Bartleman, *Azusa Street*

"Shortly after God filled me, His Spirit rested mightily upon me one morning, and He said to me, 'If you were only small enough, I could do anything with you.'"[26]

—Frank Bartleman, *Azusa Street*

Jesus said the same, "Whoever humbles himself as this little child is the greatest in the kingdom of heaven" (Matthew 18:4). The humblest is the greatest. John said of Jesus, "He must increase, but I must decrease" (John 3:30). Jesus said of John, "Among those born of women there has not risen one greater than John the Baptist" (Matthew 11:11). Gideon's army had to become small to defeat the Midianites (see Judges 7). David had to be small to defeat Goliath (see 1 Samuel 17), and Paul had to become weak for God's strength to become perfect (see 2 Corinthians 12:9).

REPENTANT TEARS

A.G. Osterberg, one of Azusa Street's faithful from the beginning, was asked, "What was the one outstanding spiritual phenomena of the Azusa Revival?" He replied, "It can be answered in one word, namely, 'tears.'" Osterberg continued, "The Azusa Revival began, where every revival should rightly begin, in repentant tears. It began in tears, it lived in tears, and when the tears ended the Azusa revival ended!"[27]

Osterberg explained: "Tears of guilt confession; tears of fault confession; tears in humble contrition; tears in humble reverence; tears of self-denial and abnegation, in expression of soul humility, until high-mindedness was brought low, and the natural supreme ego minded topmost, became the selfless last; tears of sheer gladness and heavenly joy; tears, Holy Ghost tears, intermingling testimony and praise, often overflowing upon the congregation as a benediction from the battlements of glory; a baptism of tears falling upon the congregation, all weeping until the whole service became a beseeching altar. All the mechanical arrangements in the world would be unable to arrange such a program. All the great preachers of earth's dominions combined could not accomplish it. It was inspired and divinely powered by the Holy Ghost."[28]

"High or low, rich or poor, minister, laymen, surgeon, professor, carpenter or bricklayer, all appeared humble and contrite now. A heaven sent Holy Ghost revolution-revival was doing its prescribed spiritual work. They became, therefore, a family over which the banner of Christ and Pentecost waved without blemish or shame, as pure and wholesome in their reactions and lives as the pure driven snow; one in life, purpose, unity and testimony, to spread the glorious news over lands afar; over the face of the wide world!"[29]

CHAPTER 2

WILLIAM JOSEPH SEYMOUR

William Joseph Seymour was the son of former African slaves from Centerville, Louisiana. Seymour's father, Simon, was listed in a census as a dark, mixed-race mulatto. One exception to President Abraham Lincoln's 1863 Emancipation Proclamation to free slaves was those in Southern Louisiana's sugar parishes who made up nearly half the state's population. They were considered far too numerous to suddenly be freed during the war.[30]

Centreville, Louisiana (now spelled Centerville) on Bayou Teche, occupied by the 116th New York infantry, September 1863. Frank Leslie's Illustrated Newspaper XVII (7 Nov 1863).

Photo: Shane K. Bernard/canjunculture.com.

However, one other exception was given: immediate freedom would be granted to any slave who joined the Union Army. Simon made sure

Bocage Plantation near Centerville, Louisiana, established c. 1845. This is believed to be the plantation where the parents of William Seymour lived at one time.

Photo: Flower Pentecostal Heritage Center.

he met both exceptions by joining the Union Army from Southern Louisiana's parishes. He served in the famous U.S. Colored Infantry (*Corps d'Afrique*) for three years in Louisiana and Florida. Unfortunately, Simon developed intestinal problems during the war (likely a parasite from crossing many swamps), which continued to plague him after the war.

After Simon was honorably discharged from the army in 1866, he moved to Bayou Sale where he met Phillis Salabar. They were married by a Methodist minister in Franklin, Louisiana, in 1867. Since neither Simon nor Phillis could read or write, they each signed their wedding license with an "x." Simon was a brickmaker before and after the war, and Phillis likely worked as a farmer on a rice plantation. She was described as having "very dark" skin.[31]

SEYMOUR'S UPBRINGING

William Seymour was born on May 2, 1870, the second of eleven children. Most of his siblings did not reach adulthood. Like many young African Americans in those days, Seymour had only a Bible for reading and education prior to enrolling in school, where he learned basic literacy skills. Though baptized and raised Catholic, his parents occasionally attended a nearby Baptist church while continuing to work on the plantation after being freed. Christianity held many common beliefs with the African slave religion, including belief in a divine spirit, spirit possession, invisible spirits, signs and wonders, miracles and healings, trances, visions, and dreams.

By 1877, Reconstruction of the South had ended, leaving many blacks feeling betrayed by their liberators. Many were denied basic liberties such as the right to vote, the right to obtain an education, and the right to benefit from employment. In 1883, when William was thirteen, Simon bought a four-acre farm in Verdunville near Bayou Teche,

Bayou Teche, oil on canvas painting by Joseph Rusling Meeker, 1874. Johnson Collection, Spartanburg, South Carolina.

Photo: Wikimedia/Wmpearl.

just east of Centerville. By the late 1880s, his father had grown very ill. Though he applied for disability and a military pension, it was officially denied two weeks after his death in 1891.

Having served in the Union Army, Simon was likely considered a traitor by most Southern white people. During the war, one of the Union generals described Seymour's boyhood home, St. Mary's parish, as "the obstinate proslavery parish."[32] Simon died at the age of 54, leaving his wife, 21-year-old William, and three younger surviving siblings impoverished and with little means. Later, in 1912, the family farm was ceded to the Iberia, St. Mary, and Eastern Railroad Company for right-of-way passage. Phillis would then come live with William.

SEYMOUR'S SALVATION

Like many other young Southern black men in those days, Seymour and his two younger brothers soon traveled north to seek better employment opportunities, but perhaps also to escape the ongoing scourge of indiscriminate violence. Seymour first stopped in Memphis, where he stayed with relatives, then moved on to St. Louis, where he took whatever odd jobs he could find as a porter, truck driver, bartender, or waiter. Then Seymour traveled northeast to Indianapolis, where he again served as a hotel waiter. There, he received his salvation at the Simpson Chapel Methodist Episcopal Church, a black congregation affiliated with the interracial Methodist Episcopal Church. Seymour was particularly fond of Wesley's teachings and the church's desire for interracial fellowship and outreach to all classes.

Yet, dissatisfied with how far the Methodists had strayed from their Wesleyan-Holiness roots, like denying special revelations and the physical return of Christ prior to His millennial reign, and the fact that the church was "interracial" in name only, Seymour soon joined

Daniel S. Warner's Evening Light Saints. This was a non-denominational "come-outer" Holiness group which later became the Church of God (Anderson, Indiana). Warner believed the last spiritual outpouring, the "Evening Light," was being given to the "Saints" before the close of history. Warner's commitment to address all his followers as "Saints" led him to a vigorous policy of racial and gender inclusion and outreach as well as to high Holiness standards. Warner envisioned a church that was liberated from racial, gender, and denominational discrimination and was completely unified in the Spirit—a standard and practice Seymour would soon adopt.

Also, while in Indianapolis, Seymour was influenced by the ministry of Martin Wells Knapp, founder of the International Holiness Union and Prayer League, also known as the Church of God Reformation Movement. Seymour viewed Knapp's theology as much closer to his own.

SEYMOUR'S SANCTIFICATION AND CALLING

In 1900, Seymour may also have gone to Chicago where he sat under the ministry of John Alexander Dowie (also racially inclusive) for a time, before moving on to Cincinnati. In Cincinnati, Seymour again joined the Evening Light Saints, where he received his complete sanctification experience after making two separate trips to the altar.

Seymour also attended Martin Wells Knapp's "God's Bible School" in Cincinnati, where blacks and whites could study missions, holiness, healing, and the imminent return of Christ together. Knapp taught the importance of taking visions, dreams, and internal voices seriously, while also discerning spirits to recognize which came from God. Knapp even authored a book called *Impressions*, which taught how to distinguish between impressions from God and impressions from Satan. Since Seymour had experienced similar impressions and visions from his youth, this would help form a foundation for Seymour's beliefs.

Martin Wells Knapp founded the International Holiness Union and Prayer League, and God's Bible School in Cincinnati, Ohio.

Photo: gbs.edu.

In Cincinnati, Seymour received his call to ministry and ministry credentials with the Evening Light Saints (Church of God, Anderson, Indiana) but had many doubts and reservations. Soon, the city was swept by an invasion of smallpox, which was often fatal in those days. Seymour contracted it and managed to pull through, but not until it had left him facially scarred and blind in his left eye. Seymour replaced his eye with an artificial one and wore a beard the rest of his life to help cover the scars. Seymour felt the disease had been God's judgment on him for refusing to accept his call to ministry and immediately set out as an itinerant preacher. Like many preachers in those days, Seymour supplemented his income as a traveling salesman, so as not to have to beg or receive offerings.

SEYMOUR IN HOUSTON

In 1903, Seymour left Cincinnati and moved to Houston to stay with relatives, which became his home base while he continued traveling as an itinerant preacher, mostly throughout Texas and Louisiana. During this time, Seymour also traveled to Chicago, perhaps a second time, where he met John G. Lake, a minister in John Alexander Dowie's church. While staying at the Chicago Hotel, Lake and Seymour discussed spiritual matters. By the winter of 1904-1905, Seymour felt led to attend a minister's seminar in Jackson, Mississippi, on "special revelation" and to receive spiritual advice from a "significant colored clergyman," likely C.H. Mason or C.P. Jones, the original founders of the Church of God in Christ.[33]

While in Houston, Seymour again supplemented his income as a waiter and attended a small Holiness mission pastored by Mrs. Lucy Farrow of Norfolk, Virginia. Mrs. Farrow was the niece of famous abolitionist Frederick Douglass and a worker in Charles Parham's ministry. She was also perhaps the first African American to join the modern Pentecostal movement, having been baptized in the Holy Spirit while attending Parham's school in Baxter Springs, Kansas, in 1905. Mrs. Farrow was known to the Parhams simply as "Auntie," having worked closely with them in ministry and having served as a caretaker and nanny for their children. The Parham's had asked "Auntie" to come watch their children for them during their move from Kansas to Texas that year.

Mrs. Farrow agreed, asking Seymour if he would pastor her church in her absence, and Seymour also agreed. When Mrs. Farrow returned from Kansas, having received the Holy Spirit, she also spoke with Seymour about receiving the baptism in the Holy Spirit, but Seymour was reluctant. Like most Holiness groups, the Evening Light Saints had taught that they received the Holy Spirit when they were sanctified. They also taught that speaking in tongues could be restored to the church, but considered Parham's group a "counterfeit" or "pretension" of this.[34] Later, however, after attending several of Parham's meetings, and after a period of intense prayer and honest searching, asking God to "empty him of his false ideas, and when he was emptied of every false thought and idea that he had, the Lord then made plain to him Acts 2:4, as a personal experience."[35] Seymour was now convinced the baptism in the Holy Spirit was a separate work from salvation and sanctification.

CHARLES FOX PARHAM

Much like Seymour, Charles Fox Parham believed God had called him to ministry but decided to go to college and learn medicine instead, but then developed rheumatic fever. Believing that God was chastening him for not going in the ministry, Parham promised to preach, when suddenly every organ and joint in his body was made whole. Parham quit college, returned to itinerant ministry, and soon committed his life to preaching divine healing and praying for the sick. Moving to Topeka, the Parhams opened Bethel Healing Home and began publishing the *Apostolic Faith* magazine, while offering classes for those preparing for ministry.

Charles Fox Parham was a forward-thinking minister who wanted "to know more fully the latest truths restored by the later day movements." Known as the "Father of Pentecostal theology," he became one of the principal founders of the modern Pentecostal movement by articulating its principal doctrines, including speaking in tongues as the "introductory sign" and "gift first bestowed upon the baptized."

Photo: Apostolic Archives International Inc.

In 1900, after Frank Sandford, a healing evangelist from Maine, held a series of tent meetings in Topeka, Parham decided to set out on a fact-finding mission to study other ministries.[36] He visited Dowie's ministry in Chicago, A.B. Simpson's Christian Alliance in New York, A.J. Gordon's work in Boston, and Frank Sandford's "Holy Ghost and Us Bible School" in Maine. There he observed some Bible students coming down from their prayer tower speaking in tongues, and one who claimed to be called to missions work in Africa.

BETHEL BIBLE COLLEGE

Now fully convinced that God had something more "to meet the challenge of a new century," the Parhams opened Bethel Bible College, complete with an observatory and prayer tower.[37] Thirty-four students, mostly seasoned gospel workers who trusted God for finances, enrolled. Subjects included repentance, conversion, consecration, sanctification, healing, and the imminent return of Christ. Though a consensus was reached on each subject, the question of evidence for Holy Spirit baptism proved much more difficult. So Parham asked the students to study the Bible, particularly Acts, to learn more about the biblical evidence for the baptism in the Holy Spirit. When Parham returned, he was amazed at what the students reported. While different things occurred when the Holy Spirit fell, the indisputable proof was that they spoke with other tongues.[38]

That evening at the New Year's Eve Watch Night Service, just as the new century was about to dawn, one of the students—a thirty-year-old Holiness preacher named Agnes Ozman—asked Parham to pray for her that she might receive the baptism in the Holy Spirit. Parham laid his hand on her head and prayed when a glorious halo surrounded her head and face and she began speaking in Chinese and was unable to

Erastus Stone, a man intent on building his family of five the largest mansion in the state of Kansas, eventually ran out of funds. Two years later, Rev. Parham rented the building from its new owners for his Bethel Bible College. It would soon become the site of the twentieth century's "upper room."

Photo: Flower Pentecostal Heritage Center.

speak in English for three days. When she tried to write in English to explain her experience, she wrote in Chinese.[39]

A few days later, the entire student body was in the "upper room," caught up in the Pentecostal experience. Returning from a preaching engagement, Parham saw a flicker of light, then entered the room and saw some sitting, others kneeling, and still others standing with hands raised in the air, but all were singing beautifully, as if led by an invisible conductor, Charles Wesley's hymn "Jesus, Lover of my Soul"—in tongues! One student told him, "Just before you entered, tongues of fire were sitting above their heads," perhaps explaining the flicker of light he had seen.[40] Then Parham knelt and asked God to give him the Pentecostal blessing. The Lord said if he was willing to undergo persecution, hardships, trials, slander, and scandals, the blessing was his. Parham said, "Lord, I will. Just give me this blessing." He immediately began worshiping God in other languages until morning.[41]

Soon newspaper reporters, language professors, and government interpreters converged on the school to investigate the phenomenon. Experts concluded the students had spoken in twenty-one different languages from around the world. Parham believed those who spoke in foreign languages had been equipped as missionaries, though this aspect would not hold true.

Today Parham is known as the "Father of Pentecostal theology" because his school articulated one of the principal Pentecostal doctrines—speaking in tongues as the "introductory sign" or "gift first bestowed upon the baptized."[42] Parham's laying his hands on Ozman is also known as the "touch felt round the world" that "made the Pentecostal movement of the twentieth century."[43] After the tragic death of his youngest child and the building was sold out from under him, Parham closed his Topeka operations and set out on a whirlwind tour to preach the baptism in the Holy Spirit with tongues as the initial evidence.

Three years later, in 1904, Parham was preaching at a popular health resort in El Dorado Springs, Missouri, when a prominent Galena, Kansas, citizen was miraculously healed. Parham gained a strong following after that and began recruiting young men and women to join his crusade team. In 1905, Parham preached in Old Orchard, Texas, when he again experienced a highly publicized healing incident. Parham then moved his headquarters to Melrose, Kansas, where he continued publishing his magazine *Apostolic Faith* and again sponsored a short-term Bible school. Then, after holding a series of meetings at Bryan Hall in Houston, Parham moved his headquarters to Houston, and in January 1906 opened yet another ten-week intensive Bible school. Twenty-five students enrolled, including William Seymour who, despite the "Jim Crow" segregation laws in force in Texas at the time, "was so humble and so determined to learn God's Word," Parham obliged him.[44]

THE APOSTOLIC BIBLE TRAINING SCHOOL

When Parham announced he was opening the Apostolic Bible Training School in Houston, Mrs. Farrow insisted Seymour attend. However, since Texas segregation laws at the time did not permit blacks and whites to be in the same school together, Seymour could not become a resident. However, Sarah Parham wrote, "He was so humble and so deeply interested in the study of the word that Brother Parham could not refuse him. So, he was given a place in the class and eagerly drank in the truths which were so new to him and found for his hungry soul."[45] Though some accounts place Seymour in the hallway, an adjacent room, or out on the veranda, several historical eyewitnesses saw Seymour in the classroom along with the others.

The *Apostolic Faith Report* reported in 1921, "One negro man by the name of Seymour, became a regular attendant, taking his seat in the classes: and it was here that he gained the full knowledge of the Full Gospel message." Pauline Parham, Charles Parham's daughter-in-law, also said in a 1989 lecture, "William Seymour humbly asked Bro. Parham if he could sit outside and take in the lessons, but Bro. Parham gave him a place in the class-room with the other students to learn the truths about the Pentecostal message." And again, she said, "Dad Parham, being from Kansas, was not used to such laws and customs

The Apostolic Bible Training School, 503 Rusk Avenue, Houston, Texas, 1906. The two signs hanging from the roof say, "Apostolic Faith Movement, Headquarters."

Photo: Flower Pentecostal Heritage Center.

and he welcomed Seymour into the classroom.... The account I heard from those present was that he was welcomed into the class along with everyone else."[46]

In fact, Parham recognized Seymour as a seasoned minister and allowed him even more liberty and latitude than some of the other students. Parham and Seymour preached together to the black community of Houston. Parham even let Seymour preach at the mostly white Brunner Tabernacle. Indeed, all of Parham's workers and students recognized Seymour as a faithful student. Howard Goss, an early Parham associate, distinctly remembered Seymour attending the 9:00 a.m. meetings. He also recalled the students' rigorous daily schedule saying, "We were given a thorough workout and a rigid training in prayer, fastings, consecration, Bible study and evangelistic work. Our week day schedule consisted of Bible Study in the morning, shop and jail meetings at noon, house to house visitations in the afternoon, and a six o'clock street meeting followed by an evening evangelistic service at 7:30 or 8:00 o'clock."[47]

William Joseph Seymour, the son of former African slaves from Louisiana, sat in Parham's Bible School in Houston, Texas, in 1906, where "he was given a place in the class and eagerly drank in the truths which were so new to him and found for his hungry soul." Mrs. Charles Parham, *The Life of Charles F. Parham* (1930), p. 137.

Photo: Flower Pentecostal Heritage Center.

THE LOS ANGELES CONNECTION

Another friend and church member of Lucy Farrow's, who was living with relatives in Houston at the time, was Miss Neely Terry of Los Angeles. She also attended Farrow's church (including during Seymour's pastorate) and had served as the Parhams' cook. Miss Terry returned to Los Angeles after learning that her friends and family had been kicked out of the Second Baptist Church for professing Holiness doctrine and had begun a small black Holiness mission affiliated with the Nazarene Church in the home of her cousins, Richard and Ruth Asberry. Sister Julia Hutchins had been elected their interim pastor until a permanent replacement could be found. She was hoping to eventually go to Africa and become a missionary.

When Miss Terry arrived in Los Angeles, she told the group about Pastor Seymour's strong and gentle leadership, described him as a "very godly man," and recommended him to the group.[48] Sister Hutchins, who was looking for someone who would neither be a "self-appointed leader" nor "harsh and denunciatory," immediately wrote a letter sending for Seymour, even forwarding money to help cover his train fare.

Parham, however, had great plans for Seymour to do more mission work there in Texas and begged him to stay at least until he received the Holy Spirit. Seymour had only been in the school about six weeks when he received the invitation to come to Los Angeles. Warren Carothers, another Parham associate who was also a local pastor and attorney, said everyone was "disappointed somewhat" with Seymour leaving, but excited about the prospect of the Apostolic Faith message spreading to a new region.[49]

Seymour believed it to be a "divine call" and "the leading of the Lord," and Parham, again, obliged him. He and the students helped raise enough money for his train fare and laid hands on him as Seymour knelt.[50] Then they sent him on his way, each hoping he would soon return to help with the important work in Texas. Parham even promised to send "Apostolic Faith" lapel pins for Seymour's future workers, and Seymour would later write back to receive his credentials through Parham's ministry.

Seymour departed by train for Los Angeles with a stop in Denver, where he visited the Pillar of Fire Training School, founded by the popular but controversial Wesleyan-Holiness minister, Alma White. Seymour was invited to a meal in the company of Alma White and other school officials and was asked to pray over the meal. Alma later became highly critical of Seymour after her husband, Kent White, received the baptism in the Holy Spirit and spoke in tongues under

Seymour's Los Angeles ministry, which ultimately led to their bitter separation and divorce.

Alma Bridwell White was the founder and a bishop of the Pillar of Fire Church. She was the first woman bishop of Pillar of Fire, a proponent of feminism, the Ku Klux Klan, and was involved in anti-Catholicism, antisemitism, anti-Pentecostalism, racism, and hostility toward immigrants.

Photo: Flower Pentecostal Heritage Center.

Alma later described Seymour's Denver visit saying, "He was very untidy in his appearance, wearing no collar, and had a greenish-looking brass button exposed in the band of his shirt" (likely referring to his "Apostolic Faith" button). Alma was unsure why he had even stopped there, other than for God to allow her to see "the person that the devil was going to use." She continued saying that he prayed over the meal "with a good deal of fervor," but then described him among the leading "religious fakirs and tramps" of the day, saying she even felt "serpents and other slimy creatures" creeping around her as he prayed.[51] Alma White would later become affiliated with the Ku Klux Klan.

In contrast, Alma's husband, Kent, later wrote this to his estranged wife regarding Seymour: "I believe God chose him, one of the despised race, so that man might not glory, and then let him drop out [of the picture]. Anyhow it is the Holy Spirit's personal movement, not man's.... Seymour had the Holy Spirit...and was very humble."[52]

CHAPTER 3

THE BONNIE BRAE REVIVAL

I t is a rare known fact that among the founders and first Spanish set-tlers of Los Angeles, no less than twenty-six of them were black.[53] The California Gold Rush of the late 1840s and '50s led to an increased demand for cattle to be raised on the rancheros around Los Angeles.

Dr. Larry Martin, author of *The Complete Azusa Street Library*, shared a funny story about the booming economic conditions of Los Angeles during this time. Intriguingly, the story is about a black man named "Sam" who left his job in Texas to go to California. After his trip West, he refused to go back to his job in Texas. So the master approached him saying, "Sam, you'd better come back on the job. We've just killed a new batch of hogs, and I've got some mighty fine hog-jowls [jaws] for you." Sam shook his head and replied, "Uh uh, boss. You ain't talkin' to me, no suh. I've been to Los Angeles and I don't want yo' old hog-jowls, cuz I'm eatin' high on up on de hog now!"[54]

The same thing happened to William Seymour. He left his mission work and studies in Texas to go to Los Angeles. Though Charles Par-ham and everyone else at the mission wanted him to return to Texas, after learning how ripe the City of Los Angeles was for revival, he had no desire to return to his mission work in Texas.

View of Downtown Los Angeles, looking north from Main Street, c. 1906, when Seymour arrived. Main Street is thriving with vendors, street cars, buggies, cars, cyclists, and pedestrians. California Historical Society Collection, 1860-1960.

Photo: Wikimedia/Fae.

SEYMOUR IN
LOS ANGELES

When William Seymour arrived in Los Angeles on February 22, 1906, the city was racially diverse, free of segregation laws, and in revival mode. Cecil Robeck described 1906 Los Angeles as "a fertile seedbed for new ideas and new opportunities...a city full of dreams and ambitions."[55] A 1906 advertisement in the *Los Angeles Express* clearly illustrated the economic opportunities of the day:

FOR SALE—COUNTRY PROPERTY
$1.00 Per Acre
For 160 ACRES OF GOOD VALLEY LAND
in Los Angeles county, near town and railroad,
in the artesian flowing well district.
Opportunity of your life. Don't miss it.
CALL AT ONCE.[56]

One hundred-sixty acres of "good valley" land in Los Angeles County, purchased in 1906 for $160, would be worth upwards of $5 billion in 2006. Sometimes, "the opportunity of your life" really is.

Joseph Smale, pastor of the First Baptist Church of Los Angeles, had just returned from a three-week tour with Evan Roberts in Wales and was fired up. Immediately, he ordered cottage prayer meetings to be held throughout the city in preparation for the coming revival and began hosting interdenominational Spirit-led meetings at his church. However, unwilling to let believers from other denominations lead their meetings, the church elders shut them down after only four months. So Smale and a group from the church founded The New Testament

Church of Los Angeles. Smale believed the miraculous had departed from the church because the church had departed from the faith and fully expected his members to operate in spiritual gifts.[57]

Frank Bartleman, who had been working with various Holiness missions throughout the city, also attended The New Testament Church, and began corresponding with Evan Roberts in hopes of sparking a similar revival in Los Angeles.

Meanwhile, after arriving in Los Angeles, Seymour felt a greater burden to pray for Los Angeles, stating, "Before I met Parham, such a hunger to have more of God was in my heart that I prayed for five hours a day for two and a half years. I got to Los Angeles, and there the hunger was not less but more. I prayed, 'God, what can I do?' The Spirit said, 'Pray more.' 'But Lord, I am praying five hours a day now.' I increased my hours of prayer to seven, and prayed on for a year and a half more." The Lord said to him, "There are better things to be had in the Spiritual life, but they must be sought out with faith and prayer."[58] Seymour continued, "I prayed to God to give what Parham preached, the real Holy Ghost and fire with tongues with love and power of God like the apostles had."[59]

SEYMOUR LOCKED OUT

Two days after arriving in Los Angeles, Seymour arrived at the Holiness mission, which had already outgrown the Asberrys' home on Bonnie Brae Street and moved to a small building on the corner of Ninth and Santa Fe. Nightly meetings began immediately upon Seymour's arrival. The church was eager to see and hear the man of God they had previously heard so much about. All were happy to see him. He began preaching Saturday evening February 24, then regular services on Sunday, and afternoon prayer meetings on Tuesday and Friday. Seymour spoke on a variety of subjects including regeneration, sanctification, Holy Spirit baptism, the anointing of the Spirit, and faith healing.

However, since Miss Terry had been so closely associated with Parham's ministry in Texas, Seymour assumed they also wanted to hear more about the Pentecostal blessing with the introductory sign of speaking in tongues. So, after preaching for only two weeks, he chose for one of his Sunday morning texts Acts 2:4 (KJV): *"And they were all filled with the Holy Ghost, and began to speak with other tongues, as the Spirit gave them utterance."* After admitting that he himself had not yet received the gift, Seymour emphatically taught that a person had to speak in tongues, or they were not baptized in the Holy Spirit.

Seymour did not teach Holy Spirit baptism as a work of grace for sanctification as most Holiness people believed. Instead, he taught it as an empowerment for those who were saved and sanctified, evidenced by speaking in tongues. He asked the church to meet him at 3:00 p.m. that afternoon to pray with him until "all received their Pentecost."[60] Church member Emma Cotton wrote, "Oh! What a surprise to those old saints who had claimed the baptism of the Holy Ghost for years. There they were told by the preacher they did not have the Holy Ghost; they were only sanctified."[61]

To Sister Julia Hutchins, their interim pastor, this sounded too much like the so-called "third work" doctrine which most Holiness groups had rejected as heresy. Though some received Seymour's new teaching with enthusiasm, others vehemently opposed it—especially those who had claimed the baptism in the Holy Spirit for years and were now being told by their preacher they did *not* have the Holy Ghost, they were only sanctified! After the service, church members Edward and Mattie Lee invited Seymour to their home for Sunday dinner. However, when they all returned for the afternoon service, they found Sister Hutchins had padlocked the doors! She simply could not allow Seymour to continue confusing her flock.

Now without a job, a place to live, and no money to leave town, the Lees reluctantly felt obligated to bring their unwelcome guest back home. Seemingly undaunted and not knowing anyone, Seymour simply stayed in his room and prayed daily, occasionally asking the Lees to join him in prayer. Mr. Lee was a janitor at the First National Bank and had previously himself served as a preacher when they lived in Fresno. Though at first unsure about their new houseguest, the Lees grew to like him, as did several other members of the church, who did not agree with Seymour's doctrine but nonetheless felt safe joining them for prayer.

When Sister Hutchins learned of this, she and church member W.H. McGowan called for a meeting between Seymour and President J.M. Roberts of the Southern California Holiness Association as well as other Holiness ministers. The officials made it clear that they believed sanctification and baptism in the Holy Spirit were the same, and that they already had the experience and did *not* believe speaking in tongues was for today. Seymour was then given an opportunity to defend himself and his doctrine. When confronted, Seymour simply and matter-of-factly restated Acts 2:4 and the premise that no one had received the baptism in the Holy Spirit until they spoke in tongues. As far as Seymour was concerned, their problem was not with him but with the Word of God. This would not be the first or last time Seymour's calm leadership skills would be tested.

Though President Roberts clearly stated Seymour could no longer preach his version of baptism in the Holy Spirit in the Holiness church, he also expressed how pleased he was that Seymour was seeking the baptism in the Spirit. In fact, before departing, he told Seymour, "When you receive it, please let me know, because I am interested in receiving it too."[62] Seymour later added in the first issue of *The Apostolic Faith*, "So I received it and let him know."[63]

THE BONNIE BRAE MEETINGS

After only two weeks, the cottage prayer meetings had outgrown the Lees' home, so Richard and Ruth Asberry again offered their home on Bonnie Brae Street. Only this time, they invited Brother Seymour, the stranger, to hold day and night prayer meetings. Richard was also a janitor at the Wilcox Building in Downtown Los Angeles. Though the Asberrys still did not agree with Seymour's teachings, they felt bad about what had happened, and Seymour accommodated them.

At first, the cottage prayer meetings on North Bonnie Brae Street were primarily attended by friends and neighbors. Bud Traynor, a young railroad worker, and his mother Sallie, who also lived with the Lees, joined them. William, a plasterer, and Emma Cummings and their five children joined them. Also, Miss Jennie Evans Moore, a masseuse, cook, and house servant from Austin, Texas, who lived at 217 North Bonnie Brae Street, across from the Asberrys, joined them. She would one day become Mrs. William Seymour.

Then, as news spread throughout the area, several believers from the Holiness Church on Hawthorne Street came, as did Swedish-born Emma Osterberg and her young son Arthur "A.G." Osterberg, who pastored the Full Gospel Tabernacle. Then, Frank Bartleman and several other white believers from the Peniel Holiness Mission began joining them. All that was missing now was the baptism in the Holy Spirit, and since Seymour had yet to receive it himself, he was having difficulty leading others in the experience. He did try his best to explain to them secondhand what happened when people received the Holy Spirit, but without firsthand experience, it seemed all but impossible.

During this time, Mr. Lee often prayed during his breaks at the First National Bank. On one such occasion, he received a vision of the apostles Peter and John, standing in front of him, lifting their hands to heaven, and shaking under the power of God as they spoke in other tongues. He could not wait to tell Seymour: "I know now how people act when they get the Holy Ghost." Since that vision, Mr. Lee became convinced it was a real experience and increasingly hungered for it. In fact, at dinner one evening, Mr. Lee asked Seymour to lay hands on him to receive the baptism. However, knowing what 1 Timothy 5:22 (KJV) said, "Lay hands suddenly on no man," Seymour was reluctant. But then later that evening, Seymour did lay hands on him, and Mr. Lee fell to the floor in a trance. His wife, Mattie, screamed, "What did you do to my husband?" immediately calling for an end to the proceedings. Seymour just prayed, then Mr. Lee woke up, more excited than ever to receive the Pentecostal blessing.[64]

About that same time, Jennie Moore had received a vision in which she saw three white cards, each with two names written in two languages. All total, the cards were written in French, Spanish, Latin, Greek, Hebrew, and Hindu. Though blessed by the experience, she had no idea what the vision meant, and sadly, no one else could interpret it for her.[65]

So by late March, Seymour had told the group about his good friend, Lucy Farrow, in Houston. Not only had Mrs. Farrow received the Holy Spirit, but as one of Parham's altar workers, she was also gifted to lay hands on people and had become quite successful in leading others into the experience. Immediately, they received an offering and sent for Farrow.

312 AZUSA STREET

Now, fully aware of the growing number of people attending the evening meetings and needing a place to meet for prayer in the daytime, Seymour began searching for a building. About two and a half miles away in the old downtown industrial district was an abandoned two-story

312 Azusa Street as it appeared when Seymour rented it from its original occupants, the First AME Church, in 1906. The "FOR SALE" sign is visible in the upper corner. Below the sign is the door through which most people entered the building. In the foreground is the rear of the Brown and Ford Marble and Granite Works, which everyone called the "tombstone shop."

Photo: Flower Pentecostal Heritage Center.

4,800 square-foot building on a dead-end street. Originally home to the Stevens African Methodist Episcopal Church, the first black congregation of Los Angeles, the church had since relocated to a better part of town. Since then, it had been leased as a wholesale house, warehouse, lumberyard, stockyard, tombstone shop, and most recently a stable and warehouse for hay and stock with rooms to rent upstairs.

Emma Cotton wrote, "They went out to find another meeting place, and they found old Azusa.... It seemed to have been waiting for the Lord."[66] A.G. Osterberg recalled his mother going to one of the Bonnie Brae meetings when "they announced they had found a place on a little street east of the city hall, called Azusa Street, that once was a Methodist Church and was presently used by a contractor for storage of building materials. They had learned he would surrender his occupancy, and decided to clean up the place and use it for services. They agreed that the following evening the folks would help that contractor put his stuff on trucks and move it out, then get busy and fix the lower floor for meetings."

About the only clue left that it had once been a church was the Gothic style second-story window over the front entrance. When it was a church, the sanctuary was on the second floor and the first floor housed the members' horses during services. The building was completely trashed, its doors and windows broken, and it was desperately in need of repairs. Besides that, there was no indoor plumbing, only a single outhouse behind the building that served as a restroom. To top it all off, a fire had once broken out in one of the upstairs apartments, leaving the building partially destroyed. The pitched church roof was then replaced with a flat asphalt roof. The neighborhood was not much better. Azusa Street was described as a back alley slum of the "skid row flavor," complete with saloons, stables, wholesale houses, lumber yards, and a tombstone shop next door. But the rent was only eight dollars a month and Seymour had a building. Now all he needed was the rent money.

THE PASADENA CONNECTION

That night, Seymour prayed and received his answer: the following night, after the meeting, he was to take a trolley to Pasadena. Though it was illegal for a black man to be in Pasadena after dark in those days, Seymour did not argue—he simply obeyed. The next night after the meeting, he rode the trolley to Pasadena until the Lord instructed him to get off. Then the Spirit led him to an apartment where Sister Julia Carney and several of her friends from the First Baptist Church were praying for revival and for the baptism in the Holy Spirit.

Members of the First African Methodist Episcopal Church at 312 Azusa Street, c. 1900. The original church met in the "upper room" on the second floor, while the first floor served as a stable for horses and buggies.

Photo: Flower Pentecostal Heritage Center.

Sister Carney had received the baptism experience herself two years prior, after Brother Lankford returned from Parham's school in Topeka. When Brother Lankford shared his experience with Dr. Finis Yoakum, founder of the Pisgah Home rescue mission in Los Angeles which Sister Carney had attended, Dr. Yoakum immediately embraced it, shared the experience with his church, and Sister Carney received. Though only fifteen years old and married at the time, Sister Carney felt led to move to Pasadena and share her experience with her friends. When Seymour walked up to the apartment, it was 10:30 p.m.

Normally, if a black man knocked on a door in Pasadena at 10:30 at night in 1906, the door was slammed, and the police were called. But this night the Spirit was in charge and the owner simply greeted him at the door: "Can I help you?" Seymour replied, "You're praying for

The Pasadena & Los Angeles Electric Railway in 1906, Figueroa at Marmion Way, America's first interurban railway. You can see "PASADENA" on the front of the car above the conductor.

Photo: oldhomesoflosangeles.org

revival, right?" Astonished, the ladies inside unanimously replied, "Yes!" Seymour said, "I'm the man God has sent to preach that revival." Immediately, the ladies invited Seymour in, and after some excited chatter, he preached and received an offering. The offering was more than enough to rent the warehouse. And there, "in a barn-like room on the ground floor of an old Methodist Church...about a dozen congregated each day, holding meetings on Bonnie Brae in the evening."[67]

THE BONNIE BRAE REVIVAL

On Friday, April 6, Seymour announced a ten-day fast to tarry for the blessing of baptism. Ten days would not be needed. On Monday, April 9, the third day of the fast, Mrs. Lucy Farrow, accompanied by fellow mission worker Joseph Warren, arrived from Houston. Mr. Lee came home from work that day feeling weak and sick from the fast, but he was so excited to meet Lucy Farrow. Immediately he said, "Sister, if you will lay hands on me, I believe I will get my baptism right now!" Mrs. Farrow politely refused, saying, "I cannot do it, unless the Lord says so," suggesting the Lord would tell her when it *was* time.[68]

Later at dinner, Mr. Lee told everyone he was not feeling well, and asked Seymour if he would pray for him so he could attend the evening meeting. Seymour anointed Mr. Lee with oil as Seymour and Farrow prayed, and he immediately felt better. Then Mrs. Farrow announced, "The Lord tells me to lay my hands on you for the Holy Ghost."[69] Farrow and Seymour prayed for him, and once again, he fell out of his chair as dead, and his wife, Mattie, again protested. Only this time, he began speaking in other tongues! Then he rose to his feet, raised his hands, and continued speaking in other tongues. Now overjoyed, the group continued rejoicing as they walked two blocks to the Bonnie Brae House. They could hardly wait to tell the others.

When they arrived at the Bonnie Brae House, every room in the house was packed with people praying. Seymour led the group in

The Asberry home at 214 North Bonnie Brae Street as it appeared in 1906.

Photo: Flower Pentecostal Heritage Center.

singing, testimonies, and more prayer. Then, choosing again for his text Acts 2:4, Seymour shared Mr. Lee's testimony of how he had received healing and the baptism in the Holy Spirit prior to the meeting. But before Seymour could finish, Mr. Lee raised his hands in the air and began shouting aloud in other tongues! Everyone instantly fell to the floor "as by some mighty power" and began praying for the baptism.[70]

Soon, six or seven others, including Jennie Moore, began speaking in tongues. Others, including Bud Traynor, rushed out on the front porch preaching and prophesying. Still others ran out in the street speaking in tongues. Then Willella, the Asberry's young daughter, came in the living room to see what the commotion was, and she and her brother also ran out in the street screaming and yelling as neighbors began gathering in the street to see what was happening.

THE PIANO

Jennie Moore then made her way back to the piano bench and began singing and playing the piano in a beautiful melody of tongues and interpretation. But that was not the strangest part—Jennie had never played piano or sung before! She said it felt like "a vessel broke within me and water surged up through my being." This was reminiscent of Jesus' words to the woman at the well: "For when you drink the water I give you it becomes a gushing fountain of the Holy Spirit, springing up and flooding you with endless life!"[71] When it reached her mouth, she spoke in all six languages she had seen on the cards in her vision, and after each message in tongues, there was an interpretation in English. She had also previously told the Lord, "Although I wanted to sing under the power I was willing to do whatever He willed."[72] She later wrote, "I sang under the power of the Spirit in many languages...the Spirit led me to the piano, where I played and sang under inspiration, although I had not learned to play. In these ways God is continuing to use me

The piano played by Jennie Evans Moore on April 9, 1906, when the Holy Spirit came upon her, during the Bonnie Brae Revival.

Photo: Flower Pentecostal Heritage Center.

to His glory ever since that wonderful day and I praise Him for the privilege of being a witness for Him under the Holy Ghost's power."[73]

Moore was perhaps the first black woman in Los Angeles to receive the Holy Spirit with the gift of tongues. The meeting lasted well past 10:00 p.m. Brother Seymour later said that when he came out from under the power of the Spirit, it was 10:00, and his friend, Brother Lee, was still speaking in tongues and magnifying God![74]

As a footnote to this story of Jennie Moore playing the piano, my wife and I had the wonderful privilege of visiting the Bonnie Brae House in 2017. We called ahead to make an appointment, but there was no response. So we went to take pictures outside when we saw someone leaving the house. It was the current owner. We inquired, introduced ourselves, and told her about the books I had written. She graciously invited us in without an appointment.

Immediately upon entering, I noticed a piano in the front room. I asked, "Is that *the* piano?" She said, "Yes." Then she proceeded to tell us her story. She said when she first purchased the home, she knew nothing about its history. Evidently, the previous owner said nothing. But then she kept noticing a man in the street, standing outside her house every day, praying. Finally, out of curiosity, she asked him, "Why do you stand outside my house every day praying?" He said, "You mean, you don't know?" Then he explained to her the history of the house.

Since then, she agreed to let the Church of God in Christ make the necessary renovations to her home to open it to the public by appointment only. She said she also occasionally allows special groups and visitors to stay overnight and pray. On one such occasion, one of the "Supremes" of "Diana Ross and the Supremes" fame stayed overnight.

In the middle of the night, her guest heard the piano playing, but when she went to see who was playing it, no one was there. So she went back to her room, packed her bags, and was about to leave when the owner stopped her. "Is something wrong? she asked, "Why are you leaving?" "This house has a ghost!" she replied. "I heard the piano playing, but when I went to see who was playing it, no one was there." The owner started laughing. She said, "No, that happens all the time. That's not a ghost. That's the Holy Ghost reminding us that He's getting ready to do again what He did here before!"

The next night at the Bonnie Brae Revival, the crowds had grown so large, they had to build a makeshift pulpit on the front porch for Seymour and others to preach from as the porch became their pulpit and the street their pews. Day and night the revival continued for three days. Hundreds were saved and many healed and baptized in the Holy Spirit. Even Sister Julia Hutchins came with her entire congregation and spoke in tongues. Sometimes shouts of excitement could be heard coming from the house. Other times it would fall silent. Those who entered the house often fell under the power and lay on the floor for three to five hours.

SEYMOUR'S SPIRIT BAPTISM

On Thursday, April 12, the third day of the revival, witnesses said the house shook as in the book of Acts.[75] Seymour was preaching when suddenly the foundation gave way, sending the porch crashing into the steep bank in the front yard, but miraculously, no one was injured. One eyewitness wrote, "They shouted three days and nights. It was Easter season. The people came from everywhere. By the next morning there was no way of getting near the house. As people came in they would fall under God's power; and the whole city was stirred. They shouted until the foundation of the house gave way, but no one was hurt."[76] The police were emphatic: "Either shut it down or rent a place like a regular church or auditorium. You have gotten too big to continue to meet at this home."[77] Seymour had been warned several times before.

After many had left on the last night, Seymour was praying inside when a white man came and knelt beside him to pray. After much praying and seeking for the Holy Ghost, his white friend said wearily in exhaustion, "It is not the time." Seymour replied, "Yes it is, I am not going to give up." Now continuing to pray alone, suddenly a sphere of white-hot brilliance seemed to appear, draw near, and fall upon him. Divine love melted his heart as he sank to the floor. Soon he heard unutterable words as from a great distance. Then he slowly realized the indescribably lovely language belonged to him. It poured from his innermost being. Seymour had finally received his Pentecostal blessing! At length, he arose happily with a broad smile on his face and embraced those around him.[78] Seymour later wrote, "We had prayed all night, when at four o'clock in the morning, God came through the window."[79]

CHAPTER 4

312 AZUSA STREET

Though Sister Carney and her friends had raised enough money to rent the old warehouse, much work remained with little time or money left to do it. A.G. Osterberg, pastor of the Full Gospel Tabernacle and timekeeper for the McNeil Construction Company, asked three Mexicans on his crew if they wanted overtime and donated the labor to replace the doors and windows. Mr. McNeil, owner of the construction company and a devout Catholic, donated the lumber and supplies. Sister Carney and her friends volunteered to help remove the clutter that had accumulated over the years. Sister Carney recalled how Brother Seymour assigned each volunteer an area to clean and mentioned how grateful she was for being assigned the task of cleaning up after the goats with their little droppings instead of the horses and cattle.[80]

A.G. Osterberg recalled, "When we arrived some colored ladies already were working there, and the first thing they wanted to do when those men came in was to have a prayer meeting. The next thing we knew one of the ladies had one of the workmen down on his knees and he was weeping and getting soundly converted. To the best of my knowledge that was the first convert in the Azusa Street Mission, which took place before we opened it up—and that man was a Roman Catholic."[81]

After cleanup, the volunteers gathered wooden fruit crates found behind a nearby grocery store to supplement the nail crates and nailed

2x12 redwood planks to the crates, which served as benches or pews, then spread sawdust on the floor. The rest of the seating consisted of an odd assortment of chairs, benches, and stools. Since the building had partially burned, leaving black soot on the walls, they would eventually whitewash the walls. Seymour set two wooden packing crates used for shipping shoes in the center of the room, then covered them with a cotton cloth for a makeshift pulpit. A junkman would have valued it at fifteen cents.

Joseph Warren made altar benches to run in a square around the pulpit, each consisting of a board and two chairs. However, A.G. Osterberg complained it was too flimsy and asked Mr. McNeil, who had once studied for the priesthood, if he could have some 2x16 planks. Mr. McNeil agreed and Osterberg built a slightly elevated platform in the center with some kneeling benches. When he tried to pay Mr. McNeil, he refused saying, "I would be a poor [priest if I] couldn't do that much for some colored religious folks." Osterberg later joked, calling it his "Catholic altar."[82] Later, a regular pulpit was added and "straw matting" for a floor.[83] A mailbox was hung inside the door for offerings since neither Parham nor Seymour liked to collect offerings. There was seating for thirty to forty people—it would not be enough.

The second floor, the original sanctuary, was also cleared of debris to create a long narrow "upper room" or "tarrying room" for candidates to "tarry" for the Holy Spirit and for children's church on Sundays. There were also several small former Sunday school rooms and a small kitchen, which doubled as offices and sleeping quarters for Seymour and the volunteer staff. One of them was set aside for laying hands on the sick and for special prayer for those wanting to be healed.

THE FIRST MEETING

Clara Lum, who later served as the mission's secretary, described the facility as "the most humble place I was ever in for a meeting." Others compared its rough quarters to Bethlehem's manger.[84] The first issue of *The Apostolic Faith* declared, "The meetings are held in an old Methodist church that had been converted in part into a tenement house, leaving a large, unplastered, barn-like room on the ground floor."[85] On Saturday, April 14—just two days after the porch collapsed on Bonnie Brae Street and the day before Easter—the first meeting was held at 312 Azusa Street with 10 to 20 in attendance, while evening services continued a few more nights on Bonnie Brae Street.

FREE ADVERTISING

Easter Sunday, April 15, Jennie Moore and Ruth Asberry worshiped at The New Testament Church. After Pastor Smale finished his sermon, he gave the people an opportunity to share testimonies. Jennie stood up and shared about the meetings that had been taking place on North Bonnie Brae Street. Then she announced that Baptists were receiving the Pentecostal baptism and that "Pentecost" had come to Los Angeles. She concluded her testimony with a long utterance in other tongues. Ruth Asberry then interpreted her tongues message in English. This, of course, created a great stir. Some were so frightened they started heading for the doors, others shouted praises, while a few, who had also been to the Bonnie Brae meetings, spoke in other tongues.

Pastor Smale quickly but gently stepped in before things got out of hand. Frank Bartleman, who was also there, tried to make sense of it all. Several gathered on the sidewalk after the service to discuss what had happened. That afternoon, Frank Bartleman went to the Bonnie Brae meeting to check things out for himself. He wrote, "There was a general spirit of humility manifested in the meeting. They were taken up with God. Evidently the Lord had found the little company at last, outside as always, through whom He could have His way. God had not chosen an established mission where this could be done. They were in the hands of men; the Spirit could not work. Others far more pretentious had failed. That which man esteems had been passed by once more, and the Spirit was born again in a humble 'stable' outside ecclesiastical establishment."[86]

Bartleman compared the Bonnie Brae meetings and the Azusa Street Mission to the humble stable in Bethlehem and to Martin Luther's dilapidated building in Wittenberg, writing, "In the middle of the square at Wittenberg stood an ancient wooden chapel, thirty feet long and twenty feet wide, whose walls, propped up on all sides, were falling into ruin. An old pulpit made of planks, and three feet high, received the preacher. It was in this wretched place that the preaching of the Reformation began. It was God's will that that which was to restore His glory should have the humblest surroundings. It was in this wretched enclosure that God willed, so to speak, that His well-beloved Son should be born a second time."[87] Others, referring to the building's surroundings, said, "You would hardly expect heavenly visitations there, unless you remember the stable at Bethlehem."[88]

Addie M. Cook, a leading Methodist layman of Los Angeles, wrote, "We prayed that Pentecost might come to the city of Los Angeles. We wanted it to start at First Methodist Church, but God did not start it there. I bless God that it did not start in any church in this city, but in a barn, so that we might all come and take part in it. If it had started in a fine church, poor colored people and Spanish people would not have got it, but praise God it started here. I want to warn every Methodist in Los Angeles to keep your hands off this work."[89]

That evening, Mack E. Jonas, an unsaved black man, attended the Azusa Street Mission for the very first time. He said, "I had never been in a meeting like that before."[90] Within a few days, he became the first black man to be saved at the mission and even lived upstairs at the mission for a while. The first man to be saved at the mission was fittingly one of the three Mexicans whom A.G. Osterberg had hired to help clean up the building and get it ready for its first church service. Among the countless others who were saved at the mission was a drug addict who had been in and out of prison for twenty years, a morphine addict, someone who had been twice admitted to an insane asylum, many drunks, and a burglar who had planned to rob a house before leaving the house keys at the altar of the Azusa Mission.

OPENING NIGHT AT AZUSA

A.G. Osterberg recalled the first evening meeting at Azusa Street: "The crowd that filled Azusa Street the first day it was opened came in a good measure from the Bonnie Brae prayer meetings. I would say there were about one hundred persons the first night. We had meetings every night at that time, and the crowd would almost double each night until by the end of the week the place was packed. The benches were taken out and the entire auditorium was filled with chairs…they would stand two and three deep around the walls in the doorways and windows, looking in from outside—any place close enough to hear."[91]

THE PRESS

On Tuesday, April 17, *The Los Angeles Daily Times* sent a reporter to the evening meeting on Azusa Street to investigate what was going on down at the old warehouse. The next morning, the following headline and article appeared on the front page:

WEIRD BABEL OF TONGUES

New Sect of Fanatics is Breaking Loose

Wild Scene Last Night on Azusa Street

Gurgle of Wordless Talk by a Sister

Meetings are held in a tumble-down shack on Azusa Street, near San Pedro Street, and the devotees of the weird doctrine practice the most fanatical rites, preach the wildest theories and work themselves into a state of mad excitement in their peculiar zeal. Colored people and a sprinkling of whites compose the congregation, and night is made hideous in the neighborhood by the howlings of the worshippers, who spend hours swaying forth and back in a nerve racking attitude of prayer and supplication. They claim to have the "gift of tongues" and to understand the babel.[92]

The front page of *The Los Angeles Times*, Wednesday morning, April 18, 1906.

Photo: Wikimedia/Magnus Manske.

This article, intending to ridicule them, had the opposite effect—more like free advertising. Soon, believers and cynics alike were converging on the tiny warehouse, eventually numbering in the hundreds, then thousands. Within three months, a meeting of fifteen people grew into an internationally acclaimed congregation of hundreds with thousands more attending. This would be the first of many articles to come.

THE EARTHQUAKE

That same morning, as many Los Angeles residents were receiving the news of this "new fanatical sect," another seismic event was occurring which sent shockwaves up and down California's coast. At 5:12 a.m., an estimated 7.9 magnitude earthquake—one of the most devastating in history—rocked the city of San Francisco. The quake resulted in equally devastating fires that lasted for several days as 3,000 people died and about 80 percent of San Francisco was destroyed. Buildings shook as far south as Los Angeles, where two more aftershocks were felt around noon the following day. Bartleman recorded, "While sitting at the noon meeting at Penial Hall…the floor suddenly began to move with us." Many wondered if the San Francisco quake was not somehow connected to the spiritual quake taking place in Los Angeles.[93]

Certainly, earthquakes had been recorded in Acts and in New England preempting the Great Awakening, but not many had occurred concurrently with a revival.[94] Alfred G. Garr, pastor of the Burning Bush Holiness Church in Los Angeles said, "Our church building trembled and heaved…while in other parts of the city of Los Angeles, windows were broken and chimneys were thrown down…. Will cities and individuals take heed after seeing such horrible displays of the omnipotence of the great God?"[95]

Evidently, many did take heed because the spiritual fervor in Los Angeles soon reached an all-time high. Even *The Los Angeles Herald* announced the San Francisco quake had served as a "wakeup call."[96] The only difference was, whereas in times past religious zeal resulting from

The 1906 San Francisco Earthquake and fire. "Ruins on Kearney St. near Post." From the Pillsbury Picture Co., Library of Congress Photo Collection.

Photo: Wikimedia/Fæ.

a natural disaster would quickly wane, this spiritual foment would last for years. And while the San Francisco quake was felt up and down the west coast, shockwaves from this Los Angeles revival would soon be felt around the world.

The night after the quake, only about a dozen black and white worshipers were at the Azusa Street Mission, but soon more seats were provided, and more seekers came.[97] Frank Bartleman, who attended his first meeting at Azusa Street that day, wrote, "I found the earthquake had opened many hearts…. It was used mightily in conviction, for the revival the Lord graciously brought afterward. In the early Azusa days, both heaven and hell seemed to have come to town."[98] Then he added, "Nearly every pulpit in the land was working overtime to prove that God had nothing to do with the earthquake and thus allay the fears of the people."[99] Bartleman was indignant toward preachers for being used by Satan to drown out God's voice, which was surely in the earthquake.

Just three weeks prior, Bartleman had written, printed, and distributed a tract he called "The Last Call." In it, he compared his day to Noah's day when people were warned of impending doom. After the quake, he wrote another tract simply called, "The Earthquake!!!" He distributed 25,000 copies in a few days and had to order 25,000 more. William Manley, editor of the *Household of God* and pastor of the Holiness group by the same name headquartered in Oakland, ordered another 50,000 tracts to be distributed in the East Bay where thousands had fled earthquake-torn San Francisco. Bartleman distributed his in saloons, prostitution houses, streetcars, businesses—anywhere he could find an open hand.

REGULAR SERVICES

Meanwhile, the Azusa Street Mission was now offering a regular schedule of 10:00 a.m. morning, 3:00 p.m. afternoon, and 7:30 p.m. evening services. The afternoon services were mostly just a continuation of the morning services. Worship was round the clock. African American preacher Mother Cotton described it as one seamless service that ran "three years, day and night, without a break."[100] Weekday mornings prayer and Bible study could be led by Seymour or another volunteer staff member, upstairs or downstairs.

A.G. Osterberg described the Sunday morning prayer services: "The prayer services were generally short. We would be down on our knees six or eight times in the course of a Sunday morning service, praying for special requests as they came in. Then somebody would start a chorus or Brother Seymour would bring his message. There was no minute wasted. It was alive—it was active—moving—something going on all the time. To my mind, that was what attracted a good many people— there was something doing—folks were not just sitting with folded hands waiting for someone to say or do something. There was speaking in tongues in the services, but very few ever spoke loudly. It was in undertones and usually individually.

"Brother Seymour taught from the very beginning: 'Let him who speaketh in tongues pray that he may interpret.' That had a slightly restrictive influence on those who were a little on that extreme side and wanted to get up and talk in tongues in every meeting. We didn't have that. Neither did we have interpretation expressed in words as though the interpreter spoke in the place of God—speaking in the first person. Our own people didn't do that, but sometimes strangers coming in started to, but Brother Seymour would stop them. They might refer to God in interpretation and testimony saying the Lord has spoken 'to me and told me what I should do,' but they didn't attempt to speak to the congregation as an oracle and tell the congregation what they should do."[101]

SPIRIT-LED MEETINGS

A typical meeting at Azusa Street would open with one of the elders explaining the order of service (there was no order and there was no typical service): "We have no planned program, nor are we afraid of anarchy or crooked spirits. God the Holy Spirit is able to control and protect His work. If any strange manifestations come, trust the Holy Spirit, keep in prayer, and you will see the word of wisdom go forth, a rebuke, an exhortation that will close the door on the enemy and show the victory won. God can use any member of the body, and He often gives the more abundant honor to the weaker members."[102]

Bartleman wrote, "We found early in the Azusa work that when we attempted to steady the ark, the Lord stopped working. We dared not call the attention of the people too much to the working of the Evil One. Fear would follow. We could only pray—then God gave victory. There was a presence of God with us that, through prayer, we could depend on. The leaders had limited experience, and the wonder is that the work survived at all against its powerful adversaries. But it was of God. That was the secret."[103]

Services began with someone singing a song or sharing a testimony. Many of the "sermons" were given by lay people in the form of "testimonies." The testimony meetings that preceded the preaching often continued for two hours or more as people were always standing waiting to testify. Even children between eight and twelve often stood on the altar bench and testified to the baptism in the Holy Spirit and to speaking in tongues. If a Mexican or German could not speak English, they would just speak in their own language and feel at home because the Spirit would interpret through their emotions and facial expressions and the people would respond saying, "Amen."

Then, like in early Quaker services, anyone who felt led could get up and preach or sing in English or in tongues with interpretation. Meanwhile, as with Finney's revivals, prayer was taking place continually on the second floor. And like in the camp meetings of old, anyone could be seen shouting, dancing, jerking, shaking, weeping, laughing, falling into trances, or speaking or singing in tongues. When the power of God hit, one or two would fall, or a hundred would fall at a time like dominoes or like an army slain in battle. But mostly, everyone just prayed and trusted God to direct the meetings.

If anyone stood in a meeting and spoke out of their intellect or without being "anointed" by God to speak, the Spirit would soon convict them, and they would sit down. If not, they may have heard wailing sobs coming from the audience. Or worse, Mother Jones would get up and look the speaker straight in the eye. That meant, "You're not anointed. Go sit down!" If the speaker did not understand by her look, then she would proceed to tell them.

Bartleman wrote: "There was no pride there. The services ran almost continuously. Seeking souls could be found under the power almost any hour of the day or night. The place was never closed nor empty. The people came to meet God—He was always there. Hence a continuous meeting. The meeting did not depend on the human leader. God's presence became more and more wonderful. In that old building, with its low rafters and bare floors, God broke strong men and women to pieces, and put them together again for His glory. It was a tremendous overhauling process. Pride and self-assertion, self-importance, and self-esteem could not survive there. The religious ego preached its own funeral sermon quickly."[104]

HOLY GROUND

There was a holy awe at the mission. The people did not salute or even shake hands. They met in the Spirit, not in the flesh. Bartleman continued: "Those were Holy Spirit meetings, led by the Lord. It had to start in poor surroundings to keep out the selfish, human element. All came down in humility together at His feet. They all looked alike and had all things in common, in that sense at least. The rafters were low, the tall must come down. By the time they got to Azusa, they were humbled, ready for the blessing." He added, "We avoided human contact and greeting as much as possible. We wanted to meet God first…. The Lord was liable to burst through anyone. We prayed for this continually…. It might be a child, a woman, or a man. It might be from the back seat or from the front. It made no difference…. I would rather live six months at that time than fifty years of ordinary life. But God is just the same today. Only we have changed. "[105]

Rachel Sizelove agreed: "'No flesh could glory' in His presence. As the saints would gather at the Azusa Street Mission they felt they were treading upon holy ground. Our conversation would be yea, yea, nay, nay, so sacred was the very air we breathed we did not stop to salute any man by the way, that is when we met there we did not meet and shake hands with each other, we were so shut in with God, expecting to receive fresh manna right from Heaven.

"We felt all flesh should keep silent before the Lord, and upon entering the building we would kneel at our seats or the altar, with tears dripping on the seats, as the 'Sun' of righteousness was melting our hearts." She continued, "No one dared get up and sing a song or testify except under the anointing of the Spirit.... I told how they had no piano, drums or musical instruments of any kind and no visiting or talking among the saints but a continual waiting upon God, they had no strange fire, which typifies any use of carnal means to kindle the fire of devotion and praise."[106]

A.C. Valdez, Sr., who was only ten years old himself at the time, said even the children were quiet! "In most churches kids would be running up and down the aisles or twisting and turning in their seats. Here the children, seated between their parents—even babies in their mothers' arms—were quiet. But it was not their parents who kept them still. Nobody even whispered. All the adults were praying with eyes closed. I knew the Spirit of God was there. Suddenly, people rose to their feet. Everywhere hands shot to heaven. Mine went up, and I hadn't tried to raise them. So did the hands of smaller children and even those of babies in the arms of black mothers."[107]

SPONTANEOUS ALTAR CALLS

If Seymour had a sermon, he would often throw it away and open the floor for anyone to share. Altar calls were also Spirit led. People were just invited to interact with the sermon whenever they felt led. Bartleman wrote: "No subjects or sermons were announced ahead of time, and no special speakers for such an hour. No one knew what might be coming, what God would do. All was spontaneous, ordered of the Spirit. We wanted to hear from God, through whoever he might speak. We had no 'respect of persons.'"[108]

The Apostolic Faith announced, "The meetings begin about ten o'clock in the morning and can hardly stop before ten or twelve at night, and sometimes two or three in the morning, because so many are seeking, and some are slain under the power of God. People are seeking three times a day at the altar and row after row of seats have to be emptied and filled with seekers. We cannot tell how many people have been saved, and sanctified and baptized with the Holy Ghost, and healed of all manner of sicknesses."[109]

Former Methodist minister A.W. Orwig wrote, "Sermons, testimonies, prayers and songs…were usually attended with divine unction to such a degree as to move and melt hearts in every direction. The altar of prayers was generally crowded…. Many of both classes who came out of curiosity, and some possibly to ridicule, were smitten to the floor by the power of God and often wrestled in agony and prayer until they found that for which they sought—some for pardon and others for deeper experience with God."[110]

Altar calls sometimes consisted of a group of people who would suddenly or spontaneously rush to the altar to seek God. Bartleman wrote, "Someone might be speaking. Suddenly the Spirit would fall upon the congregation. God himself would give the altar call. Men would fall all over the house, like the slain in battle, or rush for the altar en masse, to seek God. The scene often resembled a forest of fallen trees. Such a scene cannot be imitated. I never saw an altar call given in those early days. God himself would call them. And the preacher knew when to quit. When God spoke, we all obeyed. It seemed a fearful thing to hinder or grieve the Spirit. The whole place was steeped in prayer. God was in His holy temple. It was for man to keep silent."[111]

E.S. Williams, who later became an evangelist, pastor, and General Superintendent of the Assemblies of God, tried to explain the Azusa Street altar calls: "I wish I could describe what I saw. Prayer and worship were everywhere. The altar area was filled with seekers; some were kneeling; others were prone to the floor; some were speaking in tongues. Everyone was doing something; all seemingly were lost in God. I simply stood and looked, for I had never seen anything like it."[112]

THE SANCTIFICATION EXPERIENCE

Though some received salvation, sanctification, Spirit baptism, and spoke in tongues in a single service, most only received one experience at a time. The sanctification experience was believed to be, not a total eradication of the sin nature, but God removing or rendering inoperative the basic desire to sin inherited from Adam, thus making it possible for a Christian to live free from sin. This experience often included public displays of tears, groaning, crying over past sins, or what Parham called "the gymnastic contortions of the Holy Rollers, who throw fits, perform somersaults, roll and kick in the straw or dust or upon the floor of the meeting house."[113]

Since the sanctification experience often involved jerking, twisting, shaking, rolling, or groveling on the floor, the term "Holy Rollers" became popularized. One Azusa eyewitness said, "The demonstrations are not the shouting, clapping or jumping so often seen in camp meetings. There is a shaking such as the early Quakers had and which the old Methodists called the 'jerks.' It is while under the power of the Spirit you see the hands raised and hear speaking in tongues. While one sings a song learned from heaven with a shining face, the tears will be trickling down other faces."[114] Other times, sanctification could be a festive celebration complete with singing, shouting, clapping, leaping, and dancing.

THE HOLY GHOST EXPERIENCE

For many, the "baptism with the Holy Ghost" experience, which was not considered a "third work of grace" but a "gift of power" to assist the saved and sanctified believer in the ministry of the gospel, had almost the opposite effect. Alpha Rosa, an evangelist from the Cape Verde Islands, said, "The power of God came upon me until I dropped to the floor. I was under the power of God for about an hour and a half, and it was there that all pride, and self, and conceit disappeared, and I was really dead to the world, for I had Christ within in His fulness. I was baptized with the Holy Ghost and spoke in a new tongue."[115]

Glenn Cook, who had persistently tried to receive the Holy Spirit at the meetings for five weeks, said, "When I had just about given up all hope, the Holy Ghost fell on me as I lay in bed at home. I seemed to be in a trance for about twenty-four hours and the next day in the meeting began to speak in tongues."[116]

William Durham had a similar experience. He said, "Suddenly, the power of God descended upon me, and I went down under it. I have no language to describe what took place, but it was wonderful. It seemed

William Durham in 1906. After receiving the baptism in the Holy Spirit with speaking in tongues at Azusa Street in 1907, Durham transformed his Chicago North Avenue Mission into a center for Pentecostal revival in the Midwest.

Photo: Flower Pentecostal Heritage Center.

to me that my body had suddenly become porous, and that a current of electricity was being turned on me from all sides; and for two hours I lay under His mighty power, and yet I knew I was not baptized yet."[117] The following evening he again fell to the floor for two hours.

Then, on the third night, for three hours he felt God's power touching him and causing him to quake, beginning with his arms, then moving throughout his body, and finishing with his vocal organs, speaking in unknown tongues. He said, "I arose, perfectly conscious outwardly and inwardly that I was fully baptized in the Holy Ghost, and the devil can never tempt me to doubt it…. Then I had such power on me and in me as I never had before. And last but not least, I had a depth of love and sweetness in my soul that I had never even dreamed of before…a dynamo of power in me…it is fathomless, real, literal, blessed, grand. Oh, that all the world could seek and find this wonderful gift of God!"[118]

William Shepherd, a Free Methodist, said he also "fell under the mighty power of God" just two nights after Durham. The guards who came to arrest Jesus and the apostles Paul and John also fell to the ground "as dead" when in the Spirit or confronted by Christ.[119] The phrase "falling under the power" became a familiar one at Azusa Street.

WHEN TIME STOOD STILL

Meetings began at 10:00 a.m. and often lasted for hours or days. No one ever grew tired because the Spirit seemed to energize not only the meetings but also all who attended them. Fortunately, the mission was situated among shops, stables, and lumberyards, so the neighboring businesses did not complain about the all-night meetings. Even the curious and eager would come and sit for hours, listening to strange sounds, songs, and exhortations. Sounds of shouting and rejoicing could be heard and a "supernatural atmosphere" felt from blocks away.

Mrs. W.H. McGowan, a Methodist, reported that her husband worked on a team that hauled sand and gravel and would stop at noontime to watch the services at Azusa Street. One day, he became so engrossed in the meeting, when he finally looked down at his watch, it was five o'clock. Mrs. McGowan also wrote about a night meeting they both attended. She said, "One night there were five or six men and women who came in and sat down on the platform. All at once they began singing in the Spirit. I sat there spellbound. I thought I never heard such music in my life. It sounded like the angels singing."[120] According to them, time seemed to stand still at these meetings.

Kelso Glover also spoke of a night when the glory came down and he hid behind the piano, not from man but to find God. Then a flood of ecstatic utterance came over him. The next thing he remembered was someone saying, "He could go on like that all night." Finally, he opened his eyes. The place was empty, and the janitor and his wife were discussing what to do with him. Unwilling to risk losing his long-awaited experience, he closed his eyes again to gaze and praise and thank the Lord. Finally assured he would not lose his experience, he spoke in tongues all the way home.[121]

LIKE THE WELSH REVIVAL

The Spirit-led meetings at Azusa Street resembled those of the Welsh Revival, which had taken place half a world away and just one year prior. One Welsh reporter wrote that though a thousand or two would often attend the services, order reigned: "The meetings…were absolutely without any human direction or leadership. 'We must obey the

Spirit' is the watchword of Evan Roberts. Evan kept telling everyone to 'pray, obey, and surrender totally to the Spirit.' Three-fourths of the meeting consists of singing. No one uses a hymnbook. No one gives out a hymn…. People pray and sing; give testimonies; exhort as the Spirit moves them…. I have seen nothing like it."[122] Another wrote, "The revival is born along by the billowing waves of sacred songs…. It is the singing, not the preaching that is the instrument which is most efficacious in striking the hearts of men."[123]

On Monday evening, October 31, 1904, Evan Roberts, full of the Holy Spirit, commenced a series of prayer meetings at which he made urgent appeals for people to repent of their sinful state and confess Jesus Christ as their Savior and Lord. The Great 1904-05 Welsh Revival was under way, and before it ended, hundreds of thousands in Wales and across the world were affected.

Photo: welshrevival.org.

Evan always sought the Spirit's leading for a service, often remaining quiet and in the background unless prompted by the Spirit to speak, exhort, pray, or lead. Most of the time, he simply urged the people to "obey the Spirit" and then remained silent, letting others break in one after another. One time, he interrupted the singing only to say, "We may sing all night without saving. It is prayer that tells, that saves, and that brings heaven down among us. Pray, friends, pray."[124]

The Spirit always kept the meetings peaceful and orderly. When asked to reveal his revival secrets, Evan replied, "I have no secret, ask and ye shall receive." Then later, when asked again, he replied, "It is certainly beyond my power to instigate a fresh revival, for revival can alone be given by the Holy Spirit of God when the conditions are fulfilled.... Bend the church and save the world."[125]

Also, speaking in tongues was fairly new to Los Angeles but had previously occurred in Wales just a year prior. William F.P. Burton, who would become a Pentecostal pioneer in Great Britain and cofounder of the Congo Evangelistic Mission in Zaire, reported hearing speaking in tongues for the first time at the Welsh Revival.[126] John G. Lake also connected the Azusa Street Revival to the Welsh Revival, saying, "in many instances during the Welsh revival people were baptized in the Holy Ghost and spoke in tongues. In our assembly at Johannesburg there is a young Welsh missionary who testifies that he was personally acquainted with a number of these, and heard them speak in tongues during the Welsh revival.... The same wave of spirituality that touched Wales crossed the seas to America and a deeper manifestation of God took place."[127]

CHAPTER 5

THE DELUGE

By the summer of 1906, meetings were continuous day and night as thousands from all classes, races, and walks of life began crowding inside and outside the tiny 40 by 60-foot warehouse. Crowds grew to as many as 1,500 on Sundays. Many listened for hours hoping to catch a glimpse or snippet of what was happening inside.

Within two months, 500 to 700 people of all races were reportedly attending the "jammed full" meetings.[128] Others crowded in the lobby, while many more sat in the low windows or peered in through the windows and open door while standing on the boardwalk outside. *The Apostolic Faith* confirmed, "In a short time God began to manifest His power and soon the building could not contain the people."[129] About a third of those who came were pastors and evangelists. A.G. and Lillian Garr had to close their meetings at the Burning Bush Hall. Pastor Smale had to visit the mission to find his own congregation.

A.G. Osterberg recalled, "When the place was full Sunday morning, I would be safe in saying there were 750 to 800 persons inside and 400 to 500 outside. All day long on Sunday there would be a crowd, from 7:00 in the morning. There would be approximately 1500 persons around there all day."[130] Osterberg estimated as many as 21,300 attended the services and up to 800 crowded into the building at a time. *The Los Angeles Daily Times* said, "The room was crowded almost to suffocation."[131]

Bartleman wrote, "There were far more white people than black people coming. The 'color line' was washed away in the blood."[132] William Manley recounted, "About twenty-five colored people and about three hundred white people all one in the Spirit."[133] Glenn Cook said, "The crowds kept increasing until the people could not get in the building. It was on a little used side street, and soon the street was filled with people from every walk of life and every nationality." He said, "Over twenty different nationalities were present, and they were all in perfect accord and unity of the Spirit."[134]

AN ACTS 2 REPEAT

Frank Bartleman recorded several instances in which people of different nationalities who came to Azusa Street heard others speaking in their native languages without learning the languages. Sister Prince, an African American volunteer staff member, spoke in perfect German to two German-born immigrants who later testified to its authenticity. A young African American woman, who knew only English, spoke to a Reverend S.J. Mead, who had recently returned from the mission field in Africa, in the dialect of an African tribe with which he was familiar. Reverend Mead then repeated back to her the exact same words she spoke in the African dialect to the satisfaction of all who were present.[135]

Brother Burt, a missionary from India, was at the altar seeking the baptism in the Holy Spirit when he heard a white man near him speaking in an Indian dialect. His message was so assuring to Brother Burt that he immediately received his baptism, as the fire of God went through him in a most wonderful way. A few days later, Brother Burt heard a white sister speaking in another Indian dialect with which he was familiar and was able to interpret what she said.

A Reverend Joseph H. Kelley, who had recently returned to St. Louis from the mission field in the Philippines, heard about the Azusa Street Revival and came to Los Angeles to "expose the tongue deception." But soon after arriving, a little white sister spoke to him in the tongue of a hostile remote tribe in the Philippines in which he had labored. Knowing this language was unknown in this part of the world, he nearly fell off his chair. So he went upstairs and asked for a private room where he prayed for forgiveness. The next day he returned to the upper room praying for Pentecost, when another white sister spoke to him in another Filipino dialect with which he was familiar, saying, "This is that which was spoken by the prophet Joel..." (quoting from Acts 2:16.) He also was swept away by the experience.[136]

Former Methodist minister, A.W. Orwig, shared of a woman who attended the Azusa Street Mission and reportedly crossed a street one day when she saw her grocer, a Frenchman, crossing in the opposite direction. She greeted him in the French language, and, utterly surprised, he asked, "Since when have you been able to speak French?" To this she replied, "I do not know that I spoke French, for I don't understand a word of that language." To this the man answered, "You certainly spoke in very excellent French, warning me to repent of my sins and to give my heart and life to God."[137]

A.H. Post, a Baptist minister who received the Holy Spirit at Azusa Street wrote, "As you see, this Pentecost is not the gift of tongues, but, as on that Pentecost recorded in the second chapter of Acts, the gift of tongues was a sign and a powerful and practical witnessing agency."[138]

Bartleman wrote such instances "were too numerous...to mention."[139] George Studd, who joined the mission later, wrote, "Los Angeles has a cosmopolitan population and people of almost every nationality heard messages in their own language, and many remarkable conversions can be told of foreigners, who heard the Gospel in their own tongues."[140]

Studd told the story of a young Mexican who testified, "I have been here before and have laughed at you people, and did not believe in you; but I will never do so again. My wife is by my side and cannot speak or understand a word of English, but that young lady who gave her testimony a little time ago turned round and looking towards my wife with outstretched arms said in Spanish under the Spirit's power, 'Oh, come to Him, do come to Him now!' My wife is broken down in tears, and wants you to pray for me also."

Sixteen nationalities were represented in Jerusalem on the day of Pentecost, according to Acts 2, when each heard the 120 speak "the wonderful works of God" in their own native languages. Why should we doubt the Holy Spirit would do the same at Azusa Street where more than twenty nationalities were represented?[141]

THE UPPER ROOM

Teams of messengers were sent to the various trains when they arrived in Los Angeles to greet the out-of-towners who came to visit the mission. When they arrived, they would ask, "Have you received the baptism of the Holy Ghost?" If they answered, "Yes," they had a follow-up question, "Have you the sign?" If they answered "No" to the second question, they would invite them to the altar or upper room to pray with them to receive the Holy Spirit.

The upper room was where many people sought Pentecostal fullness and left speaking in tongues. A.C. Valdez, Sr. described the upper room tarrying meetings: "Everything about the Azusa Street Mission fascinated me—especially the prayer or 'tarrying room' on the second floor. Usually one hundred or more black, brown and white people prayerfully waited there for the Holy Spirit to come upon them.... Many times waves of glory would come over the tarrying room or meeting room,

William J. Seymour standing in front of the Azusa Street Mission at 312 Azusa Street.

Photo: Flower Pentecostal Heritage Center.

and people would cry out prayers of thanks or praise as they received the baptism in the Holy Spirit.

"Meetings used to go past midnight and into the early hours of the morning. Hours there seemed like minutes. Sometimes after a wave of glory, a lot of people would speak in tongues. Then a holy quietness would come over the place, followed by a chorus of prayer in languages we had never heard before. Many were slain in the Spirit, buckling to the floor, unconscious, in a beautiful Holy Spirit cloud, and the Lord gave them visions…. During the tarrying, we used to break out in songs about Jesus and the Holy Spirit, 'Fill Me Now,' 'Joy Unspeakable,' and 'Love Lifted Me.' …In between choruses, heavenly music would fill the hall, and we would break into tears."[142]

TRAVELERS FROM AFAR

The first issue of *The Apostolic Faith* went out to 5,000 and soon to over 50,000 subscribers around the world. The train station a half mile away continually unloaded passengers arriving from all over the continent as news of the revival spread through both the religious and secular press. Many rode trains more than 3,000 miles or horse-drawn wagons up to 500 miles.[143] Among the visitors were many seasoned Holiness ministers and missionaries who would soon spread the Pentecostal message around the world. Many of these pilgrims came from Africa, China, Japan, India, Canada, and the U.S.

The Santa Fe Railroad La Grande Station (1893-1939) on the corner of Santa Fe Avenue and East Second Street in Downtown Los Angeles was just a few blocks from the Azusa Street Mission. Slocum, J.E., Landscape Photographer, San Diego. California Historical Picture Collection.

Photo: Wikimedia/Lexlex.

Brother A.C. Atherton, a Presbyterian evangelist from Iowa, heard the glad tidings from Los Angeles, traveled 2,500 miles, and was slain under the power of God his first meeting. He said that one meeting paid for his entire trip. Afterward, he received the baptism in the Holy Spirit and spoke in tongues, then went home filled with a great cry to spread the good news.[144]

Many travelers from afar had to ask directions to the Apostolic Faith Mission. Common responses were, "Oh, you mean the Holy Rollers," or "It is the colored church you mean?"[145] Some reportedly fell out in the Spirit or spoke in tongues as soon as they walked across the platform or exited the train. Brother David Garcia, who lived a half mile from the station, saw this, then ran to the warehouse to get Frank Bartleman, and the two witnessed the glorious sight.[146]

THE HOLY SPIRIT TRACTOR BEAM

One train station worker said this was a regular occurrence. Others could be seen falling in the streets or speaking in tongues within blocks of the mission, while still others reported being healed before reaching the building. Many said, "the atmosphere changed," or they were "seized with conviction" when they arrived within a few blocks of the mission, and then the Holy Spirit would "pull" them along, like a tractor beam, the rest of the way.[147] A.C. Valdez, Sr., who came with his mother, wrote, "As we came within a block of the two-story, white painted building, I felt a 'pulling sensation.' I couldn't have turned away if I wanted to."[148]

Valdez further explained: "Hardly ever did the Azusa Street Mission advertise in newspapers about its services. People heard about them through word of mouth. In the same way that my mother and I felt a strong pull toward the mission, so did others. Many who came said they knew nothing about Azusa Street and the Holy Spirit meetings until they had visions of the mission and were instructed to go there. Others were moved by an invisible force to attend."[149] Another participant said, "That old Methodist Church building was a real power house. You could feel the power of God for blocks away."[150]

Valdez even shared a testimony about two would-be saboteurs who planned to disrupt the meetings: "When they were three blocks from the mission, their jaws locked so that they couldn't talk over their plan of action. They became panicky, because now they were sure that a supernatural power had done this to them. Try as they might to turn back, some force kept them walking straight to the mission, where they tiptoed inside to a bench and sat down." Valdez said, "That night the men who had planned to wreck the meeting left the mission in joy" having both been converted and filled with the Holy Spirit.[151]

M.L. Ryan, editor of a religious paper in Salem, Oregon, who would later lead a team of Azusa missionaries to China, likened the draw to Azusa Street to the star over Bethlehem. He said, "Converts from all quarters of the globe are arriving constantly not knowing why they come nor the impelling cause…they are just moved by the Spirit to go to Los Angeles and when there are directed to their destination, the Azusa Street stable."[152]

Bartleman wrote, "Conviction was mightily on the people. They would fly to pieces even on the street, almost without provocation. A very 'dead line' seemed to be drawn around 'Azusa Mission' by the Spirit."[153] Bartleman continued: "The work was getting clearer and stronger at Azusa. God was working mightily. It seemed that everyone had to go to Azusa. Missionaries were gathered there from Africa, India, and the islands of the sea. Preachers and workers had crossed the continent and come from distant lands with an irresistible drawing to Los Angeles…. They had come up for 'Pentecost,' though they little realized it. It was God's call."[154] He later added, "God has spoken to His servants in all parts of the world and has sent many of them to Los Angeles, representing every nation under heaven. Once more, as of old, they are come up for Pentecost, to go out again into all the world with the glad message of salvation."[155]

Similar occurrences happened in the Old Testament when King Saul learned that David was hiding in Naioth with Samuel's school of the prophets. He sent messengers to arrest David and bring him back.

However, upon arrival when they saw the prophets prophesying, they, too, began to prophesy. Saul sent messengers a second and a third time, but they also prophesied. After three failed attempts, King Saul decided to go to Naioth himself. He prophesied all the way there, then upon arrival, tore off his clothes and prophesied in Samuel's presence. This caused the rumor to be spread throughout the land: "Is Saul also among the prophets?"[156] Like Samuel's school of the prophets, the Azusa Street Mission became an irresistible contagion for many, and like Saul, many fell under its power and influence along the way.

COUNTERFEIT SPIRITS

Of course, evangelists, missionaries, and commoners were not the only ones drawn to Azusa Street. Before long, spiritualists, hypnotists, charlatans, or anyone else who felt they needed to bring "correction" to the movement also began converging on the meetings and trying their influence. However, whenever Seymour or one of the elders tried to step in and take control, that only drew more attention to the enemy, causing fear, and the Spirit would stop moving. So they learned to just back off, pray, and continue to let the Spirit lead the services. A West African parable likens the discerning of spirits to holding an egg. Such delicate balance is needed whenever handling a move of God.[157]

Bartleman wrote, "Presumptuous men would sometimes come among us. Especially preachers who would try to spread their opinions. But their effort was short-lived. The breath would be taken from them. Their minds would wander, their brains reel. Things would turn black before their eyes. They could not go on. I never saw one get by with it in those days. They were up against God. No one cut them off; we simply prayed—the Holy Spirit did the rest."[158]

Bartleman even called Los Angeles the "American Jerusalem" because so many sects and cults were attracted to the city. Like Simon the sorcerer in Acts, many came and tried to imitate the tongues speech that was attracting so many people. Seymour called them "the spirits." Sometimes Seymour would be upstairs resting during a service and discern that there were counterfeit spirits at work in the service downstairs. Then he would run downstairs to cast out the demons and restore order back to the service. Seymour once wrote, "God has told us in His precious Word that we should know a tree by its fruit. Wherever we find the real, we find the counterfeit also. But praise God for the real."[159]

Bartleman wrote, "Discernment was not perfect, and the Enemy got some advantage that brought reproach to the work.... The combined forces of hell were set determinedly against us in the beginning. It was not all blessing.... As always, the Devil combed the country for crooked spirits to destroy the work if possible. But the fire could not be smothered. Gradually, the tide arose in victory. From a small beginning, a very little flame was kindled.... It was soon noised abroad that God was working at Azusa, and all kinds of people began to come to the meetings. Many were curious and unbelieving, but others were hungry for God. The newspapers began to ridicule and abuse the meetings, thus giving us much free advertising. This brought the crowds. The Devil overdid himself again. Outside persecution never hurt the work. We had the most to fear from the working of evil spirits within."[160]

Dr. Larry Martin, author of *The Complete Azusa Street Library*, shared a vision a resident of Los Angeles had before this great revival came. In the vision, he saw individual fires springing up and gathering to form a solid wall of flames. Then he saw a preacher trying to put the fire out with a gunny sack, but his efforts were futile against the growing inferno. This vision was later reported in *The Apostolic Faith* with the following comment added: "The man with the wet gunny sack is here also, but his efforts only call attention to the fire."[161]

Regarding Satan's counteracting works, Frank Bartleman quoted several leaders and theologians of revivals past. He quoted John Wesley who wrote, "Be not alarmed that Satan sows tares among the wheat of Christ. It has ever been so, especially on any remarkable outpouring of the Spirit, and ever will be, until the Devil is chained for a thousand years. Till then he will always ape and endeavor to counteract the work of the Spirit of Christ."

Then quoting Adam Clark, the great biblical scholar, theologian, and commentator, Bartleman wrote, "In great revivals of religion, it is almost impossible to prevent wildfire from getting in among the true fire." Then finally quoting American theologian, Dr. Seiss, he wrote, "Never, indeed, has there been a sowing of God on earth but it has been oversown by Satan; or a growth for Christ, which the plantings of the Wicked One did not mingle with and hinder. He who sets out to find a perfect church, in which there are no unworthy elements and no disfigurations, proposes to himself a hopeless task."

Bartleman quoted yet another writer who said, "So it has been in all ages. When the religious condition of the times called for men who were willing to sacrifice all for Christ, the demand created the supply, and there have always been found a few who were willing to be regardless reckless for the Lord. An utter recklessness concerning men's opinions and other consequences is the only attitude that can meet the needs of the present times."[162]

Dr. John G. Speicher, a medical doctor who served as overseer of Zion City under John Alexander Dowie, and who had visited Azusa Street, said the same: "At Azusa Street Mission in Los Angeles I saw and heard things that broke down my prejudice completely for I became convinced that it was no other than the wonderful power of the Holy Spirit that was working through his people. Not that all that I saw was to be accepted as such, for I saw much of the human element that entered in that caused me much distress at first, but this was so insignificant when compared with the wonderful results that I soon lost sight of the human in the more marvelous manifestations of the divine."

Addie M. Cook, a former Methodist who chronicled the work in 1907, agreed, saying, "Don't pick up a few of the devil's counterfeits and hold them up before the world as a warning against this movement, and pass right by hundreds of rich, beautiful, genuine nuggets of pure gold."[163]

CHAPTER 6

PARHAM AND SEYMOUR PART WAYS

In response to the all the spiritualists coming to the meetings, Seymour began writing urgent appeals to Parham, his spiritual father, asking him to come to Los Angeles to lead "one great union revival" and to help discern between the real and the false.[164] Unfortunately, Parham had another equally urgent request on his desk at the time, begging him to come to Zion, Illinois, where Wilbur Voliva had recently replaced John Alexander Dowie, creating much bitterness, strife, and confusion. Both needs were urgent, but after seeking God, Parham urged Seymour to continue his meetings while he went to Zion before all was lost.

At the time, Parham's Apostolic Faith Movement had roughly between 8,000 and 10,000 people while Seymour's mission had between 800 and 1,000.[165] *The Apostolic Faith* magazine at Azusa Street acknowledged this fact saying, "This work began about five years ago last January, when a company of people under the leadership of Chas. Parham, who were studying God's Word, tarried for Pentecost in Topeka, Kansas. After searching through the country everywhere, they had been unable to find any Christians that had the true Pentecostal power.... Now after five years something like 13,000 people have received this gospel."[166]

Parham wrote Seymour from Tonganoxie, Kansas, stating that he expected to be in Los Angeles on September 15, and declaring to the

Charles Parham (seated front center) with his Apostolic Faith crusade team in Bryan, Texas.

Photo: Flower Pentecostal Heritage Center.

people at Azusa: "I rejoice in God over you all, my children, though I have never seen you; but since you know the Holy Spirit's power, we are baptized by one Spirit into one body. Keep together in unity till I come, then in a grand meeting let all prepare for the outside fields. I desire, unless God directs to the contrary to meet and see all who have the full gospel when I come."[167]

PARHAM IN ZION

Before Parham arrived in Zion City, Dowie had spoken against him, and he was immediately met with opposition from Voliva. However, when Zion's grand hotel manager invited Parham to hold meetings in the hotel basement, hundreds began attending. Voliva was vehement. Parham was "winning some of our most faithful people," he cried.[168] Local newspapers described Parham as having "a pleasant and convincing manner that makes his discourse almost irresistible."[169] Parham's messages also sounded much like Dowie's: "Old-time Religion, Christ's Soon Coming, Repentance, Salvation, Healing, Sanctification, Baptism of the Holy Ghost."[170]

Voliva shut down the hotel meetings and proceeded to rent every auditorium in the city, so Parham had nowhere to go. However, convinced now more than ever that Zion needed Pentecostal blessings to bring peace and restoration, Parham split up his crusade team by scheduling multiple concurrent cottage meetings in large homes throughout the city. In one such cottage meeting, F.F. Bosworth, John G. Lake, and Marie Burgess Brown—all future Pentecostal leaders—were baptized in the Holy Spirit.

Bosworth would go on to hold healing crusades in major cities across North America, John G. Lake would go on to establish major Pentecostal and divine healing works in South Africa and the Pacific Northwest, and Marie Burgess Brown would become founder of Glad Tidings Tabernacle in New York City. Cottage meeting audiences reportedly spilled out onto the porches and lawns as thousands attended. Hundreds reported being released from bitterness and despair after receiving the baptism in the Holy Spirit and speaking in tongues. Hundreds more saw visions and responded to the call to full-time ministry.

Many have criticized Parham over the years for going to Zion instead of Azusa. However, in so doing, Parham not only permanently merged the streams of divine healing and Pentecostalism together, but also by tapping into Dowie's worldwide ministry, some five hundred independent Spirit-baptized healing ministries were launched into a worldwide harvest, essentially creating a second global thrust of Pentecostalism concurrent with Azusa.

Despite his character flaws, John Alexander Dowie positively affected thousands of lives and healed countless more, setting the stage for a second global thrust of healing revivalism concurrent with Azusa Street.

Photo: Flower Pentecostal Heritage Center.

Commenting on Parham's decision, one author wrote, "His decision to go to Zion City precipitated one of the most important religious events of the twentieth century."[171] Historian Edith Blumhofer, agreed, "In the fall of 1906, two restorationist teachings converged briefly in Zion City, Illinois. The two subsequently fragmented but their brief union resulted in the emergence of a third creative force that would survive as one of the formative influences in American Pentecostalism."[172]

PARHAM IN LOS ANGELES

By the time Parham arrived in Los Angeles in October 1906, he had already heard reports about "all the stunts common in old camp meetings among colored folks" that were happening there, including "white people imitating unintelligible, crude negroisms of the Southland, and laying it on the Holy Ghost."[173] Of course, this was disturbing to Parham, who understood tongues not as ecstatic languages, but as unlearned foreign languages, and who regarded emotionalism as extreme and fanatical.

Parham wrote, "I hurried to Los Angeles, and to my utter surprise and astonishment I found conditions even worse than I had anticipated...manifestations of the flesh, spiritualistic controls, saw people practicing hypnotism at the altar over candidates seeking baptism."[174] Parham was also offended by the interracial nature of the meetings and interracial marriages, which he believed was the chief cause of the flood in Noah's day. Before entering the building, he heard "chatterings, jabberings and screams." Without being introduced, Parham walked to the front of the mission, greeted Seymour and pronounced, "God is sick at his stomach!"[175]

Finally, after being warmly introduced by Seymour as his "Father in this gospel of the Kingdom," Parham spoke only two or three times before he began denouncing what he called "hypnotists" and "spiritualists" who had taken over the meetings.[176] Then, after being told by two of Seymour's elders that he was "not wanted in that place," Charles Fox Parham, the "father" of the "Apostolic Faith Gospel Mission," was not allowed to speak again. Now thoroughly disgusted, and much like he had done in Zion City, Parham went a few blocks away to the Women's Christian Temperance Union on Broadway and began holding his own series of meetings.

Though Parham claimed that "between two and three hundred who had been possessed of awful fits and spasms and controls in the Azusa Street work were delivered, and received the real Pentecost teachings and spake with other tongues,"[177] this time the meetings were short-lived, while the Azusa Street Revival would continue for years. After his visit to Azusa Street, Parham resigned as "projector" of the Apostolic Faith Movement and simply took his place "among the brethren to push this gospel of the kingdom as a witness to all nations."[178]

PARHAM RETURNS TO ZION

After only two months in Los Angeles, Parham returned to Zion City, this time moving his family and publication there. Parham left Warren Carothers in charge of his California mission, but Carothers' racial views, as a Texas attorney, were even more extreme than Parham's. Carothers believed that hatred and animosity between the races was the work of the Holy Spirit to prevent the mixing of races. Though Parham's California work was ultimately unsuccessful, he did succeed at causing the first major division within the Apostolic Faith movement. Mimicking Paul's criticism of the Corinthian church, one Azusa critic wrote, "Some were saying 'We are with Seymour;' others were saying, 'We are with Parham;' and still others, 'We are with Bartleman.'"[179]

In Zion, Parham was again met with opposition from Voliva, and again found success in his revival meetings—so much so that some

Zion Industries at Shiloh Tabernacle, Zion City, Illinois. Library of Congress Photo Collection, Wikimedia/Tibet Nation.

Photo: Geo. R. Lawrence Co.

urged him to begin a new movement there. Parham, however, had stated he wished only to bring peace to Zion, not more confusion and division. Though Parham moved back to Kansas in 1907, he left a thriving Pentecostal ministry in Zion consisting of many former leaders from Dowie's ministry.

Even Seymour, who had visited Zion in June of that year, said it reminded him of "Old Azusa, ten months ago," saying "people here receive the baptism in their pews while the service is going on, sometimes scores of them receive it…. There are little children from six years and on up who have the baptism with the Holy Ghost."[180]

In the end though, it was Dowie's ministry that had, in large part, allowed Pentecostalism to flourish, and it was in Pentecostalism that "the real significance of Dowie's message was preserved and expanded."[181] Even as late as the 1930s, Dr. Lilian B. Yeomans, who had once been healed under Dowie's ministry, said, "Some people say that Dr. Dowie's work is dead. No! It is more alive today than ever."[182]

PARHAM'S LATTER YEARS

Later that year, Parham was preaching in San Antonio, Texas, when news hit the wires that he had been arrested on sodomy charges. Though he was soon released and nothing was ever proven, Parham immediately accused Voliva of creating an "elaborate frame" to destroy his ministry. Nevertheless, the incident would leave a permanent mark on Parham's ministry, causing many Pentecostals to this day to distance themselves, some even refusing to recognize him as their founder. But then the Lord did forewarn him before giving him the Pentecostal blessing that it would be accompanied by "persecution" and "scandal."

Over the years, Parham has also been accused of being a racist. But that's a pretty tough accusation for a Southern white man living in an era of racism who broke Jim Crow laws to accept a black student; invited a black woman, Lucy Farrow, to preach at his meetings; and often preached in black churches himself. Parham did make racist comments, labeling the extremes at Azusa Street as "darky camp meeting stunts" and later commending the Ku Klux Klan for their promotion of religion and moral values—which they apparently displayed at the time. Nevertheless, in perspective, Parham was likely neither a civil rights activist nor a rabid racist, but as a principal founder of the Pentecostal movement, helped set the tone for interracial relations in the movement—both bad and good. Parham died in 1929.

Many Pentecostals tried to distance themselves from Parham in his later years, but the Lord forewarned him that his Pentecostal blessing would come with "persecution, hardships, trials, slander, and scandals."

Photo: Flower Pentecostal Heritage Center.

A CONTRAST IN LEADERSHIP STYLES

While Parham would spend the rest of his life denouncing Seymour and the Azusa Street Revival as a case of "spiritual power prostituted" to the "awful fits and spasms" of "holy rollers and hypnotists," Seymour felt it his duty as leader of the revival to protect the movement of God at all costs—even if that meant overriding his father in the faith.[183] Seymour had learned that whenever he tried to limit God to a certain form, culture, expression, or mode, the Spirit would invariably stop moving. Indeed, Glenn Cook later said the reason he believed Seymour did not receive the baptism in the Holy Spirit in Houston was because of confusing doctrines and the "lack of love and power" in Parham's meetings.[184]

Parham argued, "The Holy Ghost does nothing that is unnatural or unseemly, and any strained exertion of the body, mind or voice is not the work of the Holy Spirit, but of some familiar spirit, or other influence. The Holy Ghost never leads us beyond the point of self-control or the control of others, while familiar spirits or fanaticism leads us both beyond self-control and the power to help others."[185]

Parham's sensibilities were also offended at seeing black men assisting white women with prayer for baptism in the Holy Spirit or laying hands on them. He even denounced their worship as a "cross between the old-fashioned Negro worship of the South, and Holy-Rollerism."[186] After Parham said, "God was sick at his stomach," he was shown the door.

The feeling was mutual. The congregation at Azusa Street was as unhappy with Parham as he was with them. A.G. Osterberg said, "We didn't like that he told us that he was above us."[187] Seymour, on the other hand, refused to say anything negative about his mentor, stating in his newsletter two months later, "We thought of having him to be our leader...before waiting on the Lord. We can be rather hasty, especially when we are very young in the power of the Holy Spirit. We are just like a baby—full of love—and were willing to accept anyone that had the baptism with the Holy Spirit as our leader. But the Lord commenced settling us down, and we saw that the Lord should be our leader."[188]

CHAPTER 7

OPPOSITION
AND CRITICS

The *Los Angeles Record* wrote, "The 'gift of tongues' craze, which started some months ago in a tumble down, barn-like building in Azusa st., this city, has caused more than one war among the various religious denominations of the city since its noisy introduction. From the beginning, the crowds that gathered nightly at Azusa st. were made up of followers of many churches and many sects. The charm mystery, which worked like wild fire among the frequenters of these motley gatherings, extended its influence to such an extent that other churches were soon feeling the effects."[189]

Like every other historical move of God, including Pentecost, the Azusa Street Revival had more than its share of critics. Some of the local Holiness churches had lost so many members they had to close their doors and join the revival by default. Others, disturbed by the growing trend, warned their members to stay away. European Pentecostal leader Donald Gee observed: "There seems to be a law which students are compelled to observe, that the last wave of spiritual revival in the church nearly always seems to offer the greatest opposition to the oncoming wave of blessing and advance."[190]

OPPOSITION MOUNTS

Some called the police, asking them to shut down the meetings. Others reported them to the Child Welfare Agency, claiming there were unsupervised children in and around the building at all hours of the day and night. Still others complained to the health department of cramped quarters and unsanitary conditions, which they felt represented a danger to public health.

During the summer months the building grew intensely hot. The air became so foul at times, one reporter said it was "necessary to stick one's nose under the benches to get a breath of fresh air."[191] The lack of ventilation was a violation of sanitary laws. And since it had been a stable just a few months prior, the first summer of 1906 was plagued by flies.

Many individual members of the Azusa Street Mission were viewed as fanatics, fined, arrested, and jailed for being "insane." The Los Angeles Police Department even assigned special officers to monitor the mission to make sure that order was maintained. Sometimes they would even interrupt services if they got too loud or ran too late. Other times, it was their critics who were arrested for disturbing the peace.

One guy named Otto Smith created a commotion when he rose to his feet during a service and lashed out about their manner of service. In court the next day he was found guilty and fined ten dollars for disturbing the peace. The judge gave him a lengthy lecture saying that even if he did not agree with what they were doing at the mission, the U.S. Constitution guaranteed the Azusa Street worshipers freedom to worship however they please, so long as they did not break the law. That would not be the only time the police had to intervene in disagreements over worship practices or theological positions at the Azusa Street Mission.

THE MOSES OF THE PENTECOSTAL MOVEMENT

Pastor Smale of The New Testament Church originally supported and joined the movement but later denounced it, closing the church's doors to the "tongue-talkers." Phineas Bresee, founder of the Pentecostal Church of the Nazarene, declared it to be a false revival—apparently without even visiting. In 1919, he had "Pentecostal" removed from the Church of the Nazarene's name, so as not to be mistakenly associated with the likes of Azusa. Some gave the work no more than six months to live.

Azusa Street historian Cecil Robeck Jr. said, "The Los Angeles Church Federation, which represented most of the city's historic Protestant churches, held meetings hoping to compete favorably with those offered at the Azusa Street Mission."[192] Ironically, the Los Angeles Church Federation, made up almost entirely of Protestants, responded to the Azusa Street Mission the same way the Catholic Church once responded to the Protestants—with a counter reformation.

Though Pastor Smale believed tongues was a spiritual gift, not evidence of Spirit baptism, and argued that many who were baptized in the Spirit never spoke in tongues, he still allowed his members to exercise the gift of tongues, prophecy, healing, miracles, and deliverance. Thus, Joseph Smale became the ideal mediator and advocate between the Azusa Street Mission and the Los Angeles Church Federation.

Bartleman called Smale the "Moses" of the Pentecostal movement because, like Moses and the promised land, he could see it without fully entering it. Smale was convinced that what was happening at Azusa Street was the Holy Spirit but kept it all at bay to ensure that decency and order was maintained at The New Testament Church. This position would soon be magnified after a sensationalized story erupted.

A SENSATIONAL STORY

Dr. Henry Sheridan Keyes was a graduate of Harvard Medical School who had established the Emergency and General Hospital of Los Angeles (now part of LAC-USC Medical Center). Dr. Keyes was also a prominent Los Angeles society leader, a board member at the First Baptist Church, and a close friend and supporter of Pastor Smale, even leaving with him to help establish The New Testament Church. Problems erupted, however, when Dr. Keyes' sixteen-year-old daughter, Lillian, went to Azusa Street and received the baptism in the Holy Spirit there. *The Los Angeles Daily Times* saw this as a perfect opportunity to sensationalize a story—daughter of prominent Los Angeles leader attends church led by African Americans.

A *Times* reporter interviewed Dr. Keyes and was shocked to learn that he not only condoned his daughter's acts but also claimed he could speak and write in tongues himself. When the reporter asked him to demonstrate, Dr. Keyes wrote in tongues on a piece of paper, then took him to meet Mr. Lucius LeNan, an employee of the Los Angeles Brick Company, who interpreted what he wrote. To verify the claim, the reporter then took the paper to Baba Bharati, an "eminent oriental scholar," who said it was not a language he knew. The next day, a sensationalized story appeared in *The Times* accusing Dr. Keyes of fanaticism.

To make matters worse, Lillian had written two stinging prophetic letters of rebuke attacking Pastor Smale, accusing him of grieving the Holy Spirit, and warning him to give up his church work. Pastor Smale was shocked and sent subsequent letters to Dr. Keyes suggesting his daughter had become a victim of fanaticism and needed deliverance from an evil spirit. Dr. Keyes, who considered Lillian "the apple of his eye" and believed the Holy Spirit was sincerely working through her, was offended. Other sensationalized stories and sketches of Dr. Keyes and Lillian, including "chicken scratch" (writing in tongues), appeared in the paper. Once, when Lillian stood to speak at The New Testament

These cartoon caricatures appeared in the Los Angeles Times, July 23, 1906, supposedly representing the types of Pentecostals at the First New Testament Church. The photo at the right is of Elmer Fisher, pastor of the Upper Room Mission.

Cartoon caricatures of early Pentecostals from *The Los Angeles Times* July 23, 1906. On the left is Dr. Henry Keyes, center is Joseph Smale, upper right is Elmer Fisher, Smale's associate, below him is Frank Bartleman and others from The New Testament Church and Azusa Street.

Photo: Flower Pentecostal
Heritage Center.

tember 18, the *Times* asked Dr. Keyes to | timately Elmer Fisher established the Up-

Church, Pastor Smale told the congregation to ignore her, then led them in a song.

The entire incident caused a rift between Pastor Smale and Dr. Keyes, who promptly left The New Testament Church, bringing Smale's associate pastor, Elmer K. Fisher, with him to establish the Upper Room Mission on South Spring Street in September 1906. Elmer Fisher, who had also received the baptism in the Holy Spirit at the Azusa Mission in June, soon joined the weekly leadership meetings at Azusa Street and became a strong supporter of the Apostolic Faith Mission for another twelve years. Lillian eventually became an Azusa Street missionary, and then a Presbyterian missionary to China with her husband, where they remained until 1954. Pastor Smale eventually left The New Testament Church to pastor an independent Baptist church until his death in 1926.

THE FALLOUT

A.C. Valdez, Sr. wrote, "Old-line churches frowned on the Azusa Street Mission's Bible teaching, 'so-called miracles,' and 'noisy meetings.' Their members who came just once to Azusa Street services, when found out, were often asked to leave their congregations. Some churches tried hard to get the City of Los Angeles to close down the Azusa Street Mission, but they failed. Individuals, too, worked to break up meetings."[193] Valdez said, "Not only did people try to break up meetings, they sometimes tried to beat up individuals who left their churches for the Azusa Street Mission."

Valdez's friend, Owen "Irish" Lee, after being baptized in the Spirit and speaking in tongues using sign language, left the Catholic Church for Azusa Street.[194] Lee was followed to the mission by a Catholic woman and her accomplice—a giant of a man who was angry he had left the Catholic Church. They brought a rope with them to Azusa Street to hang Lee from a lamppost after the meeting. When the meeting ended, they went outside where the man spat and punched Lee in the face. But Lee, who was also a streetfighter, did not strike him back. Instead, as the man was about to hit Lee again, an invisible force stopped him, jolted him, and pushed him to the gutter. A few nights later, the woman and her accomplice went back to the mission and were both saved.[195] Owen "Irish" Lee later brought Pentecost to Ireland.

THE HOLY SPIRIT, THE DEFENDER

Many others, intending to bring ridicule or correction to the meetings, after visiting gained completely new perspectives. Some were knocked to the floor where they seemed to wrestle with unseen opponents for hours only to rise later convicted of their sin and error. One such testimony was printed in *The Apostolic Faith*: "I was warned by leaders that it was of the devil, but I came and got a touch of heaven in my soul."[196] Another wrote, "Preachers go there to condemn it, but have to go back and acknowledge it is of God."[197] Countless people came to Azusa Street intending to either break up or destroy the young movement. Many "Sauls of Tarsus" felt they were doing God a favor until blinded by unseen forces on their "road to Damascus" experiences where they were suddenly faced with God Himself.

Interestingly, the name *Azusa* is derived from the Native American Tongva word *Asuksanga* which translated simply means "place of the skunk." Tongva was the language of the Uto-Aztecan tribe which once occupied Los Angeles' San Gabriel Valley, where skunks were evidently once plentiful. Skunks are also well-known for their unseen God-given defense mechanism, which can quickly overwhelm, overpower, and defeat natural enemies and predators alike. Likewise, the unseen Holy Spirit became a great defender and protector of His work at "Azusa." Even the old Jack Benny joke: the name "AZUSA" is an abbreviation for "A to Z in the USA" is befitting since everyone from "A to Z in the USA" came to Azusa Street.[198]

One foreign reporter who was asked to write a humorous story on the "circuslike" atmosphere at Azusa, met a young woman at the meeting who told him how she had received the Holy Spirit. Then she spoke in tongues to the reporter. After the meeting, the reporter asked the woman how she had learned the language of his native country. She told him she did not have a clue what she was saying. He then told her she had given an accurate account of his entire sinful life in his native tongue. He immediately renounced his sins and accepted Jesus. However, when he returned home and told his boss he could not write a false story ridiculing the movement but offered to write a truthful report instead, he was fired.

Dr. John G. Speicher, who had been part of Dowie's ministry and left Zion, Illinois, to go to Los Angeles and condemn the work, described himself as a "skeptic" and "critic" who "abominated" the Pentecostal movement. After arriving at Azusa Street, however, he testified, "I soon lost sight of the human in the more marvelous manifestations of the divine."[199]

William Manley, founder of the Household of God Holiness movement in Oakland, visited Azusa Street for the first time in August 1906. Also a skeptic at first, he said, "God had full control from first to last." The Holiness editor was so touched by the moving of the Spirit there, he told his readers, "This is the most heavenly place I ever was in. My soul is charmed and filled, and is dancing for joy. This is God. Wonderful! Wonderful!! Wonderful!!!"[200]

Manley also testified of a "boy from India, about 22 years old, who could only speak a few words in English," but after being "converted, sanctified and baptized with the Holy Spirit" had "been given the English language" and spoke "the wonderful works of God in our own tongue."[201] Similarly, many of the participants in the Welsh Revival who could not ordinarily speak Welsh reportedly had supernatural experiences during the revival in which they were able to pray, testify, or sing at length in fluent Welsh.

Methodist minister A.W. Orwig wrote, "Not all…who gladly attended the meetings and derived profit thereby, fully or at all accepted this teaching. Nor did they specifically identify themselves with the movement…what surprised me…was the presence of so many persons from the different churches…some…attending…mocked and cavilled also as on the day of Pentecost. The so called 'Holiness People,' who perhaps thought they had all there was to be obtained, found the meetings a great blessing to them. Others of this class stood aloof…because the occasional speaking with other tongues proved a stumbling block to them."[202]

HANDLING THE FALLOUT

Rachel Sizelove, who had come from the Free Methodist Church, said the Lord knew her church would not receive the Holy Spirit, which is why He sent her to Azusa Street. She said she had to die to the opinions of her church before God could baptize her with the Holy Spirit, and she did not realize in the beginning how vehemently the other churches would fight it. The Free Methodist pastor was sure that what was happening at Azusa Street "was not of God; it was just wild fire; it was fanaticism of the rankest and wildest kind."[203]

Those who did go, however, he denounced without hesitation, claiming they had "merited the displeasure of God and were often turned over to Satan who was allowed to deceive them." What was his reasoning? "Why if God had wanted to do anything new here in Los Angeles He would certainly have chosen our church in which to do it for you know that we have never compromised, and we have always laid emphasis upon separation from the world and upright living. If God had been going to pour out His Spirit as He poured out the Holy Ghost in the days of the apostles He would have done it in our church."[204] Evidently, they were *not* the humblest.

In contrast, one prominent Baptist preacher and high official at the principle church of Los Angeles stood up one Sunday afternoon at the Azusa Street Mission and publicly declared how he had wished the same holy fire and marvelous works of grace would break out in his church and other churches. That took *great* humility.

A.G. Garr, who pastored the Burning Bush Mission, did one better. He locked the doors of his mission one evening, stood on the front steps and told his people, "Do not attend here tonight. We do not have the power of God; let us go to Azusa Street Mission, where they are enjoying the presence of God." The people followed him to the mission.[205] That took even greater humility. Garr went on to become the first worldwide missionary of Azusa Street and eventually established more than a hundred churches across the U.S.

THE HOLY ROLLERS

One local paper likened Azusa Street to the recent "Holy Rollers" cult in Oregon and Washington. The cult's leader, Franz Edmund Creffield, was a German American and former Salvationist. Creffield, known to his followers as "Joshua" or "Captain Creffield," believed he was the second coming of Jesus and used his claim to commit lewd acts against his female followers. The only similarity between these "Holy Rollers" and Azusa Street was late night meetings and exuberant acts of worship. The cult made national headlines in April 1906 (the same month the Azusa Street Revival began) when Creffield was murdered by the brother of one of his female followers. His follower then murdered her own brother.

Edmund "Joshua" Creffield, a German American religious cult leader, who broke with the Salvation Army to form his own "Bride of Christ Church" in Portland, Oregon. The locals nicknamed them the "Holy Rollers" cult. Oregon State Penitentiary prison photo, c. 1906

Photo: Wikimedia/Carrite.

The enemy can always be counted on to raise up counterfeits to dissuade people from the real. This was not the first or last time the term "Holy Rollers" was used. Early Wesleyan enthusiasts were called "holy rollers" and later wore it as a badge of honor. Many in the Holiness and Pentecostal movements were eventually called "holy rollers" as well.

GREAT DEFENDERS OF THE MOVEMENT

George B. Studd, a famous British cricket player who attended the Azusa Street Revival in 1908 and kept a daily diary, was never a critic but was initially cautious. Later, he became a great defender of the movement, even helping to pay for the Azusa Street property. To those who believed speaking in tongues was false, he wrote, "If there was the spurious, there must also be the genuine; for Satan is the wisest of counterfeits, and he would certainly never trouble to imitate something which either did not exist at all, or had no value."[206]

To those who accused the Azusa Street Mission of being the "devil's work," he offered the following five-point observation refuting their claim:

1. They always honored the blood of Jesus.
2. They honored the Holy Ghost, giving Him room and expecting Him to work.
3. They were certainly missionary people.
4. They were earnestly looking for the coming of the Lord.
5. They took no collections; neither did they ask for money.

His conclusion? "That does not look like the devil's work; I only wish that every church and mission had the same solid foundation stones."[207] Studd continued, "It was not the gifts nor the outward manifestations which attracted me; but it was the grace and the Christliness which I saw on the baptized ones whom I knew.... So now these baptized people made my heart hungry for more of Jesus; and it was to Him I sought."[208]

George B. Studd was one of three famous "Studd Brothers" cricket players from Britain. He helped purchase the buildings for the Peniel and Azusa Street Missions, supported the Upper Room Mission, chronicled the Azusa Revival in 1908 through his daily diary, and became a great defender of early Pentecostalism.

Photo: Flower Pentecostal Heritage Center.

Studd also interviewed people like Reverend Gerald Bailly, a practicing Pentecostal missionary. He asked him what permanent spiritual value Holy Spirit baptism had brought to his life. Bailly replied, "Oh, so much. First, the dread I had of going back to Venezuela and taking up the work there again without more spiritual power than I had before is all gone.... Second, I never had such a personal revelation of the Lord Jesus.... Third...I...have more liberty and unction in my private devotions."

Studd then asked if speaking in tongues had recurred since his baptism and, if so, to what practical value? Bailly replied, "Yes, the Spirit has spoken a good many times since, generally when I am praying. And oh, you cannot imagine the holy awe that comes on my soul as I realize that God Himself is speaking through my throat and using my tongue; for it surely is God the Holy Ghost speaking. And I cannot tell you what an uplift comes to my faith whenever He thus speaks."[209]

Another defender of the Azusa Street Mission was Seeley D. Kinne, a veteran Holiness minister and publisher from St. Louis. He said, "[I have] been among the holiness people over thirty-two years, and heard many of the best preachers in that movement and attended some of its great camp meetings. I was in Azusa Mission soon after it opened. I knew God was there."

Kinne continued: "When Pentecostal meetings are kept in the Spirit there is ordinarily more power than we ever saw in holiness or other meetings, and often they rise into a state of worship, revelation of the Divine presence, waves of joy, victory, love and praise with which we never saw anything to compare in the past. Pages could be written of the sights and scenes, many of them surpassing description. God has indeed visited men once more in these last days. We have never seen such melting and breaking of hearts of both saved and sinner as frequently occurs in Pentecostal meetings. The outward visible glory of God is at times revealed." Like Studd, Kinne mentioned a "stronger missionary spirit" and a "deeper revelation of the personal Christ."[210]

New Testament translator A.S. Worrell wrote of Pentecostal critics: "Those who have the wisdom to distinguish between the true and the false, and have the practical common sense not to reject the whole movement because of the Satanic counterfeits that are intermingled with the genuine Pentecostal coin, those who take the good and reject the spurious, have great possibilities of usefulness before them in this movement.

"Those, however, who are suspicious and critical, and are looking for perfection in human instruments, will be likely to let the present opportunity go by unimproved; and, all unconsciously to themselves, will, most likely, enter the realm of spiritual deterioration, and find themselves losers, rather than gainers, because they have not made the most of their opportunities."[211]

And particularly to those Holiness people who rejected the movement, Worrell wrote: "It is plain to be seen that a mighty uplifting power has come into their lives; differing, in some respects, from the receiving of the Holy Ghost for character-development. It should be remembered, that the Holy Savior never did any mighty works, until the Holy Spirit came upon Him; and, what He did in His official capacity, He seems to have done in the power of the Holy Spirit.[212] And, if this was true of Jesus, surely His disciples can hope to do efficient work for Him only as they are imbued with power by the same Spirit.

"Of course, there is more or less in every Pentecostal meeting we have attended, that could be referred to Satan or to 'the flesh;' but this is exactly what was to be expected; for where the Holy Spirit works, Satan works. It is to be hoped, however, that, as the gift of discerning of spirits, and the power to cast them out, are, bestowed upon God's true, Pentecostal people, they will be able to separate the false from the true; that so the genuine Pentecostal power and blessed fruits will show forth in the lives of God's fully equipped people."[213]

THE CONTINUED FALLOUT

The Burning Bush Holiness Church of Los Angeles all but disappeared when its pastor, A.G. Garr, went to the Azusa Street Mission, then left to serve as an Apostolic Faith missionary to the world beginning in India. The Elysian Heights Nazarene Church sustained significant losses when it expelled those who had accepted the Azusa Street doctrine. The Second Pentecostal Church of the Nazarene also suffered heavy damage when its pastor left with a large percentage of the congregation after they were baptized in the Spirit. The Free Methodist Church in Hermon and Peniel Mission also sustained heavy blows. The director of the Union Rescue Mission of Downtown Los Angeles was fired after attending an Apostolic Faith camp meeting and being baptized in the Spirit.

The Azusa Street Mission's motivation was never to harm other churches but to bring unity. In fact, it was the first totally integrated

The sign on the building read, "Apostolic Faith Gospel Mission. Whoso-ever Will, May Come. Let Brotherly-love Prevail."

Photo: Flower Pentecostal Heritage Center.

church in America. The painted sign on the side of the building aptly read, "Whoso-ever Will, May Come. Let Brotherly-love Prevail." And they were serious. Brother David Garcia said if Seymour came downstairs and saw that the people had segregated themselves into racial groups, he would insist that they mix and mingle and move around before the service could continue.[214]

ERASING THE LINES

Most of the criticisms launched against the revival had to do with the blurring or erasing of lines. Since Seymour believed the Spirit of God resided in every believer, leading and guiding them and not just the leaders, he allowed anyone to speak during the services, thus erasing the traditional lines between clergy and laity. Having "Spirit-led" services also erased the boundaries of established ecclesiastical order, structure, and liturgy.

For the first few years, they did not even collect offerings. Instead, signs on the wall over the mailboxes read, "Settle with the Lord." Still, the people were taught to tithe and give freely and generously, and they did. A.C. Valdez, Sr. said he could not understand at first why metal mailboxes were nailed to the walls, yet they were always filled with coins and paper money, and though no preacher, including Seymour, asked for money, those who were blessed gave generously.[215]

Virtually everything was left to the spontaneous move of God. Since speaking in tongues as ecstatic languages was allowed, all lines of human constraint and sophistication were set aside. One critic wrote, "[They sang] in a faraway tune that sounded very unnatural and repulsive."[216] Another wrote that "some of the brightest and best" members of the church had fallen into the "fearful delusion" of speaking in tongues.[217]

BREAKING BARRIERS

There was a blurring of all economic and social barriers as rich and poor, educated and uneducated worshiped together. The mere fact that some were illiterate was considered conclusive evidence by others of their blatant error. Many intoxicated derelicts stumbled into the mission, but wealthy railroad tycoons, like Henry E. Huntington and his wife, also showed up in their beautiful buggies. Huntington was a big promoter of the City of Los Angeles and owner of the Pacific Electric Railway. Former Methodist minister, A.W. Orwig, was surprised to see so many "educated and refined" people there when he first visited. He said pastors, evangelists, foreign missionaries, and "others of high positions all took part in the services in one way or another."[218]

Henry E. Huntington, owner of the Central Pacific Railroad and Pacific Electric Railway and a major business leader and booster of Los Angeles, was no doubt curious about the great attraction on Azusa Street. George Grantham Bain Collection, Library of Congress Photograph Collection.

Photo: Wikimedia/Alexcoldcasefan.

Florence Crawford, a former Methodist class leader and prominent citizen of Los Angeles, had previously worshiped with the Presbyterians, Christian and Missionary Alliance, and The New Testament Church. She and a friend had agreed if they could ever find a people who preached the whole Word from Genesis to Revelation, they would follow them to the ends of the earth.

One day her friend knocked on her door, "Sister Crawford, I have found the people." She said, "Where are they?" "They are way down in the lower part of Los Angeles." She said, "Take me to them." So they went to Azusa Street. Crawford said it was "an old barnlike building with only an old board laid on two chairs for an altar. The floor was carpeted with sawdust; the walls and beams blackened with smoke. I looked around to see if anybody saw me go in, but I would not have cared if the whole world saw me go out. I had found a people that had the experience I wanted."[219]

Florence Crawford, along with many others, received both her sanctification and Holy Spirit baptism experience at Azusa Street. From that time on, she said her burning desire was to spread the message of Pentecost with the power and anointing of the Holy Spirit for Christian service.

Photo: Flower Pentecostal Heritage Center.

Even critics acknowledged the Pentecostal message had captured the hearts of "some of the brightest and best."[220] A.S. Worrell, a Baptist scholar, theologian, Bible translator, and president of three colleges, attended. As did Dr. Henry Keyes, founder and president of the Los Angeles Emergency and General Hospital, and Professor Carpenter, head of the math department at Los Angeles High School.

Bringing revival to the streets and marketplace also blurred the lines between religious and secular space. The age barrier was broken as youth as young as twelve years old ministered to the sick. But ultimately it was the blurring of the races and sexes that drew the most criticism. Blacks and whites mixing and men and women kissing and hugging one another were considered repulsive to many. One woman reported being incensed at the sight of a colored woman with her arms around a white man's neck while "praying for him."[221] However, for every one person who criticized the movement, it seemed a thousand more came and believed in their work—and it's no wonder after hearing the countless stories and testimonies that occurred over a span of several years.

CHAPTER 8

THE REVIVAL SPREADS

By late summer 1906, members and attendees had established several affiliated missions in Los Angeles and the surrounding areas. Many more were distributing tracts, setting up tents, renting storefronts, and holding meetings on streetcorners or near trolley stops in Pasadena, Monrovia, Sawtelle, Whittier, Anaheim, Long Beach, and San Pedro. By September, scores of evangelists had been sent to San Jose, Santa Rosa, San Francisco, San Diego, Portland, Spokane, and Seattle, and by December, Denver, Colorado Springs, Indianapolis, Minneapolis, Cleveland, Akron, Chattanooga, Norfolk, and New York.

STREET EVANGELISM

Many sang and preached on street corners, but their favorite locations were East First and San Pedro, a block and a half away, or East Second and San Pedro, a half block away from the mission. A few of the Azusa Street evangelists were arrested on charges of disturbing the peace. One was taken into custody when a witness saw an angel stand by him in court. Another lady sang all the way to jail, then shouted and prayed in jail. The authorities were anxious to release her. Another man was arrested for speaking in tongues, then spoke in tongues in court and several, including the judge, recognized the language. He was also released.

The streets of Los Angeles were ripe for revival in 1906. Broadway, looking north from Sixth Street, Los Angeles, c. 1906. The street is crowded with people, horse-drawn carriages, street vendors, and streetcars. California Historical Society Collection, 1860-1960

Photo: Wikimedia/Fæ.

Henry Prentice conducted an open-air meeting in Whittier. However, since he did not receive offerings for support, he was arrested for homelessness. After explaining Matthew 10 in court, how Jesus instructed His disciples to take neither gold nor silver, the judge became exasperated and the prosecuting attorney dropped the charges saying, he would not face him for "all the money in the United States."[222] The case was dismissed, and both the judge and attorney found their way to Azusa Street and were saved.

Henry McLain was arrested for having a prayer meeting in his home and disturbing the peace. He was convicted and chose a thirty-day jail sentence of hard labor, shoveling dirt on a Mexican chain gang. Each evening, after the meal, McLain conducted a Bible study, occasionally bursting out in tongues as the prisoners wept bitterly. On one such occasion, he opened his Bible to Isaiah 55, burst out in tongues, and read the entire chapter in Spanish. He did not know he had spoken in Spanish until they told him later. He said, "I never had such power of God on me as when I was in that jail."[223]

Abundio and Rosa de Lopez held open-air meetings after serving at the Spanish Gospel Detective Mission for Latino railroad workers and preaching outdoors at the historic *La Placita* Mexican plaza. After being baptized in the Spirit at Azusa Street, the Lopez's served as Apostolic Faith Mission street preachers, altar workers, missionaries to San Diego for a time, and pastored their own Spanish-speaking Apostolic Faith Mission nearby.

STREETCAR EVANGELISM

Since most people did not yet own automobiles in 1906, most rode the streetcar to the meetings. In fact, the growing interurban trolley system greatly aided the revival as new missions sprang up at the end of nearly each streetcar line, including Long Beach, Pasadena, Anaheim, Whittier, and Monrovia. The Monrovia mission even paid streetcar tickets for any of its members who wanted to attend a meeting or two at the Azusa Street Mission.

Sometimes groups of street evangelists met at the mission, then boarded streetcars to nearby suburbs like Whittier, San Pedro, or Long Beach and held street or tent meetings. Once, four of them were arrested in Whittier for disturbing the peace, but when word reached

A Plaza University trolley car of the Los Angeles Railway Company with two conductors c. 1906. California Historical Society Collection, 1860-1960.

Photo: Wikimedia/Fæ.

back to the mission that they had been arrested, another group of fifteen quickly rode out to take their place.

WATER BAPTISM SERVICES

At other times, hundreds took streetcars to the beach for all-day worship and baptismal services. In July 1906, some five hundred worshipers sang and shouted for joy as they took a specially chartered Salt Lake Railroad train to Terminal Island, where Pastor Seymour and Hiram Smith baptized 138 candidates in the Pacific Ocean. Seymour personally baptized 106.

That September, 85 more were baptized, then 100 more in the 1907 camp meeting. Others knocked on doors, witnessed, and prayed for the sick. Still others carried their witness into the workplace and community, where they fed and cared for the poor. Unable to compete with all this, and falling behind in missions, the Los Angeles Church Federation launched similar street meetings and campaigns in the summer of 1906.

RACIAL DIVERSITY

The Azusa Street Revival was an event. Most attendees came only for one meeting or perhaps a week or two. The Azusa Street Mission was the local congregation that hosted this revival for three years. Since Pastor Seymour envisioned a multiracial, multiethnic congregation from its inception, it became one of the most racially and culturally diverse groups in Los Angeles at the time. The mixture of African American, Latino, Armenian, Russian, Swede, German, French, Italian, Chinese, Japanese, and Native American attendees sounded much like the list of nations represented at the church's first Pentecost. Frank Ewart, who later succeeded William Durham and helped found the Oneness Pentecostal movement, said Seymour's "sweet winsome ways broke down all barriers erected by spiritual bigotry, and won the love and trust of the people to such an extent that they forgot their natural animosities."[224]

Many who arrived by train were veteran Holiness and evangelical pastors, evangelists, missionaries, and Christian workers. Seymour often recruited them to preach and minister in the meetings, despite some of them having strong personalities.

ECUMENICAL OUTREACH

About a dozen churches and missions either sprang up or reoriented themselves to identify with the Azusa Street Revival. Frank Bartleman started his Eighth and Maple Mission about six blocks from the Azusa Mission. Pastor Elmer Fisher led an offshoot of The New Testament Church called the Upper Room Mission about four blocks from Azusa at 327½ Spring Street South. Rev. Charles Kent, a former Nazarene pastor, established a mission on 51st Street. There were several other missions within blocks of the Azusa Mission and Pastor Seymour valued them all, hosting weekly leadership meetings at the Azusa Mission for them to gather.

And gather they did—for prayer, fellowship, Bible study, mutual counsel, support, and long- and short-term strategic planning. Others also participated, like A.H. Post, who had held tent meetings in Pasadena under William Manley's Household of God movement and later established a Pentecostal work in nearby Pasadena. Healing evangelist Carrie Judd Montgomery, who had visited both Azusa Street and Post's Alley Church in Pasadena, described Azusa as a place of "sweet unity of spirit" with "quiet but powerful manifestations of the Spirit of God."[225]

The Apostolic Faith, published by the Azusa Street Mission, provided progress reports and testimonies on The New Testament Church, the Russian Molokan community, the Eighth and Maple Mission, the Upper Room Mission, the People's Church, the Nazarenes in Elysian Heights, and the Vernon Mission, and invited prayer on behalf of all.

Seymour also preached in many of the affiliated churches and invited them to participate at the Azusa Street Mission as well—even in his absence. Whenever new preaching points, new congregations, or new cottage prayer meetings emerged, Seymour advertised their meetings.

Seymour envisioned Apostolic Faith missions springing up throughout the city that would work together with the Azusa Street Mission.

He was always inviting new leaders from within the mission as well as those from without to participate in the revival. He viewed every minister as a co-laborer and fellow worker in the faith, embracing their gifts and seeking to collaborate with them for the sake of the gospel and revival.

Bartleman said of his Eighth and Maple Mission: "We always recognized Azusa as having been the mother mission, and there was never any friction or jealousy between us."[226] Within four years of the opening of the Azusa Street Mission, no less than twenty-five Pentecostal churches existed in the Los Angeles area.[227] The Apostolic Faith declared: "The scenes that are daily enacted in the building on Azusa Street and at missions churches in other parts of the city are beyond description."[228]

Seymour essentially saw Los Angeles as a huge mission field that needed every available minister, ministry, church, and mission. This work was summed up in the January 1907 issue of The Apostolic Faith: "We must give God all the glory in this work. We must keep very humble at His feet. He recognizes no flesh, no color, no names. We must not glory in Azusa Mission, nor in anything but the Lord Jesus Christ by whom the world is crucified unto us and we unto the world. We stand as assemblies and missions all in perfect harmony. Azusa stands for the unity of God's people everywhere. God is uniting His people, baptizing them by one Spirit into one body."[229]

APOSTOLIC FAITH CAMP MEETINGS

In one weekly Monday morning leadership meeting in April 1907, Rachel Sizelove, Clara Lum, and R.J. Scott raised the subject of a possible camp meeting. The camp meeting committee was to begin June 1, 1907, lasting three months or as long as the Lord willed. Sizelove had had a dream the night before in which she saw many little white tents pitched at the foot of a hill in Hermon at the Arroyo Seco (means "dry stream") where she lived. She was a part of the Free Methodists Colony there and was thrilled that God wanted to bring the light of Pentecost to her people, so they could receive the baptism in the Holy Spirit.

She hastened to share her dream with the group. Brother Seymour and the saints had been praying about a camp meeting and looking for a place for the summer, since the mission could not hold all the people. R.J. Scott, a Canadian who had been baptized in the Spirit at the mission, became its chief organizer. Florence Crawford's husband, Frank, a local real estate agent and developer, helped the group locate and lease fifteen acres between Los Angeles and Pasadena in what is now Arroyo Seco Park. More than three hundred tents were pitched on the campground.

Apostolic Faith Camp Meetings began in 1907, organized by R.J. Scott, and held in the Arroyo Seco between Los Angeles and Pasadena. The campground was originally used by the Azusa Street Mission with thousands attending.

Photo: Flower Pentecostal Heritage Center.

The first camp meeting officially ran between June 1 and September 1, 1907. The tabernacle they erected seated a thousand, and thousands more were in attendance. Local newspapers reported, "'the Holy Rollers' tents extend along both sides of the arroyo for a distance of perhaps half a mile. There are hundreds of them. The tents are well kept and comfortably furnished. In them live Negroes and whites, side by side."[230] R.J. Scott made it clear to reporters the meetings and tents were well-maintained, sanitary, and orderly. Though Seymour himself never attended or led any of the first meetings, he gave others free rein to lead them.

THE AZUSA STREET STAFF

Rev. Hiram W. Smith, a former Methodist minister who came on staff, provided Seymour with much-needed wisdom and spiritual counsel. He also cosigned with Seymour many of the ministerial credentials for the many missionaries sent out by the mission.

Phoebe Sargent and Jennie Moore were eventually appointed as "city missionaries" on staff to oversee this work. Phoebe Sargent was the wife of a successful homebuilder and previously owned and operated Elysian Hospital, a local sanitarium. Jennie Moore, who often led singing at the mission, eventually became Seymour's wife. Their work was to spread the mission's work and fame throughout Southern California.

Florence Crawford was designated as "state director" and Glenn Cook as "assistant state manager." Crawford and Cook both held meetings along the West Coast and eventually in Oklahoma and Indiana as well. Seymour also traveled and held meetings in Houston, Zion City, Illinois, and various other parts of the country where revivals had broken out, including Minneapolis, Indianapolis, and Virginia.

Crawford was a great asset to the mission because of her previous rescue work and public-speaking skills. Crawford, who was originally from western Oregon, was a former class leader in the Methodist Episcopal Church of Los Angeles and active in the Women's Christian Temperance Union, which fought for women's voting rights. She had also done extensive volunteer work and was active in several other civic clubs. She had worked with the sheriffs and police departments, juvenile courts, visited local prisons and slums, and even joined the National Congress of Mothers, now the PTA (Parent-Teacher Association).

Early leaders of the Azusa Street Mission in 1906. Standing left to right: Phoebe Sargent, G.W. Evans, Jennie Moore, Glenn Cook, Florence Crawford, Thomas Junk, and Sister Prince. Seated left to right: May Evans, Hiram Smith (Mildred Crawford, daughter of Florence Crawford, on his lap), William Seymour, and Clara Lum. By 1907, most had been sent out to do mission work.

Photo: Flower Pentecostal Heritage Center.

Clara Lum was editor of *The Apostolic Faith* and Florence Crawford its co-editor. Lum had previously worked for a paper called *The Missionary World* in Shenandoah, Virginia, and was also Seymour's secretary, having previously worked as a servant in the home of Charles Parham. Glenn Cook, who was Seymour's business manager without pay and who had been publisher of *The Burning Bush* and worked for a daily newspaper, was the publication's printer and distributor. Cook also oversaw the handling of all incoming mail and correspondence.

Cook said that none of the staff received pay, yet neither did they lack funds. After he took his position at the mission, a rancher came to him and said the Lord had spoken to him in the field to come to town immediately and give him twenty dollars. After he handed him a $20 gold piece, he said the Lord told him to give him twenty dollars every month, which he continued to do for a year. Other unpaid staff members and volunteers assisted with researching articles and addressing, mailing, praying, and responding to inquiries and prayer requests. By January 1907, the Azusa office received as many as fifty letters daily and the staff did their best to answer each one personally.

Bartleman wrote: "One reason for the depth of the work at Azusa was the fact that the workers were not novices. They were largely called and prepared for years from the Holiness ranks and from the mission field, and so on. They have been burned out, tried, and proven. They were largely seasoned veterans. They had walked with God and learned deeply of His Spirit. These were pioneers, 'shock troops,' Gideon's three hundred, to spread the fire around the world, just as the disciples had been prepared by Jesus."[231]

CHAPTER 9

THE ANGELS, HEAVENLY CHOIR, BOX, GLORY, AND FLAMES

It's been said that every fresh revival brings its own hymnology, and the Azusa Street Revival was no exception. The mission's faithful sang traditional hymns. Their favorites were "The Comforter Has Come," "Heavenly Sunlight," and "Under the Blood," which they sang daily. They also learned new hymns and choruses and embraced new forms of singing in the Spirit (mostly harmonious singing in tongues). Quite often, one would rise and sing a familiar song in a new tongue.

Frank Bartleman expressed his preference by condemning any worship led by a song director as forced or contrived worship in place of Spirit-led worship. Bartleman believed some of the revival's leaders "quenched the Spirit" by later leaving well-known memorized hymns and singing in tongues to instead singing preselected songs published in hymnals and led by song leaders. To him, these were human attempts to control people and services rather than embracing the spontaneity of the Spirit.

Henry McGowan, who was fourteen at the time, said, "People were hungry for God. Special prayer meetings were going on everywhere. God had put new hope in people's hearts. They would meet early in the morning, and start singing. They had no song book or piano. But, oh, what singing! One of their main songs was 'The Comforter Has Come.'

For a long time people had been crying out for a deeper walk with God. Now it had come and people were so excited about it. They would sing for a while, and then those who had been filled with the Holy Ghost would get up and tell about it, and how wonderful it was. After some testimonies, someone would preach and tell what God had promised. Then it would start all over again, and go on almost all night. If anyone was hungry, they would leave for something to eat and then return as soon as possible."[232]

ANGELS SEEN AND HEARD

Neither songs nor singers were announced, and performances were never applauded. It was common for worshipers to see or hear bands of angels. One eyewitness described the Azusa Street meetings saying, "No instruments of music are used, none are needed. No choir, but bands of angels have been heard…. No collections are taken. No bills have been posted to advertise the meetings…. All who are in touch with God realize as soon as they enter the meetings that the Holy Ghost is the leader."[233]

Sarah Payne received the baptism in the Holy Spirit at the mission, and a few nights later, heard a legion of angels singing, "Behold, I come quickly." She said the heavenly visitors sang unbroken verses from the last chapter of Revelation and a few lines from other parts of the Bible. Once again, Los Angeles, the "City of Angels," had lived up to its name.[234]

In reference to the roots of worship at Azusa Street, Pentecostal historian Eileen Southern described all Pentecostal worship in the United States, in some sense, as the direct "heir to the shouts, hand-clapping and foot-stomping, jubilee songs, and ecstatic seizures of the plantation 'praise houses.'"[235] Vigorous hand clapping was sometimes accompanied by cows' ribs, washboards, and thimbles.

A piano and violin were later added. However, since the fiddle was often associated with dance-hall music, many believed "the fiddle had the devil in it," so the violin was soon removed. Rev. Lawrence Catly recalled that, whenever Seymour was upstairs resting while someone else was leading the meeting downstairs, he would stomp on the floor which meant "he thought the meeting was getting too loud or out of order."[236] If that did not work, he would eventually come downstairs and lead the group in prayer until things settled down.

THE RUSSIAN MOLOKANS

The Russian Molokan "Spiritual Jumpers and Leapers" who attended the meetings were already familiar with the jumping and chanting found at the mission. They commonly practiced a similar sing-song vocal prayer and praise, which they brought with them from their homeland after immigrating to the U.S. in 1905. Demos Shakarian, grandfather of the Demos Shakarian who founded the Full Gospel Business Men's Fellowship in the 1950s, and his brother-in-law, Magardich Mushegian, were walking down San Pedro Street one day in 1906, looking for a job in one of the stables, when they passed by the Azusa Street Mission and heard the familiar sounds of praying, singing, and speaking in tongues. They thought they were the only ones in Los Angeles, much less in America, who spoke in tongues at the time. They stopped, inquired, and went inside.

The "heavenly choir" (singing in tongues) was especially sweet music to the ears of the Shakarian family, which they immediately recognized as similar to their own worship. This alone convinced Demos that this was a place where his family could worship. They eventually joined the Pentecostal movement thrilled that "God was also beginning to move in America just as He had in their homeland of Armenia and in Russia."[237] Curiously, Demos Shakarian's grandson would later model the

The Shakarian family in Los Angeles, early 1900s. Seated left to right: Demos and Goolisar Shakarian with their daughter, Hamas. Standing left to right: Erchen, Lily, Isaac, Margaret, Esther, and Sirron.

Photo: Flower Pentecostal Heritage Center.

Full Gospel Business Men's Fellowship after the Azusa Street Mission by conducting ecumenical meetings for all races and denominations led largely by laymen and businessmen.

THE HEAVENLY CHOIR

During the meetings, letters and testimonies were often read about people in other parts of the world who had received the baptism in the Holy Spirit and spoke in tongues after hearing about the Azusa Street Revival. Praise would often erupt as letters were read, which led to spontaneous worship and singing in other tongues. Seymour called this "the Heavenly Choir." Whenever the heavenly choir began to sing, the power of God would increase, and an anointing would fall on the service.

The heavenly choir received near unanimous praise from all who heard it. Even a newspaper reporter who heard the "The Chorus of tongues" said, "while likewise unintelligible," it "was weirdly beautiful." *The Apostolic Faith* editor added, "people are melted to tears in hearing this singing. It is the harmony of heaven and the Holy Ghost puts music in the voices that are untrained."[238]

A.W. Orwig, a former Methodist minister who visited the Azusa Street Mission, wrote, "Especially did the enchanting strains of the so called 'Heavenly Choir,' or hymns sung under the evident direction of the Holy Spirit both as to words and tune, thrill my whole being. It was not something that could be repeated at will, but supernaturally given for each special occasion and was one of the most indisputable evidences of the presence of the power of God. Perhaps nothing so greatly impressed the people as this singing: at once inspiring a holy awe, or a feeling of indescribable wonder, especially if the hearers were in a devout attitude."[239]

William Durham agreed, saying, "I have attended many large Holiness camp meetings and conventions, but I never felt the power and glory that I felt in Azusa Street Mission, and when about twenty persons joined in singing the 'Heavenly Chorus' it was the most ravishing and unearthly music that ever fell on mortal ears. It seemed and still seems to me, I could not sing in that chorus. I know it came direct from heaven."[240]

John G. Lake said, "One of the most remarkable features of the meetings was the 'heavenly choir.' A few, or as many as 20, would sing in their unknown tongue. There was no human orchestration. It was all under the direction of the Holy Spirit. Truly, heaven had come to earth."[241]

Ernest S. Williams wrote, "Some from cultured backgrounds affirmed that they had never heard in an opera such exquisite music as when the Spirit of God would sweep over the congregation in what became known as heavenly song. Healing for the body was fervently taught, but it was not put in first place. Demons were cast out. *But worship was the principal thing.*"[242]

Glenn Cook said, "One of the great features of the meetings was the singing of heavenly anthems in the Spirit."[243] Cook said when he saw Sister Moore's "shining face and heard her sing in the Spirit, I felt as though I had never had any experience. That old building seemed to have been annexed to heaven and had become the habitation of legions of the heavenly host."[244]

Another listener said, "There was a most remarkable incident of the sweetest singing I ever heard by about half a dozen women, all in unknown tongues, in which at intervals one voice would die away in very plaintive strains, while the others carried on the song. Then the former would break out in rapid strong language, filled with unction, and other would give tones as of singing in the distance. This was most enchanting, and filled with tender love. The singing was led by Miss Moore, who never could sing before, until she was baptized with the Spirit."[245]

A.G. Osterberg recalled, "We would sing a song or chorus, and everyone would join in. Then choruses would break out here and there, and some would be singing in tongues and some in English—and the harmony was wonderful. Once in a while a soprano voice would leap out and you would hear it above the whole congregation. Then it would be mingled with other voices and it all formed a beautiful harmony. Then the singing would stop short and everyone would start praising the Lord…. No one who has ever heard a congregation singing under the unction of the Spirit could ever forget or mistake it."[246]

Frank Bartleman who once was privileged to participate in the heavenly choir wrote, "It was a spontaneous manifestation and rapture no earthly tongue can describe. In the beginning, this manifestation was wonderfully pure and powerful. We feared to try to reproduce it, as with the tongues also.... No one could understand this gift of song but those who had it.... It was exercised as the Spirit moved the possessors, either in solo fashion or by the company. It was sometimes without words, other times in tongues.

"The effect was wonderful on the people. It brought a heavenly atmosphere, as though the angels themselves were present and joining with us. And possibly they were. It seemed to still criticism and opposition, and was hard for even wicked men to gainsay or ridicule.... In fact it was the very breath of God, playing on human heart strings, or human vocal cords. The notes were wonderful in sweetness, volume and duration. In fact they were ofttimes humanly impossible. It was indeed 'singing in the Spirit.'"[247]

"Often it is a chant by one or two, or more. But the greatest effect seems to be produced when suddenly in the meeting a dozen, or perhaps a score, will burst forth in the most beautiful chords, all in harmony, and all pitches of voice. This will sometimes continue as much as half an hour, though generally a shorter time. It is under direct inspiration of the Spirit and can in no wise be produced at any other time. None can take part in this but those who have received their gift. They treasure it most sacredly.

"It is one of the most effective exercises of the Spirit in the present work. It simply cannot be described...it seems...to calm the most savage heart. It surpasses and defies the best trained choir of our land for harmony and feeling. This has been declared by most competent judges of voice culture. Besides this, the rapture the performer undergoes, especially when a number are singing in unison of spirit is beyond description. I speak this most humbly from personal experience. It is the very foretaste of the rapture that we soon shall realize when He shall call for us."[248]

Some even received gifts of singing and playing instruments in the Spirit, just as Jennie Moore had received at the beginning. One minister from England, who could never sing, was baptized in the Holy Spirit and began singing beautiful heavenly strains in other tongues.[249] The same thing happened in other locations where Azusa Street evangelists and missionaries were sent.[250]

THE PIANO AND VIOLIN

Later in 1907, Brother Charles Sines, who was a concert pianist, brought his piano. Brother Sines could sing and play any song Seymour wanted without sheet music or a hymnal. Often Brother Seymour would ask Brother Sines to start singing and playing a certain song or hymn. Other times, he would just instruct the people to "sing in the Spirit" and heaven would fill the room. Sometimes they would sing in tongues, other times without words, but virtually every time Seymour instructed them to "sing in the Spirit," something wonderful would happen.

Brother Christopher, who owned a Stradivarius violin, accompanied Sines on the piano for a while. He and Sines were great friends, having played in concerts together. However, Brother Christopher said when he played his violin "in the Spirit," he played at a level he could never have achieved even at his greatest concert. The heavenly choir was enhance by the piano and violin.[251]

PRAYER AT AZUSA STREET

Prayer also remained a centerpiece of the revival. During the services, the congregation would often be down on their knees six or eight times, praying for special prayer requests.[252] Seymour himself was a man of prayer who often sat behind the pulpit praying with a shoe crate over his head for long periods of time. The large "upper room" was dedicated to constant prayer as spontaneous, boisterous prayer often bathed the revival meetings below. In fact, after the preaching, many would retire to the upper room to pray. Then, when the preaching began again, a bell would be rung, and many would go back downstairs. This became a daily routine.

Glenn Cook wrote, "We were saturated with the spirit of love and prayer and the days passed all too swiftly." Frank Bartleman concurred saying, "There was a presence of God with us, through prayer, we could depend on."[253] Prayer also remained a constant concern among the mission staff. Clara Lum wrote about the staff working together to send *The Apostolic Faith* around the world. She said, "There is a spirit of harmony and unity in the office work. We feel the power of God as we write off these blessed reports. The offices are places of prayer and praise and the power of God comes down on the workers as they fold the paper."

Behind the mission was a small cottage where Lucy Farrow, who had served as a cook for the Parhams and others, prepared and served meals for the staff. Besides a place of gathering for meals, the cottage also served as a place of prayer where many were healed, baptized in the Spirit, or slain in the Spirit. Mrs. Farrow also had a private room in the cottage which served as her sleeping quarters.

Prayer for healing was an everyday part of the mission as people were healed in the upstairs healing room, downstairs during services, and by the youth of Azusa between services. Handkerchiefs were also brought and prayed over on behalf of the sick. *The Apostolic Faith* recorded such an incident when Sallie Traynor, an original Bonnie Brae member, prayed over one of the handkerchiefs: "The Spirit came upon her in great power and she prayed in tongues, and kissed the handkerchief three times, as the Spirit seemed to lead her. It was sent with a prayer and the brother was immediately healed."[254]

Of course, great prayer went out by Seymour, Bartleman, and many others leading up to the revival. Bartleman explains: "The present world-wide Pentecostal manifestation did not break out in a moment, like a huge prairie fire, and set the world on fire. In fact, no work of God ever appears that way. There is a necessary time for preparation. The finished article is not realized at the beginning. Men may wonder where it came from, not being conscious of the preparation, but there is always such.

"Every movement of the Spirit of God must also run the gauntlet of the Devil's forces. The Dragon stands before the bearing mother, ready to swallow up her child (Revelation 12:4). So it is with the present Pentecostal work in its beginning. The Enemy did much counterfeiting. God kept the young child well hid for a season from the Herods, until it could gain strength and discernment to resist them."[255] He added, "A spiritual atmosphere must be created, through humility and prayer, that Satan cannot live in."[256]

PROPHECY AT AZUSA STREET

Prophecy also played a key role in the revival. Seymour and others would often prophesy in the meetings. One evening Seymour retired to his apartment to rest when the Lord said to him, "Brother Durham will get the baptism tonight." He returned downstairs to the altar just in time to hear Durham speaking in tongues for the first time. Seymour then raised his hands and prophesied that wherever Durham preached, the Holy Spirit would fall on the people.[257] This prophecy was quickly fulfilled as Durham returned to Chicago to overcrowded meetings that lasted well into the night. Durham's North Avenue Mission quickly became a center for Midwestern Pentecostalism.

Many visitors and foreign residents also came to the mission and heard people prophesy in their native languages. In one such incident, a Jewish man came to Los Angeles to investigate and to build a case against speaking in tongues. As he entered the building, the service was already in progress, but then he heard people praying upstairs and went upstairs to check it out. The moment he entered the upper room, Kathleen, who was a teenager at the time, felt led to go to him and speak in tongues. She spoke to him for several minutes before the bell rang for everyone to go downstairs for the preaching. The man gently grabbed Kathleen's arm and directed her downstairs to the pulpit. As soon as order was restored, he spoke:

"I am a Jew, and I came to this city to investigate this speaking in tongues. No person in this city knows my first or my last name, as I am here under an assumed name. No one in this city knows my occupation or anything about me. I go to hear preachers for taking their sermons apart, and using them in lecturing against the Christian religion. This girl, as I entered the room, started speaking in the Hebrew language. She told me my first name and my last name, and she told me why I was in the city and what my occupation was in life, and then she called upon me to repent. She told me things about my life which it would be impossible for any person in this city to know." The man then dropped to his knees, crying and praying as his heart began to break.[258]

THE BOX

Seymour regularly sat behind two shoe crates, one on top of the other, which served as his pulpit. Rev. Lawrence Catly, who was about eleven years old at the time, said, "Seymour was often not visible to the congregation because he had a habit of putting his head inside large wooden crates, which formed the pulpit, to pray quietly."[259]

Henry McGowan, who was fourteen at the time, said Seymour "didn't do much preaching" when the services started flowing, "but spent most of his time behind this old box with his head in it praying."[260] Whenever Brother Seymour came downstairs to join a service, usually already in progress, he would remove the top shoe crate from the pulpit, which many referred to as "the box," and place it over his head.

From a natural standpoint, it looked silly and ridiculous, but for Seymour, it was a reminder of their humble surroundings and an act of humility that was highly critical to the power of God being displayed. Sometimes Seymour would sit like a statue with the box on his head for ten minutes. Other times, he would sit like that for an hour. Yet invariably, whenever Seymour removed the box from his head, the greatest miracles would take place.

In fact, "the box" became so sacred and significant that nobody dared touch it—even when Seymour was not in the room. Brother Sines

Seymour used two wooden shoe crates, like this one, for a pulpit. The top crate, he either ducked his head into or put over his head as an act of humility. The Hamilton Brown Shoe Co. was the largest shoe manufacturer in the world in 1906.

Photo: liveauctioneers.com.

noticed a glow around the box when it was on Seymour's head. He once asked Seymour what was going on inside the box when it was on his head. He said he was meditating and waiting on God. He also said whenever he spoke to God inside the box, it was a whisper in tongues, and though he could hear himself speaking in tongues, he could understand every word he was saying.[261]

When asked what led to the decline of the revival, Sister Carney said the miracles "stopped when Brother Seymour stopped putting that box over his head. When he quit coming down and putting the box on his head, it started dying."[262] Bartleman agreed saying, "While Brother Seymour kept his head inside the old empty box in Azusa all was well."[263] Brother Anderson, who was fifteen at the time, concurred stating that when Seymour quit putting the box on his head, he felt disappointed, because that meant he had surrendered to the will of the people instead of to the will of God.[264]

THE SHEKINAH GLORY

Another fascinating feature of the Azusa Street Revival was the constant, abiding, and sometimes even visible presence of God, which many said was like breathing in pure oxygen. One observer said that when Seymour came down and the heavenly choir started singing, the "Shekinah Glory" would "rise and fill the whole room, and you could breathe so much better—as if the room were filled with pure oxygen."[265] Others said it was like heaven coming down. Sometimes the visible mist was only a foot high in the room and people would lie down in it just so they could breathe in God's glory.

Jean Darnall, who would later replace Aimee Semple McPherson as pastor of Angelus Temple and who was only a toddler at the time, told how she loved to attend the meetings with her mother and crawl under

The glory of the Lord, always felt, was sometimes seen at Azusa Street. This photo of 312 Azusa Street was enhanced by Esther Eunjoo Jun.

Photo: Apostolic Faith International Headquarters
Portland, Oregon.

the pew to take a nap, only to later awaken and play with the thick mist that filled the room.[266] Sometimes Seymour would wave his foot and play with the mist. Brother Riggs said it was sometimes difficult to look down and see the floor. He and Brother Ward played hide-and-seek in it.[267] Other times, the mist would become so thick that it would rise and fill the whole building, just as when Solomon's priests in the Old Testament praised God with one unified sound and the cloud of the Lord filled the temple.[268]

Many at Azusa Street walked in the mist, sat in it, ran their hands through it, and breathed it into their lungs, but no one could capture it. Brother Christopher tried to bottle it and bring it home, but to his dismay, the bottle was empty the next morning.[269] Sister Carney said the Shekinah glory was always present and felt inside the building but was not always visible.

Mother Riggs, who was thirty-five at the time, said it glowed. Brother Anderson said whenever the Spirit started moving, the smoke-like substance began to glow even brighter. Others believed it was the other way around—whenever God's glory manifested, miracles happened. Brother Garcia later added, "We have got to get the Shekinah back if we want to see a worldwide revival."[270]

THE ROOFTOP FLAMES

Many also reported seeing the "glory over the building" at night.[271] Bartleman wrote: "It seemed a fearful thing to hinder or grieve the Spirit. The whole place was steeped in prayer, God was in His holy temple. It was for man to keep silent. The shekinah glory rested there. In fact, some claim to have seen the glory by night over the building. I do not doubt it. I have stopped more than once within two blocks of the place and prayed for strength before I dared go on. The presence of the Lord was so real."[272]

The rooftop flames that often appeared outside the building were as captivating as the glory of God inside. Many confirmed that when the greatest miracles were happening inside, flames could be seen above the building outside. The fire department was called on several occasions as passersby reported flames leaping from the rooftop. The flames could be seen as far away as La Grande Station. One said, "It looked like flames about fifty feet in the air coming down and was also going up out of the roof to meet, merge, and go through the flame coming down."[273]

A caricature of the rooftop flames at Azusa Street by Joyce C. Edwards, from *Like as of Fire: Newspapers from the Azusa Street World Wide Revival*, collected by Fred T. Corum and Rachel A. Sizelove (Washington, D.C.: Middle Atlantic Regional Press, 1991), p. 1. Dupree Holiness and Pentecostal Center.

Photo: University of Southern California Digital Library, Pentecostal and Charismatic Research Archive.

On one such occasion when the firemen arrived, Seymour, Bosworth, Lake, Smith, and Sines all ran outside to see the flames. Sister Carney remained behind but later went out to investigate. She saw John G. Lake and asked him to explain what was happening. He said, "Fire was coming down from heaven into the building, and fire was going up from the building and meeting the fire coming down."[274] Then she walked about a half a block and saw the awesome sight for herself.

CHAPTER 10

EVERYDAY HEALINGS AND NOTABLE MIRACLES

As many as a hundred people at a time were in the upper room seeking the baptism in the Spirit or divine healing. They prayed on three California redwood planks laid end to end on backless chairs. Just as in John Alexander Dowie's Zion Tabernacle, crutches, canes, pipes, and other healing "trophies" decorated the walls of the upper room. One reporter wrote, "People were healed there every day."[275] Seymour declared repeatedly in *The Apostolic Faith*: "Thank God we have a living Christ among us to heal our diseases. He will heal every case," and "O how we ought to honor the stripes of Jesus, for 'with his stripes we are healed,'" and "if Jesus bore our sicknesses, why should we bear them?"[276]

African American preacher Emma Cotton described herself as a "walking drugstore" before she came to Azusa Street. She had weak lungs and cancer. However, after prayer at Azusa Street, she was instantly healed. She later added, "For thirty-three years, I have never gone back to the doctors." Inserting again, "In those days of that great outpouring when they said God would heal you, you were healed."[277]

Florence Crawford said, "I was a wreck in my body" when she first came to Azusa Street. As a teenager in Oregon, she had been thrown from a buggy, landed on a stump, and injured her back. Like many in those days, she moved to Southern California in search of physical healing with the warmer climate. By the time she arrived at the mission, she was thin, diseased, broken, had suffered bouts of spinal meningitis and tuberculosis, and had been wearing a harness with straps and a metal plate for eleven years. Shortly after coming to the mission, she removed the brace and was completely healed. She testified, "Once diseased from the crown of my head to the soles of my feet, I was made sound and well through the blood of Jesus."[278]

MIRACLES OF HEALING AND DELIVERANCE

A.G. Osterberg said that when people requested prayer in a meeting, Seymour would say, "Let us stand and ask the Lord's help in this matter."[279] Osterberg saw his first miracle the first week the mission opened when he noticed a Catholic man with a club foot who came stumbling in. After the man walked back and forth in prayer a few times, Osterberg noticed he was no longer stumbling. However, the man was so deep in prayer he had not yet noticed himself. Then, when he suddenly realized he had been miraculously healed, he walked normally to the altar shouting, "Hallelujah!" and praising the Lord in Spanish.[280]

Lawrence Catly heard about God's power to heal at Azusa through a neighbor woman. She said, "They pray and people get well." He had tuberculosis and desperately needed a miracle. So he asked his mom to take him to the mission. She eventually took him and "God delivered him."[281]

William and Emma Cummings' ten-year-old daughter, Mattie, who came to the Bonnie Brae meetings, was deaf but soon received a supernatural healing in her ears. Both Lawrence Catly and Mattie Cummings testified of having retained their healings in an interview with Pentecostal historian, Vinson Synan, commemorating the Azusa Street Revival some seventy years later.[282]

Financial miracles and miracles of deliverance were also common-place at Azusa Street. One young man fell at the altar in front of the church, started groaning and foaming at the mouth, then barking and snarling like a dog, while his body writhed on the floor in various con-tortions. Seymour said, "Come out of him thou unclean spirit." After nearly three hours of spiritual warfare, the spirit departed, and he was immediately baptized in the Spirit and began speaking in tongues.[283]

Divine healing and deliverance were not limited to the meetings nor to the mission, however. Rachel Sizelove's daughter, Maud, was afflicted with a kidney stone and was writhing in agony for nearly twenty-four hours when Sister Sizelove sent her son, Matt, to the mission to sum-mon Seymour. Seymour came to the home, approached the suffering child's bed, opened a bottle of anointing oil, anointed the girl's head, and asked, "Little girl, do you believe God can heal you?" She nodded. Seymour did not scream, yell, or get excited but calmly prayed and believed God for healing. The girl turned over in bed, fell peacefully asleep, and slept through the night, instantly healed by God's mighty power.[284]

After serving as a Free Methodist evangelist, Rachel Sizelove was baptized in the Holy Spirit at Azusa Street in 1906. In 1907, Rachel visited her mother and siblings in Springfield, Missouri, when she had a vision of a "sparkling fountain" in the heart of Springfield. Springfield later became headquarters for the World Assemblies of God Fellowship.

Photo: Flower Pentecostal Heritage Center.

Just as the apostle Paul performed unusual miracles when aprons and handkerchiefs that had touched his body were placed on sick people, diseases were healed and demons expelled when the Azusa Street staff and volunteers laid hands and prayed over every issue of *The Apostolic Faith* before mailing them. Many reported being instantly saved, healed, or baptized in the Spirit upon receiving them.[285]

People from hundreds of miles away also mailed handkerchiefs to be prayed over. Some mornings, so many handkerchiefs came in the mail that it was impossible to pray over each one. Instead, three or four staff and volunteers would kneel around a pile of forty or fifty handkerchiefs, touching them with their fingers and praying in Jesus' name. As many as were sent out, reports came back. One woman slipped one in her demon-possessed husband's pillowcase. He rolled over in bed as if irked by needles, then awoke at midnight and said, "Wife, pray for me," and arose saved. Many others reported deliverance from alcohol, tobacco, and insanity.[286]

THE YOUTH OF AZUSA STREET

Some of the most amazing stories were told by the youth of Azusa who were privileged to pray daily for the sick before Seymour came downstairs or while he was sitting with the box on his head. Clara Lum said, "[I] have never seen the power of God manifest in so many people, nor have I ever seen such manifestations of his power."[287] Many, like Brother Riggs, who was only twelve at the time, appreciated the fact that they did not have to watch the older people do all the work and have all the fun. Liberty was given to anyone who wanted to pray for the sick, and God seemed to honor that by healing nearly everyone for whom prayer was given. Many of the Azusa Street youth were used by God in ways that most seasoned adults and ministers only dream about.

Brother Cantrell, who was twenty-one at the time, said, "Anyone who attended Azusa very long had great miracles—especially if a person attended at least once a week—you had miracles!"[288] Brother David Garcia, who was eighteen at the time, said, "When you came into Azusa, you got healed. The more you attended, the more faith you had, and the more things would happen. Because your faith was building up as you saw other people believing and you believed, soon you had no doubt when you walked up to someone that they were going to get healed. After a while it was easy to have boldness to walk up to someone and proclaim 'God is going to heal you tonight!'"[289]

Azusa was a hands-on workshop for the miraculous led by God himself. Tommy Welchel, who heard and recited many of their stories in *They Told Me Their Stories*, said, "No wonder they had such a revival, no wonder this thing went worldwide. Yes, they received the speaking in tongues and that was great, but many of the miracles that were performed were not done by big preachers. Many of those being used by God were just ordinary teenagers and young people doing extraordinary works for God."[290]

Frank Bartleman concurred in the *Way of Faith* in September 1906, "The gifts of the Spirit are being given, the church's armor restored. Surely we are in the days of restoration, the last days, wonderful and glorious days.... Demons are being cast out, the sick healed, many blessedly saved, restored, and baptized with the Holy Spirit and power.... The revival will be a worldwide one, without doubt."[291] As a bit of a disclaimer, however, since many of the Azusa youth were teenagers at the time and told their stories to a storyteller some sixty years later, inaccuracies or embellishment of names or facts may exist either on the part of the participants or the storyteller. Still, none can negate the fact that everyday healings and miracles occurred at Azusa Street.

Sister Carney

Sister Carney of Pasadena, who was only seventeen at the time, told of a woman who came in appearing to be in a lot of pain and holding a bloody bandage at the side of her head. When she asked the woman what had happened, she said she had caught her husband with another woman. When she and the other woman got in a fight, the woman bit her ear off, but she did not have the ear with her. Sister Carney pulled the bandage away slightly to confirm that she had no ear and without hesitation began to pray. Immediately the pain left, but this time when she pulled the bandage away, she saw a new ear growing before her eyes![292] She said those kinds of miracles happened two to three times a day through her alone.

Sister Carney, C.W. Ward, and Ralph Riggs led the team of youth who prayed for the sick. Brother Riggs said each of them saw six or more miracles every night.[293] Brother Sines considered Sister Carney the "ringleader," thought Brother Ward was comical to watch with his silly facial expressions, and thought Brother Anderson was kin to kangaroos the way he jumped on benches and bounced around the building observing all the miracles.

Brother Lankford

Brother Lankford, who was twenty at the time and had been one of Parham's students in Topeka, was praying for a man in a wheelchair who had been paralyzed from his waist down for two years when Sister Carney broke in: "No, no, no, that's not faith!" Then she went over to the man, picked up his legs, and put the footrests up so he could stand. Brother Lankford continued praying for him and suddenly they could hear bones cracking. The man straightened up, rose out of his wheelchair, and took off running, leaping, shouting, and dancing, as others ran with him.[294]

Another man, who had recently lost two fingers in a work accident, had heard about the miracles at Azusa Street and came expecting to be healed. Brother Lankford grabbed the man's hand and instructed him to lift it in the air, as his fiancée held the other hand. As the man's fingers began to grow out, his fiancée passed out from the sight. Then Mr. Lankford proudly walked around shouting and showing off the man's new fingers.

In yet another instance, a man brought in his wife who was hunchbacked. Brother Lankford prayed for her, they heard bones popping, and she was healed within minutes before dancing and screaming. According to Mrs. Lankford, Mr. Lankford was personally involved in more than a hundred miraculous healings that included cancer and tumors disappearing, the blind receiving sight, cleft palates and lips being healed, even missing teeth being restored.[295]

Brother Anderson

Brother Anderson said many who were blind and deaf were healed, and if he did not participate in the healing, like Zacchaeus he was standing on a bench watching others get healed. He remembered his first time praying was for a young man with a club foot. Suddenly and slowly, it started moving outward, and within minutes he was running, jumping, and shouting.

He also prayed for an older woman with a knot above her wrist. He barely touched it and said, "In the name of Jesus, be healed." Within seconds, the knot was gone, as she grabbed Brother Anderson and started dancing.

His most unusual healing happened when a young woman named "Diane" came in holding a tumor on the side of her head half the size of a basketball. It was so large the doctors could not do anything for her. Before she sat down, Brother Anderson told her to expect God to work a miracle. As several people started laying hands on her, the tumor began to shrink. She was speechless, then yelled, "I'm healed!" Diane later started her own soup kitchen for the needy of Los Angeles, which lasted for decades.[296]

Sister Mangrum

Sister Mangrum, who was twenty-two at the time, prayed for a woman with crooked legs who could barely walk. Sister Mangrum asked her, "Have you come to be healed?" She said, "I came to see what was going on. You say I can be healed? Of what?" Sister Mangrum pointed to her legs. "Well, it's worth a try." Sister Mangrum laid hands on the woman's head and felt heat coming out of her hands onto the woman. The woman started shaking and said, "Something's happening." In about two minutes, her feet and legs were straight and completely restored. The two started dancing, then the woman started dancing wildly, ran out the building, then ran back in afraid she might lose her healing. When she finally settled down, the woman asked about the mist she was seeing. Sister Mangrum said, "We call it the 'Shekinah glory.'" This woman started a rescue mission and spent the rest of her life ministering to homeless women.

Sister Mangrum prayed for another lady with a crooked nose, but after she prayed, the results were not immediate. However, later in the service, she noticed the hook was gone. She told the woman, "the hook is gone." She said, "I know the hook is gone but I don't like the little point at the end of my nose." Sister Mangrum prayed again, and before the lady left the meeting, she had a perfect nose.[297]

Brother Riggs

Brother Riggs, who was only twelve at the time, recalled a large young man who came in with alcohol on his breath. He felt led to pray for him, then realized he was also blind. He asked the man if he could see. He said, "No, that's what I came here for." After Brother Riggs prayed for him, he could instantly see, and the stench of alcohol had left him. The man sat and cried, overwhelmed by the goodness of God. He went on to plant Pentecostal churches across the Midwest.

At another time, Brother Riggs saw a husband and wife being brought in by their teenage children in wheelchairs. Both appeared to have pneumonia. He asked them, "Did you come believing God to heal you?" The husband said, "Yes." Then following the "Carney rule," Brother Riggs put up their footrests, laid hands on their foreheads, and prayed. The wife began to shake, then jumped up and started running while the husband stood, raised his hands, and screamed, "Thank you, God!" God instantly healed both.[298]

Sister Lucille

Sister Lucille McGillicuddy, whose borrowed name would one day become famous as the maiden name of Lucille Ball's *I Love Lucy* character (and was paid handsomely for it) was eighteen at the time. She also later became Aimee Semple McPherson and Sister Jean Darnall's secretary at Angelus Temple. She prayed for a woman with polio, whose one leg was four inches shorter than the other. After instructing her to remove the brace, Sister Lucille prayed, and her leg was immediately straightened. She nearly fell taking her first steps with normal legs.

Sister Lucille also had a gift for praying for people with bad teeth by placing her fingers on the bad teeth. If the tooth was missing, she placed her finger on the gum until the new tooth pushed her finger out. If the tooth was crooked, she could feel it straightening out. If the tooth was infected or decayed, the plaque or infection would loosen until she could rub it off with her handkerchief.[299]

Sister Lucille's best friend, Laura Langtroff, who was sixteen at the time, often prayed with her for elderly women and people with breathing problems. Sister Laura attended nightly and experienced at least three to four miracles each night. She had a gift for praying for women with canes or crutches.

One elderly woman came in with a staff, could barely breathe or walk, and looked like she weighed about 65 pounds. It took her three hours to walk two miles to Azusa Street. Upon arrival, she saw Sister Laura and said, "That's the woman I want to pray for me." She told Sister Laura, "I won't live through the night if God doesn't heal me. Doctors say my lungs are ate up with cancer, and I can hardly breathe. I've been losing weight for about a year." Sister Laura laid hands on her, prayed, and she immediately breathed normally. She said, "I can breathe like when I was young." She even gained about 40 pounds during the meeting, without food, simply by breathing in the Shekinah glory.[300]

When she returned to Dr. Thomas Wyatt's office, he did not recognize her and asked her to complete a new patient form. After thoroughly examining her, he confirmed her lungs were like new and that it was physically impossible for her to gain that much weight since he last saw her. Upon learning she went to Azusa Street, he went with her, and within months quit his medical practice and founded Wings of Healing, an international relief organization complete with children's homes, churches, and Bible schools.

Sister Dundee

Sister Dundee, who was twenty-two, had a gift for praying for children. A mother brought in her crippled daughter on braces and crutches. Though she had previously been prayed for, nothing happened. Sister Dundee explained to her that if she was healed, it would bring great glory to Jesus. The little girl said, "Okay. Pray for me." Sister Dundee removed the braces and crutches and said, "We've got to glorify Jesus." The girl's eyes began to well up. Sister Dundee prayed, and the girl felt something happening in her feet. Sister Dundee told her to stand and start moving. She said, "I can't!" Sister Dundee said, "You need to try." She started moving her feet up and down, then started dancing and stomping. Now realizing she was healed, she continued to dance and stomp around the building while shouting.

Sister Dundee also prayed for a baby with a bowed neck who was brought in by her mother wrapped in a blanket. When Sister Dundee prayed and saw the bowed neck straighten out, she cried. The mother asked, "Is there something wrong with my baby?" Sister Dundee pulled the blanket back to show her healed baby smiling. The mother ran rejoicing. Later, the baby's father came and was saved. He went on to pastor a large church in Los Angeles for thirty-five years.[301]

Sister Goldie

Sister Goldie, who was eighteen at the time, often prayed for people with growths or disfigurements on their faces. She learned to carry towels to catch the tumors as they fell. She estimated she had been instrumental in healing some 3,000 growths and tumors in the two years she attended the revival. Sister Goldie especially remembered a young man who had broken his arm in a ballgame at school but never went to a doctor to have it reset. His arm was crooked, but when Sister Goldie prayed, it immediately straightened.

Brother Garcia

Brother David Garcia, who was also eighteen at the time, remembered praying for two women and one man who had come in wheelchairs from a nearby nursing home. They all had crippling arthritis, and one could not talk or feed herself. Brother Garcia first laid hands on the lady who could not talk and immediately her head stopped shaking. Her first words were to Brother Garcia: "Are you Jesus?" she asked. He said, "No, but Jesus healed you!" Then she asked, "Can I get up?" Garcia said, "Yes!" She stood up, started walking, then danced a beautiful waltz for about an hour.

Then the other woman said, "I'm ready." Brother Garcia prayed for her, and she too stood up and started walking. Brother Garcia reached out to steady her, but she said, "No, leave me alone; pray for him." Then he prayed for the man, and he took off running. All three were healed! Brother Garcia also remembered praying for a blind Spanish girl whose eyes were gray. He prayed, and when she opened her eyelids, she had beautiful brown eyes. The girl started dancing, celebrating, and shouting the name of Jesus as her parents tried to keep up with her.[302]

Brother Fox

Brother Fox, who was also eighteen at the time, remembered a sign language teacher who brought his entire class of thirty-five deaf students. Brother Fox said to the teacher, "If you want to teach them to sign, why did you bring them to a place where they could get healed? You're going to be out of a job!" The teacher replied, "You're talking like they're all going to get healed." "They are!" said Brother Fox. Brother Fox then gestured to the students to join hands in a circle. Looking at the teacher, he said, "Evidently, you don't have much faith, so stand off to the side." Then, forgetting they were deaf, he instructed the students: "Now, I'm going to lay hands on this man and start with him." The teacher laughed.

Undeterred, Brother Fox whispered in the first man's ear and told the spirit to come out. He was immediately healed. Then, seeing the excitement of the man who was healed, one by one, the others were all healed within a few minutes. Yet Fox had only laid hands on one. After that, whenever a group joined hands in a circle touching each other, Brother Fox said they were all healed.[303]

He also loved praying for the deaf and mute. He said you could sometimes hear a "whishing" sound when their ears were healed. A man whose throat had been eaten with cancer could not talk. After Brother Fox prayed, nothing happened. He prayed again and the lump disappeared, and he could immediately talk. Brother Fox later became a missionary to India.

Brother Sines and Brother Christopher

Brother Sines, who was twenty-six at the time, was on the platform leading the singing when he noticed a young, crippled boy on crutches sitting off to the side. He asked why no one was ministering to him. The boy shrugged his shoulders and said, "I'm just waiting for someone to come over and pray for me." Sines asked, "Do you believe God will heal you? "Why, yes!" he said. Sines took his crutches and immediately started praying and laying hands on the boy. At first, nothing happened. Then the boy yelled, "I feel it! I feel it!" and leaped to his feet running, dancing, and shouting.[304]

Brother Christopher, who was eighteen at the time and quite shy, remembered a woman who came up to him and said, "My husband is blind, heal him." Brother Christopher said, "I can't, but I can pray for him, and Jesus will heal him." She replied, "Okay, do it!" Brother Christopher humbly prayed for the man, and he was instantly healed. Brother Christopher also remembered a young man who had burned his arm at work, which had turned gangrenous. He prayed for him and told him to go home and clean the wound, and he and came back the next night completely healed.[305]

Brother Bill Brown

Other testimonies sounded like stories ripped from the Gospels: When Brother Bill Brown, who was sixteen at the time, saw a man lying on a cot, he asked him, "Do you want to be healed? Do you want to take up your cot and carry it home?" The man smiled and said, "Yes." Brother Bill prayed for him, and immediately he got up, folded up his cot, and began worshiping God.[306] Brother Brown estimated he had participated in the healing of more than fifty blind people, all of whom were instantly healed.

NOTABLE MIRACLES

On one occasion when the flames were dancing on the rooftop, Brother Seymour approached a man with a wooden leg and asked, "What did you come here for?" The man replied, "I want you to pray for my leg. It is starting to get gangrene where the wooden leg attaches." Seymour replied, "I'm just upset because you have the wooden leg on. It would be a challenge for God to grow a leg out when the wooden leg is attached." The man immediately removed the wooden leg and stood before Seymour on his one good leg. Seymour laid hands on the man and proclaimed, "Let Thy Name be Glorified. In the Name of Jesus, I command this leg to grow out." Then he said to the man, "The gangrene is gone; you are healed." Suddenly, now with two legs, the man ran up on the platform and around the room and the crowd went wild! No one could get him to stop rejoicing and praising God. Seymour did not need to preach that night.[307]

Another time when the flames were on the roof, Seymour approached a man who had lost his arm ten years earlier in a work-related accident. The arm was totally severed at the shoulder. Brother Seymour asked the crowd, "Would you like to see God have a wonderful time here tonight? Some of you may remember the man's leg that grew out about a year ago."

Seymour then asked the one-armed man, "Can you work with just one arm?" "I'm just given minimal paying jobs and I barely make enough money to even eat," he replied. Seymour shook his head and responded, "That's not good. Are you married?" "Yes." "Got kids?" "Yes." Then turning to the crowd, he said, "This man needs to be able to make a living. This man needs to work and he needs to be able to pay his tithe." Then turning back to the man, Seymour asked teasingly, "Will you tithe if I pray for you and God gives you your arm back?" "Yes!" he exclaimed. Seymour burst out laughing. "I'm just having fun."

Then he slapped his hands on the man's shoulder and commanded the arm to grow out—and almost instantly, it grew out. The man stood in total shock, then started moving his new arm around and feeling it with his other hand, awed by the miracle. A few weeks later, the man returned, bringing two hundred people with him, and telling everyone at the meeting he had his old job back. Many who came with him also needed healing and were fully restored as different people from the crowd prayed and laid hands on them.[308]

MASS HEALINGS

Occasionally, Seymour would go to a section where everyone was in wheelchairs or on cots carried from the hospital and point to them, saying, "Everyone on the cots or wheelchairs, you're healed in the name of Jesus." Then everyone would get up and walk around fully healed![309] One time there were about a dozen cripples who looked as though they had rheumatoid arthritis. Seymour pointed to them and said, "You want to see a miracle over there? Every one of you within a few minutes are going to be up and start walking in the name of Jesus." Suddenly, bones could be heard popping everywhere as everyone rose shouting with legs, arms, and hands totally straight.[310]

Such mass healings were so frequent the youth of Azusa Street had a name for it and often tried to mimic it but were rarely successful. Brother Riggs was successful but only once. They called it "doing a Seymour." Eventually, the walls downstairs also became lined with crutches, braces, bandages, old pipes, and the like, all of which were no longer needed.

SPONTANEOUS HEALINGS

Many of the healings at Azusa Street were spontaneous. A.G. Osterberg shared one such example. He recalled a meeting when a ten- or eleven-year-old girl testified, "After relating being baptized in the Holy Spirit the preceding day, she began to weep. Still weeping, she went on in spiritual prophecy and exhortation, clearly beyond all natural ability. With the tears still streaming down her heavenly illuminated face, having climbed atop her chair, delivered such a reverential, inspired, soul moving, judgment scene descriptive message, beseeching the hearers to humble themselves under the mighty hand of God."[311]

Before long, the entire congregation, including Seymour, was weeping. Then, after ten or fifteen minutes of weeping came a period of holy laughter. After the tears and laughter subsided, the people broke out in heavenly chorus, when suddenly a Spanish brother began racing up and down the aisle weeping, laughing, and shouting simultaneously. Osterberg recalled, "We soon learned that, while he was kneeling as a good Roman Catholic…God had miraculously lengthened his shortened crippled leg."[312]

In one of the more vivid testimonies from Azusa Street, A.C. Valdez, Sr., who was only ten years old at the time, shared how his mother came home from a meeting one night and woke him out of bed, speaking in tongues as she shared her excitement of being baptized in the Holy Ghost. The next night, she invited him to join her. Valdez later described his first visit to the Azusa Street Mission:

"As we moved toward an open spot on a rear bench, I suddenly felt a chill. How could that be? It wasn't cold at all. Then the hair on my arms, legs and head began to stand on end. It felt as if I were surrounded by God. I was trembling. So was my mother and everybody else. As I looked over the congregation, another chill ran down my spine. It was as if ocean waves were moving from one end of the congregation to the other—the most thrilling sight I had ever seen.

"Wave after wave of the Spirit went through the hall, like a breeze over a corn field. Again the crowed settled back into their seats. And prayers began to buzz through the hall. Then tongues of fire suddenly appeared over the heads of some people, and a black man with a shining face leaped to his feet. Out of his mouth poured words in some language I had never heard before. I began to tremble harder than before.

"Occasionally, as Pastor Seymour prayed, his head would be so low that it disappeared behind the top wooden box. Just when quiet settled over the hall, a white woman came off the bench like a jack-in-the-box. 'Oh, My blessed Jesus,' she cried out in excitement, 'I can see. I can see.'

She placed her hands over her eyes. 'Oh, Jesus, thank you. Thank you for this miracle.' And she plunged out into the aisle and began to dance, her open palms reaching toward heaven. 'Thank you, Father. I can see. I can see!' Before the night was over, another blind person could see, the deaf could hear and the crippled could walk. It was so exciting!"[313]

A.C. Valdez, Sr. was only a young Hispanic man when he first visited Azusa Street in 1906. His testimony of his first visit with his mother remains one of the most vivid and detailed of the Azusa Street Revival.

Photo: Flower Pentecostal Heritage Center.

Other healings were not as dramatic but powerful nonetheless, such as when a little boy mounted the altar and testified, "I had a toothache and I prayed for the Lord to take it away, and He took it away."[314]

J. Narver Gortner, a former Free Methodist, concluded of the early days at Azusa, as did the apostle John, St. Augustine, and many others before him: "If all that God did were written down for our learning and edification it is doubtless true that the books would occupy many shelves and every one of them would be interesting. Some would be well nigh as interesting as the Acts of the Apostles, for if miracles, real miracles, were wrought in the days of Peter and Paul, real miracles were wrought in those early days when God in answer to prayer poured out His Holy Spirit in plenitude and power."[315]

CHAPTER 11

BROTHER SEYMOUR

Everyone at Azusa Street loved Brother Seymour. Since he never took a salary, he could often be seen walking through the crowd with five or ten dollar bills sticking out of his pants pockets, which people had placed there unbeknownst to him. Sister Carney described him as "pleasant to be around…a humble man who always had a gleam in his eye, a smile on his face, and a deep, resonating voice."[316]

Florence Crawford agreed. In fact, she said it was Seymour's voice which first attracted her to Azusa Street: "They sang a little, but that did not seem to touch my heart. They went down in prayer but that didn't move me at all…. Finally, a big colored man got up on his feet. He said, 'Hallelujah!' It just went through my soul. He waited a minute, and again he said, 'Hallelujah!' I thought, 'God, I have heard the voice from heaven. I have heard it at last…. He has the thing my heart is reaching out after. I forgot everything else, for I heard the voice of the great Shepherd of the sheep."[317]

Brother Anderson described Seymour as "one of the sweetest men I have ever met."[318] Another said he was "the meekest man I had ever met."[319] John G. Lake said, "It was God in him that attracted people."[320] Even in social settings, one could feel the anointing on Seymour. Others reported that when they touched him, a kind of electricity would shock them. Lake wrote, "God had put such a hunger into that man's heart that when the fire of God came it glorified him. I do not believe any other man in modern times had a more wonderful deluge of God in his life than God gave to that dear fellow, and the glory and power of a real Pentecost swept the world."[321]

New Testament translator A.S. Worrell, who visited the Azusa Street Mission in 1906, said, "Brother Seymour has more power with God, and more power from God, than all his critics in and out of this city. His strength is in his conscious weakness and lowliness before God; and so long as he maintains this attitude, the power of God will, no doubt, continue to flow through him."[322]

A newspaper reporter once described William Seymour thus: "Adorning his mouth is one massive gold tooth, ranked by rows of other teeth, perfectly straight and white. The beard that he wears could be called a flowing one if it was longer. It flows— what there is of it. His voice is like the roaring of a cannon, and of all his most striking characteristics, he has but one eye."

Photo: Flower Pentecostal Heritage Center.

A.C. Valdez, Sr. described Seymour as "a plain man with a short beard and a glass eye." He said, "He didn't seem like a leader to me, but when I saw what was going on, I knew he didn't have to be."[323]

Others described him as "humble," "quiet," "soft-spoken," "unassuming," and "gentle." William Durham, who visited Azusa Street in 1907, said, "He walks and talks with God. His power is in his weakness. He seems to maintain a helpless dependence on God and is as simple-hearted as a little child, and at the same time is so filled with God that you feel the love and power every time you get near him." Concerning his visit, Durham wrote, "The first thing that impressed me, was the love and unity that prevailed in the meeting, and the heavenly sweetness that filled the very air that I breathed."[324] While many Holiness leaders seemed to thrive on conflict and confrontation, Seymour was the opposite—gentle, humble, unguarded, and gracious with a disarming style of leadership.

Feisty evangelist Glenn Cook was one of several Holiness critics who went to the mission to set Seymour and his followers straight. They believed Seymour was preaching heresy and that the manifestations were not from God and told them so. But the more they criticized Seymour, the more their own hearts convicted them that Seymour was right. Before long, they were on their knees begging for forgiveness and praying to receive what Seymour had.

Cook said, "Every time he preached he would quote from Mark 16 and Acts 2:4, insisting that no one had received the baptism of the Holy Ghost unless they spoke in tongues.... But the contention was all on our part. I have never met a man who had such control over his spirit.... No amount of confusion and accusation seemed to disturb him. He would sit behind that packing case and smile at us until we were all condemned by our own activities." He said, even the Holiness people who continued to reject Seymour's preaching "had a secret reverence and admiration for this man who really lived what he had been preaching for years, a sanctified life. It was the wonderful character of this man whom God had chosen that attracted the people to keep coming to this humble meeting."[325] Seymour believed his ultimate leadership role was to empower God's people for the work of ministry.[326]

SEYMOUR'S ECUMENICISM

Pastor Seymour had a vision for shared experience and communal cooperation between various Christian groups. According to one of Seymour's signed articles in *The Apostolic Faith*, the Apostolic Faith Movement stood for "Christian unity everywhere." "We are not fighting men or churches, but seeking to displace dead forms and creeds and wild fanaticisms with living, practical Christianity. 'Love, Faith, Unity' are our watchwords, and 'Victory through the Atoning Blood' our battle cry."[327] According to the *California Eagle*, an African American newspaper in Los Angeles, pastor Seymour came to Los Angeles with the intention of founding a congregation in which members of all races would be welcome. It would be a place where everyone could make a contribution, and where they could all be accepted as equals."[328]

Azusa Street historian Cecil Robeck wrote, "For several years, under Pastor Seymour's unique ministry, the mission attracted and held the ongoing participation of African Americans, European Americans, Hispanic Americans, Asian Americans, Native Americans and others. One early leader estimated more than twenty nations were represented at the meetings. As a result, the Azusa Street Mission provides a glimpse of what is possible if we allow space for the Holy Spirit to change our hearts and minds. It may also provide a model for congregations in our own day to embrace this same kind of diversity, to demonstrate before the world the power of the gospel to break down the artificial racial and ethnic walls that otherwise divide us."[329]

The Apostolic Faith reported: "[The meetings have] been a melting time. The people are all melted together...made one lump, one bread, all one body in Christ Jesus. There is neither Jew or Gentile, bond or free, in the Azusa Street Mission. No instrument that God can use is rejected on account of color or dress or lack of education. This is why God has built up the work.... The sweetest thing is the loving harmony."[330] A.S. Worrell said the Azusa work had rediscovered the blood of Christ to the church at that time. Great emphasis was placed on Christ's blood for cleansing and for unity.

Glenn Cook concurred, "If God's people would only come together and forget about doctrines and leaders whose vision is blurred by building churches and collecting tithes, having only one objective and that to be filled with all the fulness of God, I know that God would answer prayer. Doctrines and teaching have their proper place in the gospel plan but that overpowering, drawing power of the love of God must come first and our present lukewarm condition is caused by a lack of this love that 'nothing can offend.'"[331]

Frank Bartleman added, "When God's church becomes what it should be, in love and unity, the doors will never be closed or locked. …There is no division in…true Pentecost or in true worship."[332] He continued: "Every fresh division or party in the church gives to the world a contradiction as to the oneness of the body of Christ, and the truthfulness of the Gospel. Multitudes are bowing down and burning incense to a doctrine rather than Christ…. The Spirit is laboring for the unity of believers today, for the 'one body,' that the prayer of Jesus may be answered, 'that they all may be one, that the world may believe.'"[333]

Like the Evening Light Saints, Seymour believed strongly not only in racial equality but also in gender equality. On his way to Los Angeles, Seymour visited and stayed at the headquarters of the Pillar of Fire denomination in Denver, headed by a woman, Alma White. Six of the twelve original elders and leaders of the Azusa Street Mission were women. Among their many duties, they were placed in charge of examining potential missionaries and evangelists for ordination, which played a major role in the credentialing of ministers. Indeed, many women preached and sang at the mission, participated in weekly leadership meetings, served as state directors, city missionaries, camp meeting coordinators, and many more were eventually themselves sent out as evangelists and missionaries all over the globe.

SEYMOUR'S PREACHING

Like Evan Roberts in the Welsh Revival, Seymour did not preach long or often. He wanted the Lord to "have His way" and the miracles often spoke for themselves. As Jesus once said, "Believe me...or else believe me for the sake of the works themselves."[334] However, when he did preach what he called "old-time repentance, old-time pardon, old-time sanctification, old-time power over devils and diseases, and the old-time 'baptism with the Holy Ghost and fire,'" his words changed the world.[335] He often emphasized salvation or one's need to renounce sin and accept Jesus as Savior. Seymour's sermons usually only lasted about twenty minutes but were known to have lasted up to ninety minutes.

A.G. Osterberg described Seymour as a "slow speaking, humble, unpretentious, Bible loving, God fearing minister." Regarding his preaching, he said, "He was meek and plain spoken and no orator. He spoke the common language of the uneducated class. He might preach for three-quarters of an hour with no more emotionalism than that post. He was no arm-waving thunderer, by any stretch of the imagination. The only way to explain the results is this: that his teachings were so simple that people who were opposed to organized religion fell for it. It was the simplicity that attracted them."[336]

William Manley described Seymour's preaching as "short" and "fiery" and "in the tenderest love. Not a harsh word is spoken. No denunciation of any one, except in tender love." Another witness described the response to Seymour's preaching saying, "people rise and flock to the altar. There is no urging. What kind of preaching is it that brings them? Why, the simple declaring of the Word of God. There is such power in the preaching of the Word in the Spirit that people are shaken on the benches."[337]

The meetings themselves were long and spontaneous. A reporter once described Seymour's preaching as "a jumble of Scripture and shouting."[338] Others described him as yelling when he preached. However,

More than anything else, Seymour preached love: "Pentecostal power, when you sum it all up," he said, "is just more of God's love. If it does not bring more love, it is simply a counterfeit.... Pentecost makes us love Jesus more and love our brothers more. It brings us all into one common family."

Photo: Flower Pentecostal Heritage Center.

Seymour thought of himself as more of a teacher than a preacher. His style was simple, direct, not often dynamic, but sometimes emotional. He often hurled challenges at his audience, urging them to turn from the world or leave their rigid traditions behind and seek salvation, sanctification, and the baptism in the Holy Spirit, always in that order. In fact, Seymour often used the imagery and typology of the tabernacle of Moses to teach justification, sanctification, and Spirit baptism.

SEYMOUR ON SANCTIFICATION AND SPIRIT BAPTISM

He taught, "First we come to the court of the tabernacle. This is where the sinner does his first works. Here we find the brazen altar which stands for justification.... As soon as a soul is pardoned, he is washed and the work of regeneration is wrought in his soul.... Now the believer comes to the golden altar.... Now he can consecrate himself to be sanctified. Here he finds on the altar the Blood of Jesus, which represents Christ the sanctifier of His people.... We can see that the baptism with the Holy Ghost is not a work of grace for there is no altar in the Holy of Holies. This is another step, the gift of the Holy Ghost. Instead of an altar, there is an ark of gold, which represents the Lord Jesus Christ perfected in you, for in Christ you have the experience of justification, sanctification and the baptism with the Holy Ghost."[339]

Regarding the baptism in the Holy Spirit, Seymour taught, "Many precious souls believe today that in justification they have it all, that they have already the baptism with the Holy Ghost or enduement of power; but in that day, they will find they are mistaken. They say, away with this third work. What is the difference, dear one, if it takes 300 works? We want to be ready to meet the bridegroom. The foolish virgins said to the wise, 'Give us of your oil.' This thing is going to happen. Many that are saying they have enough and are opposing, will find their lamps going out and ask the prayers of God's people. God is warning you through His servants and handmaidens to get ready; but many are going to come back to get the oil from others. Dear ones, we cannot get more than enough for ourselves. You can grasp the saints' hands but you cannot squeeze any oil out. You have to get the vessel filled for yourself."[340]

In distinguishing the baptism in the Holy Spirit from sanctification, Seymour taught, "There is a great difference between a sanctified person and one that is baptized with the Holy Ghost and fire. A sanctified person is cleansed and filled with divine love, but the one that is baptized with the Holy Ghost has the power of God on his soul and has power with God and men, power over all the kingdoms of Satan and over all his emissaries." Pentecostal historian Vinson Synan added, "With this kind of Spirit-filled people, Seymour declared that

'God can take a worm and thresh a mountain.' Indeed, God and his little flock at Azusa Street were becoming a tremendous force in world Christianity."[341]

Sadly, not a single complete sermon that Seymour preached exists today, only excerpts or fragments of sermons quoted in *The Apostolic Faith*. In the thirteen issues of *The Apostolic Faith*, only twenty sermons were directly attributed to Seymour. However, from these excerpts we know that Seymour's preaching remained consistent with the mission's doctrinal statement and that he remained true to his spiritual upbringing, which included the Wesleyan-Holiness tradition, the Evening Light Saints, Martin Wells Knapp's teachings, as well as C.P. Jones's, C.H. Mason's, and Charles Parham's teachings. Consequently, Seymour believed firmly in the importance of living dedicated lives that were free from sin and uncleanness.

SEYMOUR ON SPEAKING IN TONGUES

Since speaking in tongues was such a novelty at Azusa Street, Seymour often tried to downplay its role, saying, "Now, do not go from this meeting and talk about tongues, but try to get people saved." Seymour believed salvation to be the grand purpose of Pentecost. He wrote in his very first newsletter, "God has been working with His children mostly, getting them through to Pentecost, and laying the foundation for a mighty wave of salvation among the unconverted."[342] Likewise, in the preamble of Seymour's last known written document, *Doctrines and Discipline*, he said: "We believe God's design in raising up the Apostolic Faith Church in America was to evangelize over these lands. As a proof hereof we have seen since 1906 that time of an extraordinary work of God extended throughout all the United States and Territories and throughout the world."[343]

Like Finney, Moody, Torrey, and many others before him, Seymour preached that the real purpose of the baptism in the Holy Ghost was "to be flooded with the love of God and power for service."[344] Tongues would follow. In all of Seymour's signed articles in *The Apostolic Faith*, he gave more attention to sanctification than he did to speaking in tongues.

SEYMOUR ON KEEPING ORDER IN SERVICES

Seymour later admitted, "In the early days…we all used to break out in tongues," but then everyone had to learn "to be quieter with this gift."[345] He said, "Often when God sends a blessed wave upon us, we all may speak in tongues for awhile, but we will not keep it up while preaching service is going on, for we want to be obedient to the Word, that everything may be done decently and in order and without confusion." If someone got too loud or started pounding their seat, Seymour would tap that person on the shoulder and say, "Brother, that is the flesh."[346]

John G. Lake remembered a service in which a man kept getting up and talking every few minutes. Seymour endured but finally ran out of patience. Pointing his finger to the man, he said, "In the name of Jesus Christ, sit down." The man did not sit but fell and had to be carried out of the service. Clara Lum said Seymour possessed "true wisdom and gentleness in conducting the meetings" and everyone recognized he was "called of God and anointed for the work."[347]

In one sermon, Seymour urged: "Dear one[s] in Christ who are seeking the baptism with the Holy Ghost, do not seek for tongues but for the promise of the Father, and pray for the baptism with the Holy Ghost, and God will throw in the tongues according to Acts 2:4…. [This will] come just as freely as the air we breathe. It is nothing worked up, but it comes from the heart.... So when the Holy Ghost life comes in, the mouth opens, through the power of the Spirit in the heart. Glory to God!"[348]

Bartleman agreed saying, "I never sought tongues. My natural mind resisted the idea. This phenomenon necessarily violates human reason. It means abandonment of this faculty for the time. And this is 'foolishness' and a stone of stumbling to the natural mind or reason.... The natural reason must be yielded in the matter. There is a gulf to cross between reason and revelation, and it is this principle in experience that leads to the Pentecostal baptism.... This is why simple people usually get in first.... They are like the little boys going swimming.... They get in first because they have the least clothes to divest themselves of. We must all come 'naked' into this experience."[349]

In another sermon, Seymour wrote: "In our meetings, we have had people to come and claim that they had received the baptism with the Holy Spirit, but when they were put to the test by the Holy Spirit, they were found wanting.... Again people have imitated the gift of tongues, but how quickly the Holy Spirit would reveal to every one of the true children that had the Pentecostal baptism, and put a heavy rebuke upon the counterfeit, in tongues, until the counterfeits were silenced and condemned.... People are trying to imitate the work of the Holy Ghost these days, just as they did when the Lord sent Moses to Pharoah.... Pharoah...called for wise men and the counterfeit sorcerers and magicians of Egypt...but Aaron's rod swallowed up their rods. So the power of the Holy Ghost in God's people today condemns and swallows up the counterfeit."[350]

THE REAL EVIDENCE OF
SPIRIT BAPTISM

By May 1907, Seymour was preaching that speaking in tongues was only one of the signs of Holy Spirit baptism. He said, "Tongues are one of the signs that go with every baptized person, but it is not the real evidence of the baptism in the every day life. Your life must measure with the fruits of the Spirit."[351] He added, "If you get angry, or speak evil, or backbite, I care not how many tongues you may have, you have not the baptism with the Holy Spirit. You have lost your salvation."[352] As far as Seymour was concerned, speaking in tongues could be accepted as Bible evidence of Spirit baptism only when accompanied by godly love. Seymour preached love more than anything else, and without this spiritual fruit, he was not convinced speaking in tongues had been divinely given.

Bartleman chronicled, "Divine love was wonderfully manifest in the meetings. The people would not even allow an unkind word said against their opposers or the churches. The message was the love of God. It was sort of 'first love' (Revelation 2:4) of the early church returned. The baptism of the Holy Spirit, as we received it in the beginning, did not allow us to think, speak, or hear evil of any man. The Spirit was very sensitive, tender as a dove.... We knew the moment we had grieved the Spirit by an unkind thought or word. We seemed to live in a sea of pure divine love. The Lord fought our battles for us in those days.... The false was sifted out from the real by the Spirit of God. The Word of God itself decided absolutely all issues. The hearts of the people, both in act and motive, were searched to the very bottom.... We were on holy ground." Bartleman also quoted William and Mary Booth's son-in-law, Arthur Booth-Clibborn, who said of the apostles, "Their Calvary was complete, and so a complete Pentecost came to match it.... 'As your cross, so will your Pentecost be.'"[353]

Ironically and perhaps most of all, Charles Parham, Seymour's "father in the faith," caused him to adjust his theology concerning the baptism in the Holy Spirit with speaking in tongues as the evidence. After all, the same man who introduced him to speaking in tongues did not demonstrate much love after delivering disparaging remarks against the Azusa Street faithful. In contrast, Seymour taught, preached, and exemplified love, while emphasizing the simplicity of the Pentecostal experience for love and power for service. Neither Parham nor later William Durham's theology would allow them to accept or authenticate a Spirit-filled believer who did *not* speak in tongues. Parham had difficulties accepting or authenticating even those who did not speak in another known language. Indeed, speaking in tongues would become a doctrinal requirement for ministers in several Pentecostal denominations.

Seymour would later deal with this in his *Doctrines and Discipline*, written one month after the Assemblies of God organized. In its preface he wrote, "Wherever the doctrine of the Baptism in the Holy Spirit will only be known as the evidence of speaking in tongues, that work will be an open door for witches and spiritualists and freeloveism. That work will suffer, because all kinds of spirits can come in…. When we leave the word of God and begin to go by signs and voices we will wind up in Spiritualism."[354] Regarding speaking in tongues only as known languages, Seymour preached, "Beloved, if you do not know the language that you speak, do not puzzle yourself about it, for the Lord did not promise us He would tell us what language we were speaking, but He promised us the interpretation of what we speak."[355] In the end, Seymour valued speaking in tongues as *an* initial evidence, not as a *continuing* evidence. For that, more than tongues was required.

Again, perhaps reflecting on Parham's visit to Azusa Street, Seymour said: "If you find people that get a harsh spirit, and even talk in tongues in a harsh spirit, it is not the Holy Ghost talking. His utterances are in power and glory with blessing and sweetness…. He is a meek and humble Spirit—not a harsh Spirit." Seymour believed God did not recognize color, flesh, or name but favored the contrite. Sadly, the October 1906 issue of *The Apostolic Faith* announcing Parham's coming, declared, "Before another issue of this paper, we look for Bro. Parham in Los Angeles, a brother who is full of *divine love*."[356]

Regarding signs and manifestations overall, Seymour taught: "Keep your eyes on Jesus and not on the manifestations, not seeking to get some great thing more than somebody else. The Lord God wants you just as humble as a baby, looking for Him to fill you with more of God and power. If you get your eyes on manifestations and signs you are liable to get a counterfeit, but what you want to seek is more holiness, more of God."[357]

Ironically, most Pentecostal churches and denominations today would vehemently disagree with Seymour's theology on Holy Spirit baptism and speaking in other tongues, though they consider him "the Father of modern Pentecostalism." Instead, as Seymour's biographer Charles Fox Jr. points out, Seymour could more appropriately be considered the father or forerunner of the modern Charismatic movement since it also accepts speaking in tongues in the broader sense as one of many gifts or manifestations of the Holy Spirit.[358] In Seymour's own words, "The Pentecostal movement is too large to be confined in any denomination or sect. It works outside, drawing all together in one bond of love, one church, one body of Christ." According to Fox, "Seymour argued for the practice of divine love that set believers free to be in unity rather than in the adaption of creeds and confessions that divided Christians.... He was fully convinced that the secret to the success of the Azusa Revival was that believers were united in purpose, similar to the day of Pentecost."[359]

Seymour wrote, "O how my heart cries out to God in these days that He would make every child of His see the necessity of living in the 17th chapter of John, that we may be one in the body of Christ, as Jesus has prayed. ...But we are not willing to accept any errors, it matters not how charming and sweet they may seem to be. If they do not tally with the Word of God, we reject them." According to Seymour, speaking in tongues was *one* of the evidences, while divine love was the *key result* of Spirit baptism.[360]

Seymour continued, "Many may start in this salvation, and yet if they do not watch and keep under the Blood, they will lose the Spirit of Jesus, which is *divine love*, and have only gifts which will be as sounding brass and a tinkling cymbal, and sooner or later these will be taken away. If you want to live in the Spirit, live in the fruits of the Spirit every day."[361]

An incident was recorded in *The Apostolic Faith* in which a preacher was filled with the Holy Spirit during a service at Azusa Street. After he spoke in tongues, his wife and children became frightened, thinking their loved one had lost his mind. However, when his family sensed the divine love which the Holy Spirit placed in his heart, they said, "Papa was never so sane in his life."[362]

Seymour concluded, "Pentecostal power, when you sum it all up, is just more of God's love. If it does not bring more love, it is simply a counterfeit. Pentecost means to live right in the 13th chapter of First Corinthians, which is the standard. When you live there, you have no trouble to keep salvation. This is Bible religion. It is not a manufactured religion. Pentecost makes us love Jesus more and love our brothers more. It brings us all into one common family."[363]

SEYMOUR ON THE STATE OF THE MODERN CHURCH

Though Seymour was the legal pastor of the Azusa Street Mission, he preached that the Holy Spirit was the true and active head, bishop, and chairman of the church. He preached, "It is the office work of the Holy Spirit to preside over the entire work of God on earth (John 10:3). Jesus was our Bishop while on earth, but now He has sent the Holy Ghost, amen, to take His place—not men (John 14:16; 15:26; 16:7-14). Praise His holy name! …No religious assembly is legal without His presence and His transaction."[364]

Seymour continued, "Many people today think we need new churches…stone structures, brick structures, modern improvements, new choirs, trained singers right from the conservatories, paying from seven to fifteen hundred dollars a year for singing, fine pews, fine chandeliers, everything that could attract the human heart to win souls to the meeting house is used in this twentieth century. We find that they have reached the climax, but all of that has failed to bring divine power and salvation to precious souls."[365]

"It is found that a good many of the church people seem to be full of love, but there has always been a lack of power. We wonder why sinners are not converted, and why it is that the church is always making improvements and failing to do the work that Christ called her to do. It is because men have taken the place of Christ and the Holy Spirit…. When the Holy Ghost comes in He will cleanse out dead forms and ceremonies, and will give life and power to His ministers and preachers, in the same old church buildings. But without the Holy Ghost they are simply tombstones."[366]

"The first things in every assembly is to see that He, the Holy Ghost, is installed as the chairman. The reason why we have so many dried up missions and churches today, is because they have not the Holy Ghost as the chairman. They have some man in His place…. Wherever you find the Holy Ghost as chairman in any assembly, you will find a fruitful assembly, you will find children being born unto God."[367]

SEYMOUR'S VOCABULARY

John G. Lake said Seymour "had the funniest vocabulary. But, I want to tell you, there were doctors, lawyers, and professors, listening to the marvelous things coming from his lips. It was not what he said in words, it was what he said from his spirit to my heart that showed me he had more of God in his life than any man I had ever met up to that time."[368] Rachel Sizelove once wrote phonetically what Seymour preached. She said, "Seymour would get up and say, 'Dear lubbed on; these met'ns ah difent form any you ebber saw in all your born days. These ah Holy Ghost met'ns and no flesh can glory in the presence of our God.'"[369]

Seymour was not a highly educated man, but he was nonetheless sure of what he believed and never hesitated to voice his opinion, even when it contradicted the beliefs of those around him. Thus, Seymour was often described as speaking softly but with a strong voice. Even when correcting people, he would put a gentle hand on someone's shoulder and say, "Brother, that is the flesh." Other times his correction came by a simple look or through his "calm, strong voice."[370]

CHAPTER 12

THE DECLINE, SECOND SHOWER, AND DEMISE

In 1907, the congregation incorporated as the Apostolic Faith Mission and purchased the building from the First African Methodist Episcopal Church for $15,000 with $4,000 down. Some felt it necessary to buy the mission believing the "For Sale" sign, which remained on the building, would eventually lead to it being sold out from under them. By that time, the church had an aggressive evangelistic outreach program that hosted a weekly children's church, weekly training sessions for ministers and leaders, and coordinated small group cottage prayer meetings and four-month outdoor camp meetings.

By 1908, the Azusa Street Revival had already become a global phenomenon. Azusa Street missionaries dotted the city, region, nation, and world. In the U.S. alone, 50,000 men, women, and children were reportedly praising and magnifying God in new tongues, and not a single state was without the witness of Pentecost.[371] Spiritualists, hypnotists, critics, and the like, who had tried to exert their influence much like the circus they created, had packed up and moved on. Since speaking in tongues was no longer "new," the media was no longer interested. Even most of Los Angeles' city officials had finally decided to tolerate the group.

In the summer of 1908, camp meetings resumed at the Arroyo Seco and street preachers proclaimed their messages on the corner of

Pasadena (now Figueroa) Avenue and Avenue Sixty-four, just a block from Dr. Finis Yoakum's Pisgah Home. The camp meetings continued to run throughout the summer with large crowds in attendance, while regular services continued back at what some affectionately referred to as "the old manger home." One wrote, "The pillar of fire still rests there." Another wrote, "the meetings have been going on every day since the work started and God's Word and the Holy Spirit are just as fresh and new as ever."[372]

THE DECLINE

Only two or three official issues of *The Apostolic Faith* were published in 1908 as reports on the revival at the mission became brief or vague at best. About the biggest news was that Lucy Farrow had returned from Africa and was praying for people in the cottage at the rear of the building, and that the Azusa Street property had successfully been purchased. Clara Lum again compared the property to the "barn at Bethlehem" where Christ was born, concluding, "The Spirit falls on humble hearts and in humble missions and churches."[373]

The publication also reminded its readers that the meetings had continued nonstop since April 1906, and that many were still being saved, sanctified, healed, and baptized with the Holy Ghost, but then admitted they had suffered some losses because some people "thought the teaching on divorce was too straight." However, their doctrinal position had not changed because God wanted to use "a clean people and pure doctrine as a channel for this Pentecostal power."[374] From the beginning, Seymour had allowed those who had been divorced and remarried to engage in ministry. However, upon further searching the Scriptures, he later believed this to be wrong and took a stricter stand.

INTERNAL CONFLICTS

Among the first serious internal challenges came when Professor Carpenter, a mathematician and Azusa trustee, insisted that Seymour give full account for all the funds that had been given to missions. The money had flowed so quickly, freely, and generously, Seymour had not kept any books, not so much as "the scratch of a pen." Seymour said, "I sent it out as the Lord told me and as the need required, and before God, I never misspent or kept one cent of it." He could remember as many as fifty names and mentioned that $100 went here and $500 there but could not give a full accounting. Though Seymour had never owned property and lived and died in near poverty, this was not enough to satisfy Professor Carpenter. For many, a "different spirit" had crept into Azusa Street, which would ultimately lead to its destruction.[375]

The dispute over whether to take up offerings at Azusa Street was also a divisive issue, since it had long been a tradition at the mission not to. The first issue of *The Apostolic Faith* proclaimed, "No collections are taken for rent, no begging for money. No man's silver or gold is coveted. The silver and the gold are His own to carry on His work. He can also publish his own papers without asking for money or subscription price."[376] Despite this, early Pentecostals were extremely generous.

Rachel Sizelove recalled, "How well I remember the first time the flesh began to get in the way of the Holy Ghost, and how the burden came upon the saints that morning when Brother Seymore stood before the audience and spoke of raising money to buy the Azusa Street Mission. The Holy Ghost was grieved. You could feel it all over the audience, when they began to ask for money, and the Holy Ghost power began to leave, and instead of the Holy Ghost heavenly choir, they brought in a piano."[377] Rachel had been a Free Methodist evangelist prior to Azusa Street and the Free Methodists were "non-instrumental" at the time. Others blamed the offering collections on the "devil," comparing this to when the mission had incorporated, installed elected trustees, and became a denomination like all others. It smacked of organization.

THE REVIVAL CONTINUES

Still, the revival continued without missing a beat—praising and shouting continued, the testimonies continued, the preaching continued, the manifestations continued, salvations, healings, and Spirit baptisms continued, and the crowds continued to come. George B. Studd, a British gentleman who had worked at the Peniel Mission for years and attended the Azusa Street meetings through August 1908, kept a daily diary attesting to this fact. However, what did change by 1908 was the fact that Studd and many other white people started moving back and forth between Azusa Street and the Upper Room Mission. The Upper Room also met at least twice daily, and most eventually left the former for the latter, while Pastors Seymour and Fisher continued working closely together. Seymour's goal was never to build a megachurch but instead to build a coalition of congregations under the Apostolic Faith banner. He understood the needs of the people, the city, and the need for revival to expand, and therefore welcomed other churches.

George Studd, who had been instrumental in financing the Peniel Mission and who had helped arrange the purchase of the Azusa Street Mission, was now supporting and serving as a minister in the Upper Room Mission. In July 1908, he wrote to his friends in Britain that the Azusa Street Mission was now "entirely controlled (humanly speaking) by the coloured people, though white people still attend there."[378] According to Studd, the Upper Room was now the "strongest mission" in Los Angeles.[379]

Having returned from mission work and speaking at Azusa Street during this time, Frank Bartleman wrote, "One evening at Azusa

Mission the spirit of prayer came upon me as '*a rushing mighty wind*' (Acts 2:2). The power ran all through the building. I had been burdened for the deadness that had crept in there. The temporary leaders were frightened and did not know what to do. They telephoned for help. They had not been with us in the beginning. Brother Seymour was out of town. I was upstairs in the hallway. Others joined me in prayer. We went downstairs, and the fire broke out in the meeting. But the leaders in charge were not spiritual…. They did not understand it. God was trying to come back. They seemed afraid someone might steal the mission. The Spirit could not work. Besides, they had organized now, and I had not joined their organization."[380]

FACTORS AND PERSPECTIVES

The factors leading to the decline and ultimate demise of the Azusa Street Revival were not much different from other historical revivals. A stricter order was eventually imposed on the services, limiting the flow of the Spirit. Unity among the various races, classes, and ideologies began to wane. Measures to formalize were introduced: purchasing the building, becoming incorporated, putting an official name on the building—even setting up a "throne" for Elder Seymour. Wholesale rejection by the Christian community—especially the Holiness movement—finally caught up with them. Plus, much as the Holiness movement had once been perceived by Methodists, many early Pentecostals either saw themselves or were perceived by others as being part of a spiritual aristocracy. Additionally, one reporter declared speaking in tongues was on the decline and was being replaced by other activities like "ground and lofty tumbling," "grasshopper activities," and "Holy jumping."[381]

Perhaps the best perspective on what led to the demise of the Azusa Street Revival came from Mattie Cummings, who was ten years old when the revival began, and whose family attended the original Bonnie

Brae cottage meetings. When asked why the Azusa Street Revival broke up, she said, "Because men became proud. They thought they could do things instead of the Holy Spirit doing things, and any time that men become proud like they did at that particular time, it just breaks something up."[382] Perhaps they who "were the humblest" eventually let pride enter in.

Sister Carney's perspective was even simpler: the revival "stopped when Brother Seymour stopped putting that box over his head," another loss of humility.[383] A.G. Osterberg's perspective was similar: "When the tears ended the Azusa revival ended!"[384] Seymour's take on the revival's demise was included in his preface to the mission's *Doctrines and Discipline*: "Very soon division arose through some of our brethren, and the Holy Spirit was grieved."[385] Perhaps this is why *one who sows discord among brethren* is considered an "abomination" in the Old Testament and a "carnal," "warped," "sinful," and "self-condemned" person in the New Testament.[386]

Bartleman summarized: "As the movement began to wane, platforms were built higher, coattails were worn longer, choirs were organized, and string bands came into existence to 'jazz' the people. The kings came back once more to their thrones, restored to sovereignty. We were no longer brethren. Then the divisions multiplied. While Brother Seymour kept his head inside the old empty box in Azusa all was well. They later built a throne for him also. Now we have not one hierarchy, but many."[387]

He added: "If ever men shall seek to control, corner, or own this work of God, either for their own glory or for that of an organization, we shall find the Spirit refusing to work. The glory will depart."[388] Bartleman was also offended when the "Apostolic Faith Mission" sign was painted on the building, which he described as evidence of a "party" or denominational spirit. Despite Bartleman's criticisms and lack of support for Azusa, when he left for a mission trip at the end of 1908, Azusa was the only mission in Los Angeles that gave him an offering.[389]

THE BIGGEST BLOW

The biggest blow to the mission came when Seymour married Jennie Evans Moore in 1908. Jennie, who was on staff, suggested it was the Lord's will for them to marry and Seymour agreed. Clara Lum, who was also on staff, did not agree. Lum, along with Florence Crawford and many other early Pentecostals, believed that Christ's return was imminent and that there was no time for marriage. Being single was preferred over marriage, and for married couples, abstinence was preferred. As one participant explained, "Those were wonderful days—days of Heaven on earth. We expected Jesus to come back to earth in 1908, it was so great."[390]

Florence Crawford founded and led the Apostolic Faith work in Portland, Oregon, from 1907 to 1936. After being saved, sanctified, and baptized in the Holy Spirit at Azusa Street, she became an undaunted leader whose message and ministry reached hearts and lives the world over.

Photo: Flower Pentecostal Heritage Center.

Both Lum and Crawford rejected Seymour's marriage on these grounds, believing he had compromised his sanctification and fallen into disbelief rather than staying focused on holy living and preparing for Christ's return. Crawford was previously divorced and had left her current husband and children in Highland Park to carry the revival tour on the road. When she finally settled in Portland, her children joined her, but she never returned to her husband. According to Crawford, the act of marriage was a fleshly act.[391]

Seymour vehemently disagreed, stating in *The Apostolic Faith*: "Wives have left husbands and gone off claiming that the Lord has called her to do mission work and to leave the little children at home to fare the best they can.... Dearly beloved, let us respect homes and families."[392] In another message, Seymour wrote that marriage is "honorable in all" and "the forbidding of marriage is a doctrine of devils."[393] In yet another he wrote, "It is no sin to marry. 'Marriage is honorable and the bed undefiled, but whoremongers and adulterers God will judge.' Heb. 13.4. There are those today in marriage life, since they have received sanctification and some the baptism with the Holy Ghost, who have come to think that is a sin for them to live as husband and wife."[394]

Bishop Ithiel Clemmons of the Church of God in Christ recalled having a conversation with C.H. Mason in 1948. Mason told him Clara Lum had fallen in love with Pastor Seymour and sought a marriage proposal from him. Seymour then went to Mason for advice and Mason urged him not to marry a white woman given the current state of racial relations in America. However, Seymour wanted to marry, and so chose Jennie Evans Moore.[395] Crawford and Lum may have viewed Seymour's refusal to marry a white woman as yielding to the pressure of racism or an aversion to living the "interracial miracle" he so frequently preached from the pulpit. Thus, lost love and vindictiveness may also have played a role in what happened next.

In June 1908, Lum suddenly left her position as ministry secretary to join Crawford in Portland, Oregon, taking the entire ministry publication including its 50,000 subscribers with her. The July/August 1908 issue of *The Apostolic Faith* went out exactly as before, only with a different return address. The paper simply stated, "We have moved the paper which the Lord laid on us to begin in Los Angeles to Portland, Oregon, which will now be its headquarters."[396] No further explanation was provided.

The paper included continued reports and testimonies of the revival spreading around the world with thoughts and words from Pastor Seymour—conveniently without mentioning his name. Page three contained an article entitled, "How Pentecost Came to Portland, Ore." Consequently, few questioned it and began sending their money and stamp offerings to: APOSTOLIC FAITH, PORTLAND, OREGON. Literally overnight, Seymour had lost his worldwide influence and support. His plans to build churches, rescue missions, foreign missions, schools, and colleges—all gone.

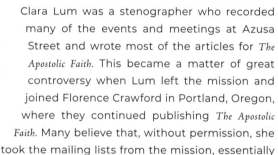

Clara Lum was a stenographer who recorded many of the events and meetings at Azusa Street and wrote most of the articles for *The Apostolic Faith*. This became a matter of great controversy when Lum left the mission and joined Florence Crawford in Portland, Oregon, where they continued publishing *The Apostolic Faith*. Many believe that, without permission, she took the mailing lists from the mission, essentially crippling the mission's contact with the world and its ability to raise funds, thus greatly contributing to the end of the revival.

Photo: Flower Pentecostal Heritage Center.

Crawford later claimed she broke ties with Seymour because of rumors Seymour had compromised his Wesleyan-Holiness belief on sanctification. Whether she heard these rumors from Lum, Cook, others, or fabricated them on her own, the fact remains that she never confirmed these rumors with Seymour, and Seymour never changed his beliefs regarding sanctification. Nevertheless, the Portland Apostolic Faith Mission accused the Azusa Street Mission of letting "down the standard of holiness" by ceasing to teach sanctification as a second work of grace.[397]

Crawford believed, since Seymour had failed both God and the movement, and since she had kept the faith and exposed the error, it was her God-given duty to relocate, carry on the name, and lead the "Apostolic Faith movement" into the future. She also claimed the Lord had told her during an outreach mission in Minneapolis, "If you will go back to Portland, Oregon, and stay there, I will make that place the headquarters of the Apostolic Faith work, and I will raise up the standard of the Gospel in that city."[398] She even claimed that the Azusa Street Mission had turned over the responsibility of publishing *The Apostolic Faith* to her, and that she and Lum had only taken two copies of the subscriber list, leaving twenty other copies of the list in Los Angeles.

According to Seymour, Lum became dissatisfied with the Azusa Street Mission, took an unauthorized leave of absence, violated her trust, and took the mission's newspaper to Portland with her.[399] Lum said she left to attend the Apostolic Faith camp meeting in Portland. This Crawford sponsored without Seymour's blessing, essentially creating a competing organization, while removing Seymour as its leader. Lum still met her June publishing deadline using the Los Angeles address, but from Portland, and without the official masthead. In fact, she promised to publish multiple issues from Portland since she planned to remain there for several months.

Seymour reportedly wrote in a lost or never-published October/November 1908 issue of *The Apostolic Faith* that Lum had taken the paper: "I must for the salvation of souls let it be known that the editor is still in Los Angeles...and will not remove *The Apostolic Faith* from Los Angeles, without letting subscribers and field workers know. This was a sad thing to our hearts for a worker to attempt to take the paper which is the property of the Azusa Street Mission to another city without consent, after being warned by the elders not to do so."[400]

FAILED RECOVERY ATTEMPTS

Seymour's failed attempt to recover the publication, by traveling to Portland later that year with several trustees, clearly revealed that Lum had permanently (not temporarily as Lum claimed) moved the paper to Portland without permission. Crawford's son, Raymond, said later in 1954 that Lum had used the camp meeting as a cover while all along planning to move to Portland to work with Crawford.[401] Premeditated or not, the effect was the same. Crawford and Lum refused to return the paper.

In a rare and uncharacteristic move by Seymour, as he left the Portland mission visibly saddened and without agreement or reconciliation, he saw E.S. Williams, a future General Superintendent of the Assemblies of God, on the stairs. Immediately recognizing him as one of the many ministers ordained and sent out by the Azusa Street Mission, and knowing this also meant he was receiving the coveted minister's railroad discount, Seymour asked, "Are you going to continue to preach here?" Williams replied, "Yes." Seymour said, "I'll have the railroad take away your clergy book." "If that is necessary," Williams replied. Seymour followed through with his threat, further revealing the depth of pain he must have felt from this incident.[402]

In 1909, since Crawford had not yet incorporated her work in Portland, Jennie Evans Moore, Malinda Mitchell, and Edward Doak filed articles of incorporation that legally established the Portland Apostolic Faith Mission as an "auxiliary" body to the Los Angeles Apostolic Faith Mission. This not only established that the Portland mission legally belonged to the Los Angeles mission, but also that the same board responsible for establishing the mission's publication was responsible for establishing the Portland mission. The board, which included Mrs. Seymour—possibly the worst emissary they could have sent considering Crawford and Lum's position—traveled to Portland to speak with the postmaster with proof that the publication belonged to them. This attempt also failed.

Crawford intervened and the postal service refused to accept the articles of incorporation as proof the publication legally belonged to the Los Angeles mission. After all, Crawford was well known in Portland; Seymour was not. The Portland paper printed a weak apology in 1910 stating, "This paper would be No. 21 from the beginning in Los Angeles, but it is No. 7 of Portland. We said it was moved from Los Angeles when we should have stated we were starting a new Apostolic Faith in Portland."[403] Crawford later recalled fond memories of her days at Azusa Street.

THE DECLINE CONTINUES

Though the Azusa Street Revival continued unhindered at least through August 1908, Seymour's marriage, Clum's departure, and the loss of the mission's publication weighed heavily on its future. By the beginning of 1909, the mission was in steady decline. Holiness layman and itinerant printer Ned Caswell wrote in his diary on March 7, 1909, "Seymour is fatter. Crowd was smaller, but still good."[404] Greek scholar and translator W.B. Godbey, who visited Los Angeles in 1909, found the city overall "electrified" with the Pentecostal movement and said the meetings at Azusa were still running night and day without intermission.[405]

In September 1909, Frank Bartleman, who had just returned to Los Angeles from a mission trip in Honolulu, wrote, "Azusa had lost out greatly since we left. 'How are the mighty fallen' (2 Samuel 1:19) came to me most forcibly. But the Spirit came upon three of us mightily in prayer one evening there. He assured us He was going to bring the power back to Azusa Mission again as at the beginning."[406]

The Upper Room Mission was one of more than a dozen churches and missions in Los Angeles that reoriented themselves to identify with the Azusa Street Revival. Pastor Elmer Fisher led this offshoot of The New Testament Church only four blocks from Azusa at 327½ Spring Street. Seymour valued them all, hosting weekly leadership meetings at the Azusa Mission to gather, pray, fellowship, study, counsel, support, and strategize.

Photo: Flower Pentecostal Heritage Center.

Caswell wrote in his diary on October 10, 1909, "Only a few old-timers and not much stirring."[407] Bartleman said, "The meetings had to run in appointed order." Some Mexicans wished to speak but "the leader deliberately refused to let them testify, crushing them ruthlessly. It was like murdering the Spirit of God.... Every meeting was now programmed from start to finish." "A spirit of dictatorship" had taken over the meetings. There was no room for the Holy Spirit to break in.[408] The numbers had dropped so dramatically that Seymour was forced to go on a cross-country preaching tour just to keep the now dwindling mission afloat. Leaving his wife and two young men in charge, he traveled from Maine to San Diego, preaching the Pentecostal message.

Canadian minister A.W. Frodsham, who visited Azusa Street in late 1910 to early 1911, described blacks and whites continuing to "worship freely together." He also said, though the mission had not been flourishing as of late, "now there are signs of abundance of rain, and many are being blessed."[409]

In contrast, Frodsham described the meetings in the Upper Room Mission much like the early days of Azusa: "The meetings are open, and the power of God is manifest in various ways.... Sometimes the meetings run one into the other, and do not close till late. The hall holds about 300 to 350, and it is well filled all day Sunday. Meetings are held every night except Mondays.... There are manifestations of the Spirit, heavenly choir, etc., but all of the flesh is kept out as much as possible. They are strong on the Word and prayer."[410]

Pastor Elmer Fisher's daughter, Ruth, also wrote of blind eyes and deaf ears being opened, tongues being loosened, others being delivered of insanity, and many being healed of all manner of sickness and disease at the Upper Room. She even recalled joining in the heavenly choir for two hours when she was baptized in the Spirit one afternoon.[411] By 1911, the Upper Room Mission was thriving as the Azusa Street Mission continued to wane.

THE SECOND SHOWER

When Holiness evangelist and pastor William H. Durham first heard about the work of God at Azusa Street from his North Avenue Mission in Chicago, he told his congregation, "That is the work of God."[412] Later, he heard someone preach that speaking in tongues was the Bible evidence of the baptism in the Holy Spirit, but not understanding it, he rejected it. However, when he saw that those who spoke in tongues had something he did not, he became a seeker. He went to Los Angeles in February 1907 and received his Pentecostal experience within a few weeks. After remaining awhile in A.G. Osterberg's home, Durham preached in Colorado Springs, Denver, and Des Moines on his way home to Chicago.

In Colorado Springs, he recounted preaching three times to "a crowded house, and the power of God was on the people, fifty came to the altar, and several came through and spoke in tongues."[413] He added, "The Spirit falls like rain wherever I preach His Word, and it seems there is no effort on my part."[414] He arrived home to the largest attendance in the history of the North Avenue Mission, with more people coming to the altar than they could handle.

However, when Durham returned to Los Angeles on a preaching mission in February 1911, the story was completely different. He found the Pentecostal work in that city to be in total disarray and decided to relocate his ministry from Chicago to Los Angeles—the birthplace of modern Pentecostalism. As far as he was concerned, all the movement's leaders in that city had proven incompetent and all who had been touched by the revival had since lost faith.

One reason, Durham diagnosed, was that many of these congregations still believed in sanctification. Durham had recently challenged this Wesleyan teaching at a Chicago Pentecostal convention in 1910. There, he sought to nullify sanctification as a second work, teaching instead that sanctification was a gradual process appropriated over the course of one's life, not an instantaneous experience. Durham invited Parham's associate Howard Goss to the conference, and Goss agreed with Durham, infuriating Parham.

Upon arriving in Los Angeles, Durham first approached the Upper Room Mission with his new doctrine. Fisher refused to listen, and

Durham was furious. Then he held several successful meetings at the Azusa Street Mission with about a dozen people in attendance. The two young elders Seymour had left in charge remembered Durham had been baptized in the Spirit at Azusa Street and had given a marvelous testimony there, so they invited him to continue preaching. Durham preached two and a half months. All seats were soon filled with hundreds more having to be turned away. It was like old times again. Many visiting ministers who had come during the "glory days" returned for a second visit, and many of the original participants returned. Bartleman called it, "the second shower of the 'latter rain,'" saying, "the fire began to fall at old Azusa as at the beginning."[415]

Durham was "a man of impressive personality" and a "pulpit prodigy" who could easily induce his audiences into fits of shouting and jerking, known as "the Durham jerks," but with one glaring doctrinal difference—Durham vehemently opposed the Wesleyan-Holiness "second work" doctrine of sanctification, stating there was only salvation and baptism in the Holy Spirit.[416] Durham believed Christ's work on the cross was a "Finished Work," a term coined by him, and that sanctification was received at conversion. However, holiness was something to be progressively worked out over the course of one's life, not some instantaneous experience.

Though some in the Holiness camp who often felt alienated or backslidden welcomed Durham's new teaching like a breath of fresh air, the two men Seymour left in charge, troubled by the teaching's popularity, contacted Seymour, who immediately returned home.

DURHAM AND SEYMOUR

For several days, Seymour sat quietly listening to Durham. Then, on Sunday evening, April 30, Durham asked for a show of hands from those who supported the continuation of the revival under his leadership. The response was overwhelming. Then he asked how many supported Seymour. According to Durham, "ten or less" supported Seymour.[417] Seymour continued to sit quietly.

At last, Seymour met with Durham, asking him to stop preaching his "finished work" at Azusa, proceeding to inform him Azusa "was his work."[418] Contrary to Crawford's accusations, Seymour had never compromised his Wesleyan-Holiness position on sanctification. Crawford had accused him of compromising; Durham accused him of *not* compromising. The following day, unable to reach an agreement with Durham, Seymour met with his board. It had been years since Parham had visited Azusa Street and the doors had been padlocked. Though Louis Osterberg and four other board members pleaded with Seymour not to, Seymour padlocked the doors. Osterberg, a long-time friend and original supporter, resigned.

After accusing Seymour of "scheming" to regain control of his own pulpit, much like Parham, Durham went across town and secured a temporary mission on Kohler Street the following Sunday. Only this time, the crowds followed. Frank Bartleman, another long-time friend and supporter of Seymour, secured the facility for Durham. Later, Durham opened the much larger Full Gospel Assembly on the corner of Seventh and Los Angeles Streets to crowds of several hundred, mostly from the Upper Room Mission, and a few from Azusa Street.

Thousands were reportedly saved, baptized, and healed, while the Azusa Mission lay virtually deserted. Not satisfied with emptying the Azusa mission, Durham continued to criticize what he called Seymour's "failures and blunders," saying it was his "unpleasant duty" to do so. To add insult to injury, Durham declared, "the power of God had entirely left [Seymour], and that he was no longer worthy of the confidence and respect of the saints."[419]

RACIAL DIVISIONS

Though Seymour never publicly attacked Durham, and though Durham eventually left Los Angeles, Charles Parham did not hesitate to attack Durham. Also incensed by Durham's doctrine, Parham prayed in January 1912 that God would reveal to the world whose teachings were right by taking the life of the teacher who was in error. Durham died of tuberculosis later that summer. Still, Durham's "finished work" doctrine would soon split the movement, mostly along racial lines, with many black Pentecostals holding to the "second work" doctrine of sanctification, and many white Pentecostals accepting Durham's "finished work" doctrine. Thus, Bartleman's "color line was washed away in the blood" became Charles Fox Jr.'s "color line was re-drawn by whites," thanks in part to Durham's finished work doctrine.[420]

In 1911, William Durham transferred most of his ministry to Los Angeles, the birthplace of modern Pentecostalism, due to internal problems at his Chicago mission. After drawing crowds at the Azusa Street Mission and being ejected for his "Finished Work" doctrine, which repudiated sanctification as a second work, Durham secured a large building in Los Angeles with thousands more being saved, baptized, and healed. Durham soon returned to Chicago, contracted pneumonia, and died in Los Angeles in 1912.

Photo: Flower Pentecostal Heritage Center.

Also, as Durham's schism further decreased Seymour's influence in the early Pentecostal movement, Durham's "finished work" doctrine eventually became the dominant Pentecostal position. Even Alexander Boddy from Sunderland, England, who visited the Azusa Mission in 1912, noted that American racial divisions were becoming "increasingly acute" because "whites [had] determined to keep their position as [the] dominant race."[421] Professor Douglas J. Nelson at the University of Birmingham, England, echoed this: "Now, with Seymour humiliated, rejected, and forgotten, whites openly embraced the old racial attitude, along with ideological controversy. Insofar as Seymour disappeared the color line reappeared."[422]

After Durham's death, the number of people following his teachings only increased. This was evidenced by R.J. Scott's announcement of another camp meeting at the Arroyo Seco in 1913, which soon became the historic Apostolic Faith World Wide Camp Meeting in which he invited Maria Woodworth-Etter as a featured speaker. Though Seymour had begun the original Apostolic Faith camp meeting at the Arroyo Seco, he received no special invitation to this one. And though he attended this one, he was neither seated on the platform nor recognized. And though Mrs. Etter desired that these meetings promote unity, a second major doctrinal dispute developed. Evidently, schism begets more schism.

Some asserted that the appropriate "apostolic" water baptism was by immersion "in the name of Jesus." Others held to the traditional Trinitarian view of baptizing in the name of the Father, the Son, and the Holy Spirit. Among those adopting this new Oneness position were Pastor Pendleton of the Eighth and Maple Mission and George Studd of the Upper Room Mission, which had now moved to a larger, former dance hall between Spring and Broadway and Fifth and Sixth Streets that seated hundreds.

To further complicate matters, according to Frank Bartleman and several Latino families who once flocked to the Azusa Street Mission, by late 1909, there was a fallout among "some poor illiterate Mexicans" whose expulsion was compared to "murdering the Spirit of God."[423] Seymour was accused of rejecting them by no longer permitting them to speak. However, since Seymour would not have rejected them for any other than doctrinal reasons, and since several Latino Azusa participants had conducted "Jesus' name" only baptisms that year, while Seymour held to the Trinitarian view, doctrinal differences yet again played a role in the demise of the interracial experiment.

CHAPTER 13

THE AZUSA STREET LEGACY

The two men who had tried to take over Seymour's ministry—Parham in October 1906 and Durham in February 1911—were both white. The two women who apparently succeeded in taking away Seymour's ministry—Lum and Crawford in June 1908—were also white. Even the doctrinal attempts to hijack the Apostolic Faith movement—Durham in 1911 and the World Wide Apostolic Faith Camp Meeting in 1913—all involved white people, and each hurt Seymour deeply. Then, when mostly white ministers in the mostly black Church of God in Christ left to form the mostly white Assemblies of God in 1914, Seymour was understandably no longer willing to trust white Pentecostal leaders.

In May 1914, the Azusa Street Apostolic Faith Mission held a business meeting amending its articles of incorporation stating that the bishop, vice-bishop, and all trustees were to be people "of color." Then in 1915, citing growing racism, Seymour compiled *The Doctrines and Discipline of the Azusa Street Apostolic Faith Mission*. In it, Seymour explained how he had been invited to come to Los Angeles. As he and his friends sought God, a revival broke out that quickly spread around the world:

"But very soon division arose through some of our brethren, and the Holy Spirit was grieved. We want all our white brethren and white sisters to feel free in our churches and missions, in spite of all the trouble we have had with some of our white brethren in causing diversion [sic], and spreading wild fire and fanaticism."[424] Seymour placed much of the blame for these divisions on his "white brethren," while acknowledging that some African Americans had played a role in the "apostolic" Oneness debate.

Seymour regrettably and reluctantly changed the mission's constitution, stating that all its officers must be people of color, making it clear that he did this "not for discrimination, but for peace. To keep down race war in the Churches and friction, so they can have greater liberty and freedom in the Holy Spirit."[425] Yet he never grew bitter, adding that he looked forward to a day when such restrictions would no longer be necessary.

The document also declared that Seymour was "bishop" and that his successor would always be "a man of color."[426] Thus, a distinction was also made between male and female roles. Though Seymour had permitted women ministers, he did not permit them to ordain, baptize, or now succeed him as bishop. Though the latter would be tested when his wife, Jennie, would take his place after his death, perhaps Clara Lum and Florence Crawford played a role in this decision. By this time, less than twenty people regularly attended the mission, and most of them were among the original seekers at the Bonne Brae House.

A couple years later, Seymour called for a meeting of all Pentecostal leaders in the Los Angeles area for the purpose of restoring unity to the young Pentecostal movement. Two leaders showed up. Speaking of himself in the third person, a disappointed Seymour later wrote: "He has done what little he could do to help the movement."[427]

SEYMOUR'S FINAL YEARS

Sadly, Seymour spent the last ten years of his life struggling to keep the small mission afloat while occasionally traveling and attending ministers' conferences with little notice or recognition. He was, how-ever, a frequent visitor at the annual convocations of the Church of God in Christ, where he was treated as an honored guest and as a dear friend of Bishop Mason.

Seymour's final years at the mission grew increasingly difficult. Ser-vices were now once a week. Seymour taught with a blackboard and chalk. Occasionally visitors from the glory days would stop by. Money was scarce. Sometimes two offerings had to be taken to cover missions, and Jennie was forced to return to secular employment.

In 1918, Pentecostal Healing Evangelist Aimee Semple McPherson arrived in California. Seymour attended her first campaign. At the meeting, he told a friend, "he had not been feeling completely well" and that his "heart had been hurting him."[428] In 1920, the Azusa Mission held an anniversary service and Bible conference. The meetings were much more liturgical than the original revival meetings, complete with printed programs, traditional hymns, and black spirituals.

Another convention was held in Los Angeles in 1922. John Mat-thews, a noted critic of the Pentecostal movement, noticed an aged black man in the audience. When he inquired as to his identity, he was informed the visitor was William Seymour, the "man who had intro-duced 'tongues' on the Western Coast." Matthews described Seymour as "worn, tired, decrepit." Yet his vision had never changed. His last message was "a plea for love among the brethren everywhere."[429]

On September 28, 1922, Seymour spent his last day with Jennie, praying, singing, praising God, and making plans for the work of the mission. Later that afternoon, as Seymour dictated a letter, he com-plained of chest pains and shortness of breath. Doctor Walter M. Boyd was called to the mission. He had had two heart attacks that day. Sey-mour's last known words were, "I love my Jesus so."[430] He died in his wife's arms at 5:00 p.m. He was 52. His funeral was attended by about 200 people, mostly black. He was buried in Evergreen Cemetery in East

Seymour's burial place covered with luscious green grass in an otherwise barren cemetery. When a cemetery worker was asked why, he replied, "It's always been like this. We don't know why." Jesus said, "Most assuredly, I say to you, unless a grain of wheat falls into the ground and dies, it remains alone; but if it dies, it produces much grain" (John 12:24). Seymour died thinking he was a failure and alone. Today, the world is full of William Seymours.

Photo: Ken Fish of Orbis Ministries (orbisministries.org), used by permission.

Los Angeles. His simple headstone reads, "Our pastor." Jennie was later buried next to him.

Though the cause of Seymour's death was listed as "a heart attack," biographer Charles Fox Jr. wondered if it had not been a broken heart. Seymour's understanding of Pentecost as a multi-ethnic, multi-cultural movement under the banner of love, as in Acts, was never fully embraced by his contemporaries. Sadly, Seymour's message of divine love, interracial equality, and unity was quickly forgotten as a preoccupation with speaking in tongues instead became the defining mark of the movement.

Fox added, "One can only imagine the kind of legacy that Pentecostals could have had had they adhered to his message of love and racial harmony. Perhaps they would have been known more for helping take the lead in breaking down racial barriers in the United States."[431]

YET ANOTHER ATTEMPTED TAKEOVER

After William Seymour's death, Jennie continued pastoring the church until 1933. Swedish Pentecostal leader Lewi Pethrus visited the mission in 1924 and reported that the work of the mission continued.[432] In 1930, a seventy-eight-year-old white man named Ruthford D. Griffith and his wife joined the mission. Claiming to be a Coptic priest, an African missionary, and a pastor of African American congregations, he began offering his preaching services to Jennie in exchange for temporary housing adjacent to her upstairs apartment. Jennie agreed.

Later, however, Griffith began asserting that Jennie was in violation of the mission's *Doctrines and Discipline*, which clearly stated that the mission's leader was to be "a man." Thus, he needed to replace her as pastor and began recruiting others to vote for him. Then, after declaring

William and Jennie Seymour in 1912. After Seymour died in 1922, Jennie pastored the Azusa Street Mission and continued her husband's work, even after losing the mission in 1931. She died in 1936 and was buried next to him.

Photo: Flower Pentecostal Heritage Center.

himself the new bishop of the mission, he intimidated and even forced Jennie and her smaller group of worshipers to worship in the smaller upstairs room, while he preached in the main sanctuary downstairs. This was now the third time a white man had tried to take over the mission.

By January 1931, tensions had grown so high, the two factions were throwing hymnals at each other. The police were called, and the mission was padlocked. Jennie sought justice, Griffith sought control, and several court battles ensued. Jennie and the remaining members, many of whom were also original members, met back in the Asberry's home on North Bonnie Brae Street, where the revival had begun some twenty-five years earlier.

A lower court initially ruled in favor of Griffith, but then a higher court overruled that decision in favor of Mrs. Seymour. It was too late. Weary of the legal battle, Los Angeles officials had by then decided to take advantage of the controversy to condemn the building and declare it a fire hazard. They first offered it to the Assemblies of God, but they

The Azusa Street Mission in 1928. After being declared a fire hazard, the building was demolished in early July 1931. Many scholars and historians agree that something happened here that changed the face of Christianity worldwide.

Photo: Flower Pentecostal Heritage Center.

declined, stating, "We are not interested in relics." The Assemblies of God has since regretted that decision many times over. However, not before the building was demolished.[433]

Frank Bartleman visited the demolition site, took the numbers "312," and proudly displayed them on the wall of his Los Angeles home. Jennie, unable to make payments or pay back taxes on the property, sold it to a Los Angeles bank. The bank foreclosed on the property in 1936 and Jennie passed away later that year. In 1938, Security First National Bank turned the property into a parking lot. Today, it remains part of the parking lot for the Japanese American Cultural and Community Center in Noguchi Plaza.

AZUSA'S LEGACY

On April 9–26, 1936, the thirtieth anniversary of the Azusa Street Revival, a joint celebration was held at Saints Home Church and Angelus Temple, both in Los Angeles. Emma Cotton managed the event, while A.G. Osterberg, Frank Bartleman, and other Azusa faithful joined Aimee Semple McPherson and twenty other pastors in sponsoring the event. Emma Cotton testified, "While I write this, my soul is lifted up, because I saw the house in its first glory and when I remember those days, I feel like going down into the dust of humility, if only to bring back that old-time power, I am willing to give my life."[434] Emma Cotton later held credentials with the Church of God in Christ and became a dear friend to Aimee Semple McPherson.

A much larger and spectacular event was held at Angelus Temple on the revival's fiftieth anniversary in 1956 with Oral Roberts, William Branham, Jack Coe, Gordon Lindsey, and many others hosting services and thousands more attending. A.C. Valdez, who went to Azusa Street as a young man, shared his incredible testimony at this event.

A similar Azusa Street Centennial celebration was held at the Los Angeles Convention Center and Memorial Coliseum in Los Angeles April 22–29, 2006, which featured many evangelical and Charismatic leaders including T.D. Jakes, Benny Hinn, Juanita Bynum, Kenneth Copeland, Creflo Dollar, Frederick K.C. Price, Charles Blake, Paula White, and many more.

In 1975, Howard University students in Washington D.C. named their ecumenical Pentecostal campus ministry "William Seymour Pentecostal Fellowship." In 1997, the Church of God in Christ refurbished the Bonnie Brae House and opened it to the public. In 1998, Azusa scholar Cecil M. Robeck led a "Walk of Remembrance" on the site of 312 Azusa Street, erecting a memorial wall and historical marker to commemorate the revival. Also in 1998, the Assemblies of God dedicated its

The Golden Anniversary celebration of the Azusa Street Revival was held at Angelus Temple in 1956 with Oral Roberts, William Branham, and A.C. Valdez sharing his incredible testimony.

Photo: Flower Pentecostal Heritage Center.

first permanent home for their denominational seminary in Springfield, Missouri, in honor of William Seymour, naming its chapel the "William J. Seymour Chapel," featuring a stained-glass depiction of Seymour and the fire that fell at Azusa Street. The memorial plague reads:

> **William J. Seymour, pastor of the Azusa Street Mission, played a formative role in the worldwide expansion of the Pentecostal movement. The ministry of the son of former slaves was marked by sound judgment, spiritual balance, personal integrity, and faithfulness. He encouraged every member of his congregation to minister, to testify, and to share the gospel whenever God led them, regardless of race, class, gender, or age.**

He demonstrated the value of racial unity and cultural harmony, exhorting his congregation to seek God about all things, to exhibit the fruit of the Spirit even as they exercised the Spirit's gifts, and to measure all doctrine and experience by the word of God. He remains an eloquent model for Pentecostal ministry.

In 1999, the Azusa Street Memorial Committee erected a similar memorial plaque at the site of the old mission in Noguchi Plaza. It reads:

This plaque commemorates the site of the Azusa Street Mission, which was located at 312 Azusa Street. Formally known as the Apostolic Faith Mission, it served as a fountainhead for the international Pentecostal movement from 1906–1931. Pastor William J. Seymour oversaw the "Azusa Street Revival." He preached a message of salvation, holiness, and power, welcomed visitors from around the world, transformed the congregation into a multicultural center of worship, and commissioned pastors, evangelists, and missionaries to take the message of "Pentecost" (Acts 2:1–41) to the world. Today, members of the Pentecostal-charismatic movement number half a billion worldwide.[435]

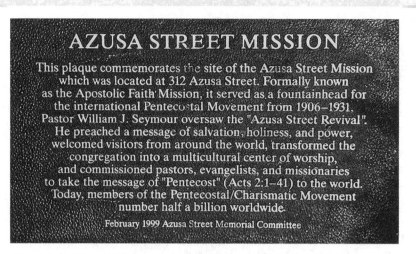

AZUSA STREET MISSION

This plaque commemorates the site of the Azusa Street Mission which was located at 312 Azusa Street. Formally known as the Apostolic Faith Mission, it served as a fountainhead for the international Pentecostal Movement from 1906–1931. Pastor William J. Seymour oversaw the "Azusa Street Revival". He preached a message of salvation, holiness, and power, welcomed visitors from around the world, transformed the congregation into a multicultural center of worship, and commissioned pastors, evangelists, and missionaries to take the message of "Pentecost" (Acts 2:1–41) to the world. Today, members of the Pentecostal/Charismatic Movement number half a billion worldwide.

February 1999 Azusa Street Memorial Committee

The Azusa Street Mission plague, as it appears in Noguchi Plaza.

Photo: Flower Pentecostal Heritage Center.

The hundreds of congregations in the Los Angeles area that claim to have emerged from the Azusa Street Mission and remain a part of that movement today include West Angeles Church of God in Christ, the Cathedral of Faith, the City of Refuge, Faithful Central Bible Church, and Church on the Way.

CONCLUDING THOUGHTS

Cecil Robeck, who has perhaps studied the Azusa Street Revival more than any other, wrote: "The Azusa Street faithful tried to show us what it looked like to live according to Zechariah's prophecy, 'Not by might, nor by power, but by my Spirit, saith the Lord of hosts.'"[436]

Bartleman concluded, "Before the Azusa outpouring, everything had settled down in concrete form, bound by man. Nothing could move for God. Dynamite—the power of the Holy Spirit—was necessary to free this mass. And this God furnished. The whole mass was set free once more. Our Year of Jubilee had come."[437] "We hoped and believed that the revival would last without cessation until Jesus should come. It doubtless would, and should, if men would not fail God, but we drift back continually in the old ecclesiastical concepts, forms, and ceremonies. Thus history sadly repeats itself."[438]

A.G. Osterberg further concluded, "The sooner we become 'of one accord'—the sooner we do away with boundaries, lines and labels, personal and national ambitions and bickering—the sooner we humble ourselves to fit in wherever the plan of God can use us—the sooner we shall be able to bring back the King."[439]

SEYMOUR'S LEGACY

Today many believe that "barn-like," "tumble-down shack" on Azusa Street to be the birthplace of modern Pentecostalism, earning Seymour the title "Father of modern Pentecostalism."[440] But perhaps Sydney Ahlstrom—the acclaimed church historian from Yale—summed it up best when he described Seymour as "the most influential black leader in American religious history."[441] Ahlstrom wrote in his 1972 award-winning book *A Religious History of the American People,* "Seymour exerted a greater influence upon American Christianity than any other Black Leader" and *Christian History* magazine named Seymour, along with Billy Graham, C.S. Lewis, Mother Teresa, and Martin Luther King Jr., as one of the top ten Christians of the twentieth century.[442]

Likening Seymour to John Wesley who once said, "I look upon all the world as my parish," *The Pentecostal Herald* wrote of Seymour's death in 1922, "The world was his parish."[443] Seymour indeed led an interracial revival that changed the world. And he did it as a black man in 1906—an infamous year in American history when more black men were lynched than any other year.[444]

Interestingly, the name "William Seymour" phonetically asks a question: "Will-you-see-more?" Was it a coincidence that God chose this man to lead this third movement in Christianity after Catholicism and Protestantism called Pentecostalism? Or can we envision yet another great movement before the return of Christ? Will you see more?

Brother David Garcia said Seymour prophesied in 1909 or 1910 that in about a hundred years there would be a return of the Shekinah Glory and a revival that would surpass the works of God at Azusa. It has also been said that Charles Parham prophesied the same.[445]

CHAPTER 14

THE PILGRIMS OF AZUSA STREET

Nearly all Pentecostal groups today—directly or indirectly—can trace their lineage back to Azusa Street. In time, anyone who visited Azusa Street became part of an honorary class of citizens called "the pilgrims of Los Angeles"—a sort of "Who's Who" in Pentecost—and was treated with veneration and respect in Pentecostal circles worldwide.[446]

Adolpha de Rosa and Harmon Clifford went to Oakland. A.H. Post went to Santa Barbara. Brigido Perez to San Diego. Florence Crawford, Ophelia Wiley, Lulu Miller, C.W. Solkeld, G.W. Evans, Thomas Junk, and others went to Portland, Oregon. Crawford started her own Apostolic Faith movement there in the Pacific Northwest. Ophelia Wiley and Thomas Junk also went to Seattle.

Glenn Cook held meetings along the West Coast and later went to Lamont, Oklahoma, Chicago, and Indianapolis before touring the country and rebaptizing the faithful in the "apostolic" way of Oneness Pentecostalism. William Durham returned to his North Avenue Mission in Chicago, founding the Pentecostal movement in the Midwest and Canada. Elsie Robinson went to Onawa, Michigan. Iva Campbell took Pentecost to Akron, Cleveland, and Alliance, Ohio. Rachel Sizelove, a former Free Methodist evangelist, took the Pentecostal message to Springfield, Missouri, where she began several cottage meetings. There she saw a vision of a sparkling fountain that filled the whole land with "living water." This "fountain" is now the international headquarters for the General Council of the Assemblies of God.[447]

Elder Sturdevant left Los Angeles in 1906 to establish the first Pentecostal church in New York City on his way to Africa. Edward Vinton received a vision of a building in Cambridge, Massachusetts. Following the Holy Spirit, he and his wife rented a former Presbyterian church on Hampshire Street and established a Pentecostal mission there. Adolpha de Rosa and Lucy Leatherman also preached in Greenwich, Connecticut.

C.H. Mason took the Pentecostal message back to Tennessee and to the Deep South. G.B. Cashwell brought Azusa back to North Carolina before also touring the South. F.W. Williams, who was saved and baptized in the Spirit at the Bonne Brae meetings, likewise traveled, preached, and planted churches throughout the South. Lee Hall took the Pentecostal message to northern Arkansas in the Ozarks.

CHILDREN RECEIVE PENTECOST

As news of the Azusa Street Revival spread, William Seymour himself was invited to take the revival to other parts of the country. Much like the apostle Paul, Seymour traveled, evangelized, established churches, and ordained ministers. In November 1906, he went to Oakland, then later San Francisco and San Jose. By spring 1907, he went back to Houston, Texas, the South, and the Midwest. By the summer of 1907, Seymour continued retracing some of his earlier travels to Chicago, Indianapolis, and Cincinnati, then on to New York, Baltimore, and Washington D.C.

While ministering outside Chicago in John Alexander Dowie's Zion City with Thomas Hezmalhalch, Seymour reported back to the Azusa mission: "People here receive the baptism in their pews while the service is still going on and sometimes scores of them receive it. It is the sweetest thing you want to see. It reminds me of old Azusa ten months ago. The people that receive the baptism seem so happy, they remind me of our people at home. There are little children from six years and on up who have the baptism with the Holy Ghost, just as we have it in Los Angeles. Praise our God. This is another Azusa. It would do you good to hear these people speak under the power of the Holy Ghost. Some of them converse in tongues. Brother Tom has never lost the spirit of the Azusa. He is still fired up the same as ever. Everywhere I have traveled among our baptized souls they seem to have such joy and freedom in the Holy Ghost."[448]

Dr. John G. Speicher, then overseer of Zion City, also testified of the work of Azusa Street when it hit Zion City: "Recently under the leadership of an evangelist, familiarly called Brother Tom, who comes from Los Angeles and who has been used mightily in many places in the conversion of sinners, there has come a greater freedom in speaking in tongues, and also a number of persons are claiming the power of interpretation.

"More wonderful even than the tongues is the way the Holy Spirit falls upon many of the people, even young children who put to shame the best preachers in the church in the way they stand before the people and preach the everlasting gospel. O, the power, the grandeur, the beauty of a child of six or ten years of age breaking forth in scriptural language and pleading with the people to turn to God with all their hearts for Jesus is coming soon! Then to go into tongues in such a beautiful way. And sometimes tots speak for half an hour at a time, and it is all praise to God for the wonderful love of Jesus. This is the whole burden of their talk. Praise! Praise! Praise! The power of the blood! And pleading for their loved ones. O, how sublime! O, how pitiful! Truly the saying of Paul has come to pass… 'God hath chosen the foolish things of the world to confound the wise.'"[449]

Dr. John G. Speicher was a physician, pastor, and church overseer in Zion City, Illinois. A bitter skeptic of early Pentecostalism, he visited Azusa Street, where he said, "I saw and heard things that broke down my prejudice completely for I became convinced that it was none other than the wonderful power of the Holy Spirit that was working through this people."

Photo: Flower Pentecostal Heritage Center.

Speicher even spoke of how this affected his own children. His sixteen-year-old daughter spoke in more than twenty languages for thirty minutes, a few of which he recognized as German, French, and Dutch, but especially, he said, she spoke beautifully in French. Then his eleven-year-old son, who also spoke in tongues, interpreted what she said in English.[450]

Similar reports came in from Oakland, Colorado Springs, and elsewhere where Azusa Street evangelists had traveled. In Colorado Springs, a six-year-old and eight-year-old spoke in tongues and a twelve-year-old girl preached and sang in the Indian language.[451] In Oakland, Carrie Judd Montgomery reported: "What has impressed us most of all in the Oakland meetings is the great work of grace on children, one little girl only nine years old, being so baptized with the Holy Spirit, that her face seemed, to look like an angel's, and the wisdom and sweetness which she displayed in dealing with another child to lead her to Christ, we have never seen surpassed."[452] All this was reminiscent of the French Prophets in Southern France, who experienced an extraordinary phenomena among their children who prophesied and delivered eloquent discourses in French and other languages unknown to them in the late seventeenth century.

SEYMOUR'S TRAVELS

Sarah Cripe, a wealthy "massage doctor," invited Seymour and other Pentecostal leaders to Indianapolis to preach and to stay rent-free in her home. She wrote, "Brother Seymour is a good man…he is the discoverer of this great faith. He met with a little band in a stable in Los Angeles and discovered the wonderful power. And now just to think… is coming right here to be with us." Later, Seymour would also minister with his friend, John G. Lake, in the Pacific Northwest to crowds of more than 10,000 "who shook and trembled and cried to God."[453]

Even when Seymour was neglected or forgotten in Los Angeles, he was still well-received across the country. In what would be among Seymour's last missionary journeys in 1921, he preached several weeks at the Christian and Missionary Alliance Church in Columbus, Ohio. There, a Columbus resident, Mrs. George Aycock, *née* Pepsico, gave us perhaps a final glimpse of Seymour preaching: "The glow would be on that man's face. He looked like an angel from heaven. So many wanted to hear him, they had heard of him…He was no man to exalt himself, but a humble man. When you'd meet him at the door you could feel… he was a real man of God…He didn't talk much. He was not a conversationalist. He'd get off about the Lord, being true to God."[454] Evidently, Seymour remained humble throughout his life.

F.F. Bosworth, John G. Lake, Thomas Hezmalhalch, A.D. Adams, and an entourage from Zion City made the spiritual pilgrimage to Azusa Street in 1907. Bosworth took the Pentecostal message to Dallas, then to other major cities like Chicago, Pittsburgh, Toronto, and Ottawa through his healing revivals. He also became a radio pioneer and later

Azusa Street pilgrims in 1907. Seated left to right: William J. Seymour and John G. Lake. Standing left to right: John A.D. Adams, F.F. Bosworth, and Thomas Hezmalhalch. Lake was an elder in Zion City and Bosworth was director of the award-winning Zion City Band. All four had been influenced by both Dowie and Seymour.

Photo: Flower Pentecostal Heritage Center.

came out of retirement to help William Branham during the postwar healing revival. Lake took Pentecost to South Africa where he founded two major denominations, then to the Pacific Northwest including Portland, Oregon and Spokane, Washington. Thomas Hezmalhalch went to Denver, Chicago, and Indianapolis before moving on to South Africa with Lake. John A.D. Adams went to Australia and New Zealand.

Lucy Farrow went to her home in Norfolk, Virginia, where 150 in nearby Portsmouth received the baptism in the Holy Spirit. She and Sister Hutchins then left for Liberia, Africa. Lucy Leatherman went to Jerusalem where she ministered to the Arabic population. Owen "Irish" Lee went to Ireland.

Sharon Stands-Over-Bull, a pastor and elder in the Crow Nation of Southeastern Montana, recalled how her grandmother received the baptism in the Holy Spirit at Azusa Street in 1906 and brought it back to the Crow Reservation. Her son, Russell, said, "Whole communities were touched by the fire of the Holy Spirit, and the Crows eventually became known throughout Indian Country as the center for Pentecost. This was the capital for Pentecost, and still is considered that by many neighboring tribes." It remains to this day possibly "the biggest church in the Indian community throughout the U.S."[455]

G.B. CASHWELL

Gaston Barnibas "G.B." Cashwell was a prodigal son raised in Sampson County, North Carolina, whose family would have voted him "least likely to become a preacher." Always the prankster, Cashwell once asked a man in Georgia to write a letter to his grandfather, telling him he was dead. The joke was on him, and the letter, prophetic. Cashwell soon encountered an evangelist there in Georgia and was converted—the old Cashwell was dead and the new one was now alive.

Cashwell became a minister in the Methodist Episcopal Church South where he came under the influence of A.B. Crumpler. Crumpler later left the Methodist Church, founding the North Carolina Holiness Association in Dunn, North Carolina, in 1897, and the Pentecostal Holiness Church in 1900. Cashwell joined Crumpler's Holiness Church in 1903. In 1906, Cashwell heard about the Azusa Street Revival in *The Way of Faith* Holiness paper published out of Columbia, South Carolina. Frank Bartleman, who was a regular contributor to the publication, wrote testimonies that created an intense hunger in Cashwell's heart.

Hoping to receive this new Pentecostal experience, Cashwell rode a train three thousand miles to Los Angeles. However, being a white man from the segregated South, he was not comfortable in a mostly black church led by a black pastor and was considering leaving. In his hotel room, Cashwell said he had to undergo a "crucifixion" and "die, to many things" before God could give him the victory over racism.[456]

Now returning to the mission, he went to the upper room and invited Pastor Seymour and several young black men to lay hands on him. Immediately, chills ran up and down his spine. He continued his quest for the baptism in the Holy Spirit there in the upper room several more days but with no results.

Then, while praying upstairs one day, he suddenly felt led to go downstairs to one of the meetings. Clara Lum was reading some excerpts of letters from T.B. Barratt and others from around the world who had received the baptism in the Holy Spirit. He said, "Before I knew it, I began to speak in tongues and praise God...He filled me with His Spirit and love, and I am feasting and drinking at the fountain continually and speak as the Spirit gives utterance both in my own language and in the unknown tongue."[457] The good folks at Azusa Street even purchased Cashwell a new suit and a train ticket back home.

Wasting no time, when Cashwell returned to Dunn, he rented a three-story tobacco warehouse and immediately began holding revival meetings. This revival has since been called "Azusa Street East." Cashwell invited ministers from Crumpler's Holiness churches, Fire-Baptized Holiness churches, and Free Will Baptist churches. The meetings lasted more than a month as thousands, including many ministers, jammed the old warehouse seeking the new experience.

G.B. Cashwell, a Holiness minister from Dunn, North Carolina, received his Pentecostal experience at Azusa Street in 1906 and immediately returned home to hold revival meetings in a rented tobacco warehouse before touring the South and converting several Holiness denominations to Pentecostalism. He is known as the "Apostle of Pentecost to the South."

Photo: Flower Pentecostal Heritage Center.

One minister reported, "I went to the Holiness Church to services here today and heard Brother G.B. Cashwell preach. He has been to California and got Pentecost and speaks in an unknown tongue. Some seeking the same experience here."[458] One Free Will Baptist minister who attended returned home one evening and his children greeted him at the door: "Papa, Papa, have you got the tongues?" "No, but I want it worse than anything in all the world," he replied. A few nights later, he also received "the tongues."[459]

From Dunn, Cashwell toured the South, holding revivals in Tennessee, South Carolina, North Carolina, Virginia, Georgia, and Alabama, firmly establishing himself as the "Apostle of Pentecost to the South."[460] Huge crowds gathered to hear him preach and to receive the new experience. Then, in February 1907, Joseph Hillary King, overseer of the

Fire-Baptized Holiness Churches, received the Pentecostal experience. In April, N.J. Holmes, a former Presbyterian minister from Greenville, South Carolina, also received the baptism and spoke in tongues. In June, Cashwell preached in Alabama where M.M. Pinson and H.G. Rodgers received the baptism in the Holy Spirit. They would soon become instrumental in the founding of the Assemblies of God.

Also in Alabama, A.J. Tomlinson heard and invited Cashwell to speak at the Church of God's General Assembly in Cleveland, Tennessee. At the close of the General Assembly meetings in January 1908, Tomlinson slipped out of his chair "in a heap on the rostrum...at Cashwell's feet" and received his Pentecostal experience. The Church of God was now an official part of the Pentecostal movement.[461]

Also, by 1908, most of Crumpler's Holiness Church ministers had received the Pentecostal experience, except Crumpler, who opposed it and was soon forced to withdraw from the organization he had founded. "Pentecostal" was added back to the name that year, reconstructing the "Pentecostal Holiness Church." In 1911, the denomination merged with the Fire-Baptized Holiness Church, and in 1915 with N.J. Holmes's former Presbyterian churches based out of Greenville, South Carolina, each time retaining the title "Pentecostal Holiness Church." In 1959, the Pentecostal Free Will Baptists in Dunn, North Carolina, broke off from the Free Will Baptists to also join the Pentecostal movement.

C.H. MASON

Charles Harrison "C.H." Mason was raised in a Missionary Baptist Church in Memphis. At the age of twelve, he accepted Christ, after which he experienced many visions and dreams. He prayed that God would give him "a religion like the one he had heard about from the old slaves and had been demonstrated in their lives."[462] His parents moved to Arkansas in 1879, hoping to avoid the yellow fever break-out in Memphis. They were too late. Mason's father succumbed, then Mason developed fever and chills, but later the "glory of God" appeared, and he was instantly and completely healed. Mason then received his call to ministry, and after reading former slave and Holiness evange-list Amanda Smith's autobiography, accepted the Holiness doctrine of sanctification. The following year, he met C.P. Jones in Jackson, Missis-sippi, and the two, along with others, founded the Church of God in Christ in 1897.

Then, "Led by the Spirit to go to Los Angeles," Mason visited Azusa Street in March 1907, accompanied by fellow ministers J.A. Jeter and D.J. Young. Mason sat by himself the first night. Jeter was critical of some things happening in the services. Mason said, the first time "I heard some speak in tongues, I knew it was right." After Seymour fin-ished preaching the second night, he said, "All those that want to be sanctified or baptized with the Holy Ghost, go to the upper room, and those that want to be healed, go to the prayer room, and all those that want to be justified, come to the altar."[463] Mason and his friends went to the altar.

Seymour and Mason knew each other, having previously met in Jack-son, Mississippi, in 1905, where Seymour attended a minister's seminar on millennial teachings and special revelations taught by Mason and C.P. Jones. So, Seymour sent for Mason and his friends to come to his upstairs room. There, he welcomed his brethren from the South, and told them God would do great things for them but also cautioned them not to run around the city looking for worldly pleasures, but to "seek the pleasure of the Lord."[464]

Charles Harrison Mason, founder of America's largest Pentecostal church, the Church of God in Christ (COGIC), traveled the nation and world preaching to interracial audiences in COGIC and non-COGIC churches. He licensed several white Pentecostal ministers and preached at the founding meeting of the Assemblies of God in 1914.

Photo: Benjamin Jimerson-Phillips "Bishop C H Mason Gather."

Seymour's words were prophetic as Mason later admitted to having temptations while visiting Los Angeles, especially after running into a woman he had met elsewhere. Nevertheless, Mason returned to the altar that evening, when he said, "there came a light which enveloped my entire being above the brightness of the sun. When I opened my mouth to say 'Glory,' a flame touched my tongue which ran down me. My language changed and no word could I speak in my own tongue. Oh! I was filled with the Glory of the Lord. My soul was then satisfied."[465]

After five weeks with Seymour and the Azusa faithful, Mason returned to Memphis with his new Pentecostal experience. He then learned that Azusa minister Glenn Cook had already preached at his church and that many had already spoken in tongues. However, his denominational overseer, C.P. Jones, did not agree with this new teaching. The church soon split, half going with Mason and half with Jones. After two years of court battles, Mason's group retained the name "Church of God in Christ," and Jones's group formed the Church of Christ (Holiness) USA. The only difference was their definition of baptism in the Holy Spirit.

By 2010, Jones's Holiness denomination had reported a membership of 14,000, while Mason's Pentecostal church reported 5 million.

GLENN COOK

Glenn Cook left Azusa Street in December 1906 and went to Lamont, Oklahoma, where he held a series of cottage prayer meetings before moving on to Chicago and Indianapolis. In Indianapolis he held meetings at the Union Gospel Tabernacle. Cook wrote to the Azusa Street Mission telling them of his work there. Within days, his work was on the lips of many in that city, and within months some had begun to speak in tongues. *The Indianapolis Star*, attempting to poke fun at their new language, called them "Gliggy Bluks." Cook went back to Los Angeles for a short time, leaving Thomas Hezmalhalch, another Azusa Street missionary, in charge. By April, Cook and Hezmalhalch, with the help of local news coverage, had 150 people attending as Union Gospel Tabernacle moved to Murphy League Hall.

Glenn Cook seated on a platform at Murphy Hall in Indianapolis in 1907. A Baptist minister from Indianapolis, he worked for a newspaper in Los Angeles before leaving to work full-time without pay for William Seymour. In 1907, Cook brought the message of Pentecost to Indianapolis, which quickly became an epicenter for the new movement. In 1914, Cook joined the Oneness Pentecostal movement, traveling throughout the Midwest and South, proclaiming the "Jesus' name" message and re-baptizing many in Jesus' name, including G.T. Haywood, future bishop of the Pentecostal Assemblies of the World.

Photo: Flower Pentecostal Heritage Center.

By June, Seymour and William and Emma Cummings had arrived in Indianapolis. Cook turned the service over to Seymour who, "in a voice that shook the church," led the group in singing "The Comforter Has Come," a favorite hymn of Azusa Street. One visiting reporter in this meeting gave one of the most complete descriptions of Seymour ever written: "This founder of the sect stands full six feet in height. He wears a rubber collar, decorated by no sign of a necktie. Adorning his mouth is one massive gold tooth, ranked by rows of other teeth, perfectly straight and white. The beard that he wears could be called a flowing one if it was longer. It flows—what there is of it. His voice is like the roaring of a cannon, and of all his most striking characteristics, he has but one eye."[466] *The Indianapolis News* wrote that the "Gliggy Bluks" were a "sect in which the color line is not drawn."[467] Undercover detectives were sent to see if any charges could be brought against Cook and Seymour.

Soon the crowds grew so large two meetings had to be held with Seymour preaching to the larger assembly upstairs and Cook speaking in the main hall. At one point, Cook requested: "Will some one please go down and stop the crowd that's comin' in so that no will get hurt?"[468]

Then, Joseph Hillary King, leader of the Fire-Baptized Holiness Church, preached at their meetings. Troublemakers also came to the meetings, but Cook asked the local police for protection. Seymour and Cook then held a baptismal service in Full Creek as 200 people watched thirteen people get baptized. Then the group returned to Murphy Hall, where Seymour conducted a foot-washing service while singing "Leaning on the Everlasting Arms." Then Seymour left Indianapolis, while Cook stayed on as pastor of the new Pentecostal congregation. Cook then led meetings at the Good News Mission, which later merged with the Apostolic Faith Mission to become the Christian Assembly.

"GLIGGY BLUKS" CONVENE.

One Woman Receives "Message" at Opening Session.

The ten-day pentecostal convention of the Apostolic Faith (Gliggy Bluks) at Pernial Temple, Eleventh street and Senate avenue, opened yesterday with delegates, both white and colored, from Indiana and several adjoining states. In the evening the Rev. Garfield T. Haywood, colored, called attention to the purpose of the organization, and scored those who ridicule it. He said "professors and school teachers don't go into this because they have too much sense, and the Lord wants people who have no more sense than to believe in Him." He condemned the medical profession, and said that they called it "practicing medicine" because the doctors wanted to practice upon the people. During the evening several persons were "moved" to engage in that weird chant which they say only the "saved" understand. One woman delivered a "message" to the people.

The "Gliggy Bluks" was an Indianapolis press nickname for early Pentecostals who came from Azusa Street in Los Angeles to Indianapolis in 1907. It was meant to poke fun at their new language. Updates on the "Gliggy Bluks" movement frequented *The Indianapolis News* and *The Indianapolis Star* between 1907 and 1913. "G T Haywood Gliggy Bluks," *The Indianapolis Star* (06 November 1911), p. 3.

Photo: : clipped by jnl63 30 Jun 2019: newspapers
.com/clip/33408827/g-t-haywood-gliggy-bluks.

IVEY CAMPBELL

Ivey Campbell helped establish the Broadway Mission in East Liverpool, Ohio. Then, moving to Los Angeles, she joined the Holiness Church of Los Angeles before visiting the Azusa Street Mission and being baptized in the Holy Spirit. Soon, she returned home to Ohio to share her testimony, and was asked to speak at the Broadway Mission. Most were skeptical. However, news of her testimony traveled to nearby communities that had also heard of the Azusa Street Revival. For example, Claudius McKinney, pastor of the South Street Mission in Akron, Ohio, who had been praying for revival, invited Miss Campbell to hold a series of meetings. In another example, Levi Lupton, a Quaker evangelist and head of a missionary school in nearby Alliance, Ohio, had received copies of *The Apostolic Faith*. Both were excited about Miss Campbell's arrival and Lupton joined the meetings.

Within a month, forty people had been baptized in the Spirit and spoke in tongues. Campbell simply told them what she had seen and experienced at Azusa Street and their need for salvation, sanctification, and baptism in the Spirit. She also delivered messages in other tongues, then interpreted what she had shared. Virtually overnight the revival became the talk of the town as crowds gathered. The services at the South Street Mission sounded much like those at the Azusa Street Mission. Again, newspapers mocked the meetings, neighbors complained, and the police were called out for protection. Still, the revival continued to increase. Miss Campbell moved on to preach in other churches in Pennsylvania and Ohio, while Levi Lupton received the baptism in the Spirit and eventually joined his missionary school to the Azusa Street Mission.

THE ASSEMBLIES OF GOD

Between 1907 and 1910, several ministers began distancing themselves from Parham's Apostolic Faith movement over questions concerning Parham's moral character. Now in need of an established church name to ordain ministers and receive clergy railroad discounts, a gentlemen's agreement was made with C.H. Mason to use the name Church of God in Christ. This new "white" Church of God in Christ group included E.N. Bell, Howard A. Goss, D.C.O. Opperman, and Arch P. Collins. Bell was a former Baptist pastor from Fort Worth who had been converted to Pentecostalism under William Durham's Chicago ministry. Others would later join from John Alexander Dowie's Chicago ministry and various denominational backgrounds including Methodist, Presbyterian, and Christian and Missionary Alliance.

Meanwhile, a second group of white ministers had formed in Alabama led by H.G. Rodgers, a Cashwell convert. By 1911, Durham's "Finished Work" doctrine had spread through the ranks of these

The First General Council of the Assemblies of God, Hot Springs, Arkansas, April 2–12, 1914. The first executive presbyters are kneeling front left to right: J.W. Welch, M.M. Pinson, T.K. Leonard, J. Roswell Flower, Cyrus Fockler, Howard A. Goss, E.N. Bell, and D.C.O. Opperman.

Photo: Flower Pentecostal Heritage Center.

independent ministers, who began voicing a need to unify under the new doctrinal position. Bell and Rodgers' groups merged in Mississippi in 1912, creating a mostly white body of 352 ministers. The call was made for a general council to meet the first week of April 1914 at the Grand Opera House in Hot Springs, Arkansas. Mason, who called the group "the White work" of the Church of God in Christ, was invited to preach. Mason's choir sang before Mason preached and gave his blessings and prayers to the new organization.

Their purpose was fivefold: 1) formulate an agreed-upon Pentecostal doctrine, 2) consolidate Pentecostal works, 3) support Pentecostal missions, 4) establish Pentecostal Bible schools, and 5) preserve the fruit of Pentecost in the nation and the world. A keynote address was given by M.M. Pinson on "the finished work of Calvary," and Bell was elected first general superintendent. A congregational form of government and

"Finished Work" doctrine was adopted, clearly defining sanctification as a progressive work. Though no one intended to create a new denomination, in essence, that is what happened. The group soon incorporated under the name General Council of the Assemblies of God. Today, the World Assemblies of God Fellowship is the world's largest Pentecostal denomination with more than 67 million members and a presence in more than 212 countries, making it the sixth largest Christian denomination overall worldwide.[469]

Fearing too much denominational control in the Assemblies of God, John C. Sinclair, who had succeeded William Durham as pastor of the Chicago North Avenue Mission, formed the Pentecostal Assemblies of the USA in 1916, which later became the Pentecostal Church of God. When the Church of God (Cleveland, Tennessee) split in 1923 over concerns about A.J. Tomlinson's theocratic rule and alleged mishandling of funds, the Tomlinson Church of God was formed, which later became the Church of God of Prophecy. By the 1930s, many other Pentecostal denominations and independent groups were springing up as well.

ONENESS PENTECOSTALS

During the first "World Wide" Apostolic Faith Camp Meeting in the Arroyo Seco near Los Angeles in 1913, an outdoor baptismal service was scheduled. R.E. McAlister, a Canadian minister who had been baptized in the Spirit at Azusa Street, was invited to teach. McAlister preached that the acceptable "apostolic" way to baptize was in the name of Jesus because "the apostles invariably baptized their converts once in the name of Jesus Christ" instead of the traditional "Father, Son, and Holy Spirit."[470] It was another shot heard round the world.

One man who heard that statement, John G. Scheppe, ran through the camp early the next morning shouting that God had revealed to

Glenn Cook (left) rebaptizes L.V. Roberts at a Oneness outdoor baptismal service in Indianapolis, March 6, 1915. This was said to have been the first Jesus' Name service east of the Mississippi.

Photo: Flower Pentecostal Heritage Center.

him the truth of baptism in the name of the Lord Jesus Christ. Another man who heard that statement was Frank J. Ewart, an Australian Baptist minister who had assisted William Durham with his Los Angeles ministry and succeeded him there after his death. Ewart spent a year formulating his ideas before preaching his first "Jesus' Name" sermon in 1914.

It was an age-old argument supposedly settled at Nicaea in 325. According to "Oneness" teaching, "Father" and "Holy Spirit" were mere titles designating different aspects of Christ's personality, thus requiring anyone baptized according to traditional Trinitarian beliefs to be "re-baptized in the name of Jesus." Ewart also took Durham's "Finished Work" doctrine a step further by declaring that salvation, sanctification, and baptism in the Holy Spirit with speaking in tongues all constituted one event that may be received at water baptism when done properly.

Among Ewart's first converts were Azusa Street pilgrims Glenn Cook and Frank Bartleman. Together, Ewart and Cook set out on a campaign to "re-baptize" the entire Pentecostal movement. However, when Cook converted Garfield T. Haywood—a leading black pastor and his 465-member church in Indianapolis—shockwaves reverberated throughout the young movement. Still, by 1916, and after much infighting, the Trinitarians had won the day. The Assemblies of God adopted its Statement of Fundamental Truths, which unequivocally supported Trinitarianism, and 156 Oneness preachers were forced to leave and form their own fellowships. Many of them reformed and reorganized under the Pentecostal Assemblies of the World with Oneness Pentecostal teachings and Haywood as their leader.

In 380, these Oneness preachers would have been judged "demented and insane" and excommunicated as heretics, but in 1916, they simply reorganized under a new doctrinal position.[471] In 1924, the Oneness churches split down racial lines to form an all-white denomination called the United Pentecostal Church, which later merged with another Oneness group in 1945, forming the United Pentecostal Church International (UPCI). It has since become more ethnically diverse. Over the years, at least sixteen other Oneness denominations have emerged, and today Oneness Pentecostals have approximately 24 million adherents worldwide.[472]

CHAPTER 15

BEGINNING OF A WORLDWIDE REVIVAL

One preacher who visited Azusa Street in 1906 said, "The Lord has shown me that this movement will soon blow over."[473] It did—all over the world! In fact, the revival spread to the rest of the world with such rapidity, it is difficult to imagine. Henry McGowan said, "News of what was going on soon spread all over the world like a prairie fire."[474] Another brother testified at the mission: "The Lord showed me a few years ago that out of California would come a movement that would startle the world, and here is the prophecy fulfilled."[475] The many ministers who attended the Azusa Street Revival became part of a worldwide network of Pentecostal missionaries.

The first issue of *The Apostolic Faith* printed at Azusa Street made this clarion call: "The Apostolic Faith Movement…stands for the restoration of the faith once delivered unto the saints—the old time religion, camp meetings, revivals, missions, street and prison work and Christian unity everywhere."[476] Subsequent issues declared, "Beginning of a Worldwide Revival," "Pentecost Both Sides the Ocean."[477] Outbreaks of tongues were reported in London, Stockholm, Oslo, Calcutta, Africa, Canada, Hawaii, China, Denmark, Australia, and Jerusalem.

The greatest Azusa Street missionary of all was *The Apostolic Faith*, which went out to subscribers around the world all at once. Countless received the Pentecostal experience simply upon receiving or reading it. One subscriber reported receiving *and* reading it, then said, "The Spirit

The front page of *The Apostolic Faith, Vol. 1 No. 1*, September 1906. Headline reads: "Pentecost Has Come: Los Angeles Being Visited by a Revival of Bible Salvation and Pentecost as Recorded in the Book of Acts." The newspaper was the greatest Azusa Street missionary with some 50,000 subscribers worldwide and reports of salvations, baptisms in the Holy Spirit, and healings continually coming in.

Photo: Flower Pentecostal Heritage Center.

witnessed with my spirit that it was the true teachings of the gospel." T.B. Barratt, a Methodist pastor from Norway who read about the revival in *The Apostolic Faith* while in New York, received the baptism in the Holy Spirit, then brought it back to northern Europe and helped spread it throughout the world.

THE FIRST APOSTOLIC FAITH MISSIONARIES

The first missionary to arrive at Azusa Street and then return to the mission field was Andrew G. Johnson. He went to Colorado, Chicago, and New York before departing for Spain, Jerusalem, Sweden, and Norway. In Norway, T.B. Barratt, a Methodist pastor, came to one of Johnson's meetings and began asking questions about the outpouring in Los Angeles. Mr. Johnson was followed by a dozen others. Seymour said, "Missionaries are going almost every day."[478] A.G. and Lillian Garr were the first non-missionaries to leave Azusa Street and go on the mission field. They went to India, Ceylon (now Sri Lanka), and Hong Kong before returning and traveling throughout the U.S. and Canada planting churches.

Alexander Boddy received T.B. Barratt at his church in Sunderland, England, which then became a center for British Pentecostalism around the world. Frank Bartleman circled the globe once and Europe twice. M.L. Ryan went to Spokane, Washington, China, and Japan. Others went to India, China, Japan, Hong Kong, and the Philippines. Some founded Pentecostal churches; others founded entire denominations.

Parham clearly believed and taught that the restoration of the gift of tongues in the last days had been given to equip missionaries with foreign languages to bring about God's end-time global harvest before the return of Christ. Seymour was not so convinced. Seymour wrote in *The Apostolic Faith,* "Some think they must go out because they have the tongues but those are good for Los Angeles or anywhere else. The Lord will lead you by His small voice."[479]

In time, however, Parham also grew cautious, sending few if any missionaries. Seymour did the exact opposite. Only testing on the mission field could finally answer this question. And that is why the Azusa Street Mission became the birthplace of modern, global Pentecostalism. Many who initially responded to the call, thinking they were gifted at speaking in a foreign language, returned home disillusioned. Others adapted, learned languages in conventional ways, or simply became what Pentecostal historian Vinson Synan called "missionaries of the one-way ticket" by successfully carrying the torch of Pentecost to the ends of the earth.[480]

HEARTY SEND-OFFS

Alfred and Lillian Garr were the first non-missionaries to leave Azusa Street. After Alfred was baptized in the Spirit at Azusa Street, he spoke in tongues for hours when a British Indian came and asked him, "How did you learn my mother tongue?" "I do not know your mother tongue," Garr replied. But the man continued, "This is the first time I have heard my mother tongue since I left India." Alfred believed he had received the Hindustani language.

Lillian, who nearly left him, thinking he had become fanatical, agreed to go with him to one meeting at Azusa Street when the glory of God broke over her soul and she, too, spoke in tongues. She believed she had received the Chinese language. A week later, they offered themselves as the first missionaries of the Apostolic Faith Mission. One man immediately stood and cried, saying, "I have five hundred dollars I want to give you to go to India." Then a lady stood up with two hundred dollars, and another with a hundred dollars. Within fifteen minutes, they had received twelve hundred dollars cash for their journey.[481]

The congregation at Azusa Street often accompanied new missionaries to the train station, singing and shouting all the way. Then they held a public sendoff meeting at the station. Most bought one-way tickets, because they believed Jesus would return before they would need to return home. If He did not, they believed God would provide the funds overseas. Their faith at the Azusa Mission was simple and boundless.

Pastor Seymour and his staff did everything they could to honor those who believed they had received the divine call, even helping them to discern their call and identify and test their gifts. They issued credentials, then blessed them with just enough money to get them wherever God had called them. The number of missionaries this tiny mission was able to send was staggering. More than twenty within the first year and many more the following year. In the beginning, Frank Bartleman said he could visit virtually every Pentecostal work in Western and Eastern Europe, the Middle East, and Asia. Lucy Leatherman was equally well-traveled in Europe, Asia, the Middle East, and South America.

VETERAN MISSIONARIES

Another category of Azusa Street missionaries were veterans in the field who had come to Azusa Street and who wanted to be sent back out as Apostolic Faith or Pentecostal missionaries. Samuel and Ardella Mead, retired Methodist missionaries to Angola, decided to return to the mission field after being baptized in the Spirit at Azusa Street. They brought Robert and Myrtle Schideler, another Azusa Street missionary couple, with them. George and Mary Berg, veteran Holiness missionaries to India, had returned to America after Mary's health declined. However, after being healed and baptized in the Spirit at Azusa Street, they returned to India for a successful second term. Paul Bettex had been a missionary in South America and his future wife, Nellie, a missionary to China. After meeting and being baptized in the Spirit at Azusa Street, they both went to Canton, China, where they were married in 1910.

ALFRED AND LILLIAN GARR

The Azusa Street Mission also produced several long-term missionaries with no previous missionary experience. A.H. Post traveled to London, South Africa, Ceylon, and Hong Kong before returning home to get his family and serve in Alexandria, Egypt. Alfred and Lillian Garr left for Calcutta, India, in January 1907 with Maria Gardener, an African American woman at the mission who agreed to serve as a nursemaid to their three-year-old daughter. When they arrived in Calcutta, they had lost all their baggage and were heartbroken. The following day, a British Army Officer named Captain Angel Smith said God had told him to give these new missionaries a substantial sum of money. He was the first person in India they led into the baptism in the Holy Spirit.

One of the most well-known missionary couples to come out of the Azusa Street Revival was Alfred and Lillian Garr. The Garrs met and married at Asbury College in Kentucky, served several years as evangelists and church planters for the Burning Bush Holiness group, before pastoring the Los Angeles mission. After receiving their Pentecostal experience at Azusa Street, they shut down the mission and invited their members to join them at Azusa Street. They were the first Apostolic Faith missionaries to the U.S., India, Hong Kong, and China.

Photos: Flower Pentecostal Heritage Center.

Since *The Apostolic Faith* publication had arrived in India before them, the missionaries who had read its reports were anxious to hear about the Garrs' experience at Azusa Street, so they invited them to a missionary convention. Otto Stockmeier, a Swiss missionary and proponent of the "Overcoming Life" movement in England, spoke first, then gave them the floor. After sharing their testimony with the missionaries, Max Wood Moorhead, a Presbyterian and Secretary of the Young Men's Christian Association (YMCA) in Ceylon, decided to continue the meetings another two months past the convention. As the Garrs continued to minister, many were baptized in the Spirit and spoke in tongues with manifestations like at Azusa Street. The Garrs quickly realized their gift of tongues did not work the way they thought, yet they never abandoned the practice of speaking in tongues. Consequently, many missionaries closed their doors to the Garrs.

Nevertheless, the Garrs believed their primary mission as missionary evangelists was to challenge, encourage, and support existing missionaries in their quest for the baptism in the Holy Spirit. When Pandita Ramabai, founder of the world-famous Mukti Mission and mother of Pentecostalism in India, heard the Garrs were in Calcutta, she immediately invited them to Mukti, and within two weeks some 800 girls at the mission had received the baptism in the Holy Spirit and spoken in tongues.

Over the next few months, the Garrs held similar meetings in Bombay, India, and Colombo, Ceylon, where a thousand more reportedly spoke in tongues. The Garrs also traveled to Hong Kong twice after being invited by several single women missionaries there. Then they traveled stateside, planting more than a hundred Pentecostal churches in the U.S. and Canada. After Lillian's death, Alfred was remarried to Hannah Erickson and the two continued traveling and planting churches before finally establishing a Pentecostal work in Charlotte, North Carolina.

PENTECOSTAL MISSIONARY CRITICISMS

Most of the Azusa Street missionaries were short-term—six months to a year. Some left permanent fruit, others died within weeks of malaria or faced fierce opposition from mostly Protestant, evangelical, and Holiness groups. Jesse Penn Lewis, the infamous Holiness author who perhaps single-handedly brought an end to the Welsh Revival, published similar articles attacking the Apostolic Faith movement as being led by demons instead of the Holy Spirit. Presbyterian theologian Arthur T. Pierson also wrote a series of articles stating that wherever tongues had appeared on mission fields, problems had occurred. A Pietist-Holiness group in Germany issued a similar statement in its "Berlin Declaration," saying the Apostolic Faith movement was "not from on high, but from below."[482] Besides the gift of tongues, S.C. Todd, working with the Bible Missionary Society in Macao, China, complained that Apostolic Faith missionaries were insensitive and abusive toward anyone who disagreed with them.

Even some Azusa Street missionaries eventually started chiming in on the complaints against other early Pentecostal missionaries. John G. Lake wrote a letter to the Upper Room Mission in Los Angeles complaining that missionaries were being sent to the foreign field without any advanced preparation or ongoing support from the mission. Lake heartily welcomed "REAL MISSIONARIES," but warned that the mission field was not the place for those who had "all the answers" or who came to introduce their new American ideas without any respect for the local culture. Azusa Street missionary Antoinette Moomau in Shanghai, China, gave similar warnings, saying, "More than the baptism of the Spirit is needed to come to a foreign field."[483]

T.B. BARRATT

Thomas Ball "T.B." Barratt, a Methodist minister from Norway, was staying at the Alliance House in New York in 1906, where he was raising funds for his city mission in Oslo, Norway, when he stumbled on a copy of *The Apostolic Faith*. Immediately recognizing the Azusa Street Revival as the long-awaited latter-day outpouring, Barratt began corresponding by letter with the Azusa Street staff and praying up to twelve hours a day for his own Pentecostal experience. Glenn Cook and Clara Lum both sent him words of encouragement.

Then Lucy Leatherman, a physician's wife and graduate of Nyack Bible College in New York, who had received the baptism in the Holy Spirit at the Azusa Mission and who had assisted Florence Crawford on the West Coast, traveled back to New York. There, she was assembling a group of Azusa Street missionaries at the Alliance House and at the Union Holiness Mission, pastored by Elder Sturdevant, also from Azusa Street. When T.B. Barratt met Lucy Leatherman, he had a ton of questions.

So Mrs. Leatherman referred him to Maude Williams, who had a small mission there in New York. At the mission, Barratt asked Lucy Leatherman and another Norwegian gentleman to lay hands on him, when an unusual brightness like "a tongue of fire" came over his head. Barratt felt filled with light and overcome with a newfound spiritual power and burden for global evangelism as he prayed in heavenly languages. Barratt not only reportedly shouted and spoke in "seven or eight languages," but also burst into "a beautiful baritone solo using one of the most pure and delightful languages" until 4:00 a.m.[484]

After staying at the Union Holiness Mission with the Azusa Street missionaries bound for Africa, Barratt sailed with them to Liverpool, England, before returning to Norway. Barratt then rented a gymnasium in Oslo that seated 2,000 and began the first modern Pentecostal meetings in Europe. He reported, "Folk from all denominations are rushing to the meetings. A number have received their Pentecost and are speaking in tongues.... Many are seeking salvation and souls are being gloriously saved. Hundreds are seeking a clean heart, and the fire is falling on the purified sacrifice. People who have attended the meetings are taking the fire with them to the towns round about."[485]

Thomas Ball "T.B." Barratt was a British-born Norwegian pastor and founding figure of the Pentecostal movement in Europe. Barratt rented a room in A.B. Simpson's guesthouse in Manhattan, New York, in 1906 to raise funds for missions. The guesthouse was a temporary residence for missionaries waiting to travel by ship to mission fields on other continents. There, he received news of the Azusa Street Revival and was baptized in the Holy Spirit. Barratt then brought the movement to Norway, Europe, India, and beyond. Originally a Methodist pastor, he left the church to establish Filadelfia Church in Kristiania (Oslo), Norway's largest church.

Photo: lokalhistorie/borgerskolen.no.

After Barratt's membership with the Methodist Church terminated, he founded Filadelfia Church in Oslo, which soon became Norway's largest church. Barratt also began publishing his own periodical in six languages while continuing to hold revival meetings throughout northern Europe. Among those attending Barratt's revival meetings were Lewi Pethrus of Sweden and Alexander Boddy, Vicar of All Saints' Parish in Sunderland, England. Boddy later visited and spoke at the Azusa Street Mission in 1912, which he described as "a sort of 'Mecca' still to Pentecostal travellers."[486] Pethrus became pastor of Filadelfia Church of Stockholm, which soon became Sweden's largest church with a host of Pentecostal missionaries around the world.

Barratt then spoke at Boddy's church in Sunderland, when another revival broke out with thousands more attending. Among those attendees were George Jeffreys and Smith Wigglesworth. Wigglesworth would go on to become a British healing evangelist, apostle of faith, and a Pentecostal pioneer who would spread the Pentecostal message globally. George Jeffries would soon preach with signs following in churches, conventions, and camp meetings across the U.K. and Ireland and, before his death, influence South African evangelist Reinhard Bonnke. Reinhard Bonnke would then go on to preach to some 120 million Africans and lead some 55 million to salvation and many more millions to healing in Christ.

SOUTH AFRICAN MISSIONARIES

Another group of Azusa Street missionaries left for South Africa in 1908. Thomas Hezmalhalch, a hymnist, soloist, and pastor of the First Holiness Church in Pasadena, received the baptism in the Spirit and spoke in tongues at Azusa Street before leading an Apostolic Faith congregation in Indianapolis and holding a series of meetings in Zion, Illinois.

Jacob and Lily Lehman left their home in Monrovia, California, to become missionaries for a time in South Africa, where they learned the Zulu language. Returning to Southern California in 1906, they heard of the Azusa Street Mission, went and were baptized in the Spirit, then moved to Indianapolis, where they attended the mission Cook and Hezmalhalch pioneered.

John G. Lake was an ordained Methodist minister who became an elder in John Alexander Dowie's Catholic Apostolic Church in Zion, Illinois, after he and his family had been healed under Dowie's ministry. Lake had also owned a lucrative insurance business and had had a seat on the Chicago Board of Trade. Lake visited Azusa Street in 1907, having met Seymour in Zion and received the baptism in the Spirit under Charles Parham's ministry there.

In 1908, all three men took part in a missionary convention in Indianapolis where they had agreed to become missionaries to South Africa and move their families there. Within days of their arrival in Capetown, they conducted their first service at the Congregational American Mission in Doorfontein, where 500 people attended. Their Pentecostal worship style was immediately accepted as 250 prayed and wept aloud at once, confessed their sins, and removed their charms and idols while the American missionaries looked on in astonishment.

John G. Lake led a small team of Pentecostal missionaries to South Africa in 1908. Within days, a revival broke out among the Zulus as multitudes were saved, healed, and baptized in the Holy Spirit. In 1912, Lake returned to America, having converted some 100,000 Africans, and founding two denominations—the Apostolic Faith Mission, South Africa's largest Pentecostal church, and Zion Christian Church, South Africa's largest church overall and second largest in the continent. Lake also founded several churches and healing homes in Portland, Oregon, and Spokane, Washington, where a reported 100,000 healings occurred between 1915 and 1920.

Photo: Flower Pentecostal Heritage Center.

John Alexander Dowie had also established several Zion churches in South Africa, which clearly helped pave the way for these missionaries. Within weeks of Lake's arrival, P.L. le Roux took a leave of absence and asked Lake to fill his pulpit for him. Again, more than five hundred Zulus, the largest ethnic group in South Africa, attended his first Sunday service. Once the Zionists heard Lake's message, they immediately received the baptism in the Spirit. Soon revival broke out, as powerful demonstrations accompanied the preaching of the Word and multitudes were saved, healed, and Spirit baptized. Lake wrote, "From the very start it was as though a spiritual cyclone had struck."[487]

This former Presbyterian church quickly became the "Central Tabernacle" of the Apostolic Faith Mission in South Africa with Thomas Hezmalhalch as president, John G. Lake as vice president, and Jacob Lehman as treasurer. Both Lehman and Hezmalhalch eventually returned to Southern California, leaving Lake as head of the mission. Though racially diverse in the beginning, the church eventually became segregated as nearly all churches became caught up in the national apartheid movement. However, later in the twentieth century, when South African Pentecostals revolted against apartheid, they again traced their roots back to Azusa Street, writing:

"In the Azusa Street Revival we find the legitimacy to continue our witness as Pentecostals. It was here that God called to himself a prophetic movement in an oppressive society that belied the dignity of black people. It was here that God called to himself a humble people to be his witnesses in a hostile world. It was here that powerless people were baptized in the Holy Spirit and endued with power to preach the good news of Jesus Christ, with 'signs following.' It is in this tradition that we come bearing a Relevant Pentecostal Witness."[488]

By the time Lake had returned to America in 1912, he had converted some 100,000 Africans and founded two denominations—one black and one white. Former South African Prime Minister Cecil Rhodes wrote, "Lake's message swept Africa. He has done more toward South Africa's future peace than any other man." Indian nationalist leader Mahatma Ghandi reportedly said of Lake, "Dr. Lake's teachings will eventually be accepted by the entire world."[489] Today, the Apostolic Faith Mission is South Africa's largest Pentecostal church with more than a million members, and the Zion Christian Church is South

Africa's largest and fastest growing church and second largest in the continent with between 2 and 6 million members.[490]

Later in the twentieth century, as European nations began withdrawing their colonial occupation of Africa, many believed that would be the end of Christianity in Africa. Instead, Africa has seen phenomenal church growth coming largely from the Pentecostal works and Independent African Churches. And all "Zion," "Apostolic," and "Apostolic Faith" churches and denominations can trace their roots back to a tiny shack filled with humble people on a dead-end street in Los Angeles called Azusa Street.

CHAPTER 16

UNLOCKING AZUSA FIRE
BY RICK JOYNER

The Azusa Street Revival, which began in 1906, was the most exciting act of God in the last two thousand years. The account is so amazing that, without question, had it taken place in the first century, it would have been highlighted in the Book of Acts. Even today, many Christians are skeptical when they hear about the miracles that took place at Azusa Street. How could a converted stable turned mission at 312 Azusa Street in Los Angeles be described along with 1600 Pennsylvania Avenue in Washington, D.C. (the White House) as one of the two most famous addresses in the world?

Still, the event was so widely corroborated, even in secular newspapers and journals around the world, we must conclude that this was an extraordinary time when the Lord wanted to show what He can do with even the humblest people who give their lives to Him. This revival was but a foretaste of an even greater move of God soon to come—the one the Lord called "the harvest" (see Matthew 13:39), which will come at the end of this age. Therefore, we must understand this revival to be encouraged but also to prepare. God will do it again, only bigger!

AN EARTH-SHAKING REVIVAL

The whole world was shaken by this revival, and we must understand how and why. When God moves, the earth will shake, as it did when He descended on Mount Sinai and in California in April 1906. The greater the move of God, the greater the shaking. Revival is serious business; it is not a spiritual amusement park; it is the presence of the King. Part of preparing is to understand this. That the greatest move of God will soon be upon us is both the greatest hope and gravest warning:

> And His voice shook the earth then, but now He has promised, saying, "Yet once more I will shake not only the earth, but also the heaven." This expression, "Yet once more," denotes the removing of those things which can be shaken, as of created things, so that those things which cannot be shaken may remain (Hebrews 12:26-27 NASB).

True revival is a holy and fearful thing. However, revival is a good kind of fear. If we will embrace the pure and holy fear of God, we will fear nothing else. The fear of God is the foundation of true faith. Every move of God has an enemy, and the enemy's main weapon is the bad kind of fear. In the days ahead, there will be an increasing conflict between faith and fear. Any move of God will be both the most wonderful experience and the most serious event.

Every true move of God in history has had an impact on the church and, to some degree, the whole church. The one that is coming will bring the most rapid and radical changes the church has ever experienced. More will be accomplished in the next few decades than in the last five centuries. Are we ready? As usual, those who cheer the most at this prospect will be the most negatively affected by it, especially those who presume God sees everything the way they do.

As stated, when true revival breaks out, there are often earthquakes, and history now attests to this. However, those earthquakes are the result of the way the Lord moved at that time. Today, people chafe at such a notion, yet these revivals received more coverage in the world press than the earthquakes that accompanied them.

Like the 1906 San Francisco earthquake, the Azusa Revival erupted with little warning. Like a tsunami, it came from a different direction and caught the world off-balance. The revival then profoundly impacted and changed the church worldwide as few have. It set the church on a course for which few could foresee or prepare. This resulted in some of the greatest growth, spiritual advances, and conflicts since the first century. Its impact was so great that it is not possible to understand the modern church without understanding this revival.

It caused the greatest transformation of church life since the Reformation and, according to some, since the first century. However, it did not bring the church to its full purpose. It was merely part of "the beginning of birth pangs" as Jesus and Paul prophesied (see Matthew 24:8; Romans 8:22). There have been other great spiritual contractions since, which have relentlessly helped move the church toward the greatest move of God ever to come on earth—the gospel of the kingdom preached with kingdom power.

WAVES OF THE SPIRIT

Moves of God are also called "waves" because they often behave like waves. Catching and riding a wave of the Holy Spirit is like surfing. To catch and ride a wave, you need to discern the pattern of waves and where they are breaking, then position yourself to move in the right direction at the right time. The same is required for catching waves of the Spirit.

On May 11, 1992, I had a prophetic experience in which I saw the church as a surfer floating on a short surfboard. He was gazing at the beach, lazily drifting, and dreaming of the "big one." While drifting, however, the very wave he was dreaming about drew closer, yet he seemed oblivious. I knew, unless he quickly awoke out of his dream state, it would break on top of him and the result would not be pretty, but pretty serious! I also knew his board was too short for the huge wave that was coming.

By the time he heard and saw the wave, it was too late. What had been his dream became his nightmare because he was unprepared. The wave flipped him over, hurled him to the bottom several times, and broke his board. I feared for his life. He did survive but with many cuts, bruises, and a few broken bones.

I watched him lie on the beach in great pain. Soon, the fear of possibly dying passed and a deep wisdom replaced it. He gazed back at the sea. Though hurt, broken, and barely moving, an awesome resolve came over him. I knew he would return to ride the waves again.

Then I saw him in a hospital room looking out the window at the ocean, still gazing at the sea. Only instead of dreaming, he was now planning. Next, I saw him standing on the beach, healed and in far better shape than before. Next to him was the largest surfboard I had ever seen. He was now ready and prepared to catch the big one!

Though the sea was calm, we both knew the biggest wave of all was on the horizon. We could feel it coming. This time, he was ready, though fear began to arise within him. I knew if he did not quickly dismiss that fear and start moving, it would be too late, and he would again miss the great wave.

Then I looked around and saw many other surfers standing on the beach. They looked like professional bodybuilders, and all had short surfboards, like the other surfer. However, they did not seem interested in catching this wave, just standing on the beach and looking good (though they looked grotesque to everyone else but themselves). I also knew they were not as strong as the true surfer, who had a natural physique. The vision ended.

PROPHETIC INTERPRETATION

In previous great awakenings and revivals, few individuals anticipated the moves of the Spirit. Consequently, many existing churches and ministries were damaged by their lack of preparation for them. Some even had to resist the revival and fight the wave of the Spirit to survive.

Today, there is a near universal expectation of an impending revival, yet little is being done to prepare for it. Though we know it's coming, many would rather just dream about it than prepare. The coming wave of the Spirit is much bigger than anything we have dreamed of, yet because many are dreaming and not watching and preparing, they are placing themselves in serious jeopardy. The short surfboards were obviously inadequate for such a large wave. This speaks of the inadequacy of our current church ministries and outreaches. Though many can see or sense what's coming, they will not have the means or the ability to ride the wave.

Since I received this vision in 1992, many parts of the world have experienced great moves of God. These moves of God have had a remarkable impact on nations and continents. Still, many churches that longed and prayed for these moves of God suffered like the unprepared surfer. Their nets were inadequate to hold the great catch, and though they bore much fruit, much was needlessly lost.

As for other parts of the world, like Europe and North America, which have not yet experienced these great moves of God, they are about to experience them. But also like this surfer, the Western Church may get nothing more than a good beating or learning experience from them. Though the church has been hearing from the Lord regarding the coming ingathering, it has not heeded those words or taken the necessary steps to prepare. Still, the beating will bring wisdom and resolve for the next one. The time spent recovering from our injuries from the impending wave must be spent planning for the next one, then our plans must be turned to action.

To ride the coming wave, we must become stronger. Strength comes from exercising. When the surfer returned to the beach, he had the physique of a natural bodybuilder, not for show. Likewise, the body of Christ must be built up for strength and endurance, not for show. Every muscle, limb, and individual part of the body must be properly exercised to full strength. For decades, we have preached the Ephesians 4, equipping-of-the-saints-for-works-of-service model; now we must do it. Many will be involved in this "spiritual bodybuilding," but only for show or to impress others instead of to prepare for the next wave. They will not have the proper equipment or even notice the encroaching wave. We must get our attention off how we look to each other and on how we appear before God. Those who build their congregations for show may look grotesque to outsiders and lack the proper skills to ride the wave. They won't even be in the water, much less in place when the wave comes.

Though the surfer who was injured in the first wave was prepared for the next wave, the enemy used that negative experience to strike fear in his heart to hinder his preparation. All our work and preparation will come to nought if we are not committed to getting back in the water and walking by faith and not fear.

THE COMING HARVEST

Though the worldwide church has experienced many remarkable awakenings, revivals, and great harvests over the last few decades, the greatest is yet to come. However, we must look forward and not backward. The Azusa Street Revival is a part of history, but also tied to a prophetic vision for the future.

As we see in Matthew 13:30, the harvest begins with the tares. Many revelations of sin and wrongdoing in the church have been the work of the Holy Spirit to prepare us for the coming ingathering. However, there are still many tares and stumbling blocks to be rooted out before the great and final harvest begins.

Every time the Lord has shown me a vision of the coming harvest, He has shown it to me in two great waves. There may be more than two, but I know there will at least be two. The first will be so great that nearly everyone will think it is the great harvest, but there will be at least one more coming after, that is much greater. In fact, the millions of new believers who will come in the first wave will become the laborers in the second wave, but they must be properly equipped and prepared.

The present church structure is more like a spectator sport than its biblical counterpart with few doing and the rest cheering. This model will not survive much longer. The coming waves of the Spirit will badly damage or destroy these models that are not fulfilling the Ephesians 4 mandate for true ministry. The first wave will be a blessing to those churches and ministries who have equipped the saints for ministry but also a judgment to those who are not properly equipped or just dreaming.

Surfing is not the safest sport. Placing yourself in the domain of the most fearsome predator on earth (sharks) and riding waves (which can also kill you) is not for the timid. Likewise, true Christianity is not for the timid. Those who are ruled by fear more than faith will soon be found out and will not be part of the greatest move of God on earth.

Like sharks, the devil and his minions will swarm toward any move of God to pick off anyone they can, while scaring off the rest. True spiritual advances cannot go far among the fearful and timid. It takes great faith and courage to participate in true revival. However, for those led by the Spirit and walking in faith and not fear, even the smallest or shortest wave is worth every risk. Those unwilling to take those risks are unworthy of revival.

Every true move of God has been a restoration of something lost by the church since the first century. Revivals revive that which is dead, sleeping, or needing resurrection. The Lord will always be with any two or three gathered in His name, but the "manifest presence of the Lord" will forever change us. Moses was a good example of this. He spent forty years as a lowly shepherd and probably considered himself washed up and finished, but after one encounter with the manifest presence of the Lord, this washed-up old man became a spiritual giant who delivered a nation. The Azusa Street Revival was likewise such an encounter that transformed and released some of the greatest men and women of God on earth, possibly since Acts.

TRUE TRANSFORMATION

Throughout history, the slightest breakthrough of the presence of the Lord not only sparked revivals and brought transformation to the church but also sent shockwaves through society. The greater the manifestation of His presence, the greater the revival. The more profound the transformation, the more powerful the shockwaves.

Church historians trace transformations of the church to illuminations of certain lost or overlooked biblical truths. The truth sets us free, but the Truth is also a Person. Therefore, encounters with God truly transform us much more than ideas. Facts can change minds, but the manifest presence of the Lord changes hearts and minds. True revivals come only when we seek the Person of Truth, Jesus Christ.

According to Matthew 22:29, error is when we do not know the Scriptures *and* the power of God. Those who know only the Scriptures are in error because they do not know His power. Those who know only His power are in error because they do not know the Scriptures. If we love the Scriptures or the power more than Him, these also can become idols. We must have both, and the coming harvest will be a marriage of both.

One moment in the manifest presence of the Lord will transform us more than years of preaching and teaching. Preaching and teaching is only the scaffolding of the building; the building is the Lord. We seek to grow up in Him. What good is a glorious temple if God is not in it? When God is in the temple, no one is focused on the temple. This is what true revivalists seek: the Lord and His manifest presence. Once we experience this, we are forever ruined for anything else.

The Azusa Street story is about those who sought God and found Him. This encounter sent spiritual tidal waves and tsunamis around the world. The glory of this revival astonished the world but also brought judgment on those who were not rightly positioned when it came. Like tsunamis, when God moves, everything not on high ground is in danger of destruction. The churches and movements that had fallen from their high calling were washed away. This will be repeated. This is not only history but also prophecy.

The Azusa story includes some of the most exciting testimonies of God's works in this age and is filled with many important principles, methods, and insights into God's ways, but the most important is the principle that God yearns to be sought. Those who seek Him find Him, and those who find Him cannot help but love Him. The love of God is the greatest treasure and most powerful force on earth. Faith can move mountains, but love can move nations. May our love for God increase and become contagious with a genuine, authentic passion for Him.

To experience revival, we must seek the approval of God more than men. The degree to which we are unconcerned about what others think will be the degree to which God can use us. We must have a higher concern for how heaven sees us than how those with a distorted vision see us. The greatest testimony in heaven is to be known as one who loves God. This is our highest calling. This is the main thing. He is worthy of being loved. When we set our hearts on loving Him, revival will come.

When relating to Almighty God, the One who created the world with a word, anything He decides to breathe on will have consequences beyond human comprehension. Since He is God, He can take the humblest prayer meeting and use it to shake the world. Since He delights in using humble, weak, and even foolish people, one meeting can have historic consequences. Thus, we should never doubt the potential of even the humblest gathering of those who know Him. Wherever two or three are gathered in His name, anything is possible.

Every great spiritual pioneer used to ignite a great move of God has at first appeared reckless or dangerous to the church to which they were sent. William Seymour was no exception to this. He wanted God so bad that he didn't care what anyone else thought. He could not live within the present limits of the time, so he pushed back on those limits. His abandonment to the Spirit then benefited multiplied millions.

From the beginning, Azusa broke many norms to an astonishingly unique degree. Even in its first meetings, the seeds of the great movements birthed out of it could be seen. The leaders of Azusa were inexperienced in leadership but seasoned in faith. They trusted God to make up for their lack, so long as they maintained their humility. It survived every onslaught and religious deception. Christian and missionary leaders came from afar and God touched all who came sincerely seeking His grace.

CONTINUAL AWE AND WONDER

It is often said of the Azusa Revival and the first-century church that the people experienced continual awe and wonder at all that God did. Every day was afire with His great acts. There was great interest and focus on the Holy Spirit and His gifts, but by far the main emphasis was loving God. He was among them in tangible ways, day and night. They simply sought and loved God like few others before them or since.

One remarkable characteristic from the beginning of this revival was the diversity of people who were drawn. Some considered this unprecedented since Pentecost, and soon remarkable healings, miracles, and dramatic conversions were taking place daily. Such diversity was considered as much a marvel as the other extraordinary miracles. Twenty nationalities were counted, and no one cared because they all came seeking to experience God and to be filled with His Spirit.

The church at that time was so dry that each testimony was like sparks on dry wood and the flames ignited fast. Newspaper articles fanned the flames with an even greater intensity. Testimonies from the Welsh Revival had stirred thousands to seek the Lord for a similar American revival, and the deplorable spiritual state of the country made her ready for it. This fire spread wider and faster than possibly any previous or subsequent revival in America.

We do not see to believe; we believe to see. Basic Pentecostal theology is: "Jesus Christ is the same yesterday, today, and forever" (Hebrews 13:8). He does everything today He did in Scripture. Since true Pentecostals believe in His present-day workings, they see them. Those who do not see them may begin to wonder where they have gone wrong. To Pentecostals, it is blasphemy to even think that God wrote one book, then retired. Since they have a living relationship with a living God, they see Him and His great works.

This was the experience at Azusa Street. Believers were in constant awe of God in their midst. Many forgot to eat or sleep, sometimes days at a time, because they were so caught up in the Lord's presence. They were simply afraid they would miss something if they slept. Like manna from heaven, they expected a fresh experience with the Lord every day. Faith built on faith until this humble mission became a window of heaven.

Those who were baptized with the Holy Spirit started seeing each other through the eyes of the Spirit instead of their fleshly, outward appearances. The more we see through the eyes of the Spirit, the closer we will come to the Lord's ultimate purpose for His church: "a house of prayer for all nations" (Mark 11:17). The gift of tongues (languages) also seemed to help people who were otherwise different, accept one another in the Lord.

At the height of the Azusa Revival, Seymour prophesied, "We are on the verge of the greatest miracle the world has ever seen." This "miracle" to which he referred was a true love and unity of races and creeds, which he considered fundamental to Christianity. He did not live to see the completion of this dream, but ultimately expected it to be accomplished.

A CONTINUING HOLY SPIRIT MOVEMENT

As this Holy Spirit movement has continued in many forms, it is not only possible but inevitable that Seymour's dream will come true. And when it does, Seymour will be considered the one who sowed the seeds for this greatest of all miracles. Possibly more than any man in history, he promoted that which, alone, can bring this to pass—the fullness of the Holy Spirit in our midst. When we are truly filled with the Spirit, we will see and know each other after the Spirit and become one.

Above all, the Holy Spirit came to testify of Jesus. He alone can convict us of our sins and lead us into all truth. When the Holy Spirit is truly manifested in our midst, we do not see the world in black and white; we see only the glory of the Son. He was sent to help us see as God sees. "Man looks at the outward appearance, but the Lord looks at the heart" (1 Samuel 16:7). God sees us not as we are, but as we will become through the blood of His Son. We must see each other the same way. Racism is an ultimate stronghold and sure sign of evil's grip, while true spiritual maturity will always result in unity.

The apostle Paul said, "tongues are for a sign" (1 Corinthians 14:22) and that sign was given at Pentecost. That day, men from every nation heard the glories of God in their own languages. This was the first time since the Tower of Babel and the scattering of languages that this happened. This sign meant that, through the Spirit and the church, all will be regathered as one.

As fractured and divided as the Pentecostal Movement is today, it has the calling and destiny to bring unity to the church and to the world. This fire still burns, though perhaps now only a flicker. It will ignite again into a mighty blaze that will burn all wood, hay, and stubble and purify all gold, silver, and precious stones (see 1 Corinthians 3:12).

This explosion that began at Pentecost and Azusa will continue so long as the Spirit is free to move as He wills and the people who sit before Him are willing to be as one. When Azusa drifted from this, it also drifted from its power source. "Where the Spirit of the Lord is, there is liberty" (2 Corinthians 3:17) and unity. We all look the same to the Lord. The blood of Jesus indeed washes away all color lines.

The Lord so loves diversity He made every snowflake, leaf, tree, and human different. God made men in His image and gave different aspects of His nature to the different races. We need each other to become a complete reflection of Him. That is why His house must be "a house of prayer for all nations." The word *nations* here is the Greek word *ethnos* from where we get our English word *ethnic*. The church will never become what it was created to be until the Lord's house includes all ethnic groups.

SEYMOUR'S LEADERSHIP

Another aspect of Seymour's remarkable leadership was his ability to discern, trust, and give the Holy Spirit the freedom He requires. Despite constant pressure from world-renowned church leaders who came from around the globe to impose their "needed" order and direction on the young revival, Seymour stayed the course and allowed the Spirit to move on His own. Like Evan Roberts, who led the great Welsh Revival before him, Seymour's greatest leadership quality was his ability to follow the Spirit.

Seymour and Roberts both believed the Holy Spirit required freedom to move through whomever He chose, including the humblest. This sometimes brought embarrassment as some took advantage of this liberty, but mostly it allowed the Holy Spirit to do marvelous things among them. If we really want the Holy Spirit, we must let Him lead. After all, He is God. Many give lip service to the leading of the Spirit yet are unwilling to let Him. Seymour was willing.

This kind of "hands off" leadership has been the hallmark of the world's great revivals, yet outside revival, this rarely works. God moves in different ways at different times. In times of dramatic and unique demonstrations of His sovereignty, it is best to stay out of His way. Other times, He seems to delight in working in and through people. Thus, we should always be in a state of submitting our will to His and following His leading. The more we do this, the more He will manifest His presence.

AZUSA'S INFLUENCE

Over the last two millennia, the church has experienced revivals, renewals, reformations, and movements. Some have spurred the church to spiritual advancement. However, in its far-reaching impact on both the church and the world, none have equaled Azusa Street. A hundred years later, its influence is still being felt and continues to increase. The seed of nearly every subsequent revival can be traced back to it. Just as an oak tree can be found in the genetic code of an acorn, the pattern for the church today can be found at Azusa Street. This is why understanding is crucial.

Though subsequent movements have inevitably been called "new," they are all progressive restorations of biblical truth. At the turn of the twentieth century, remnants of the great restoration movements of the past merged forming a critical mass. This resulted in a gospel explosion that shook the world and ignited powerful changes in how Christianity manifests itself on earth.

Without question, the Azusa Street Revival was one of the greatest revivals in history, and it could be argued it has not ended but has continued in many forms and places. Thus, William Seymour should rightly be considered one of the greatest Christian leaders of all time. To call what happened at Azusa Street just a "revival" is to obscure its impact and importance. It *was* a revival but also a renewal movement that resulted in an accelerated reformation. Its influence has now spanned every denomination and movement. The great worldwide revivals now taking place are the result of an increasing devotion to a relationship with Jesus, which is the result of an increasing receptivity to the Holy Spirit, who was sent to lead us to Jesus. This worldwide receptivity to the Holy Spirit was sown into the world through Azusa Street.

THE ATOMIC AGE OF THE SPIRIT

The beginning of the twentieth century marked the rapid increase in knowledge that the Lord predicted would come at the end of this age. It took nearly six thousand years of recorded history for man's knowledge to double. It then took only a few decades to double again. Now it is doubling every two years! As the apostle Paul wrote, "the spiritual is not first, but the natural" (1 Corinthians 15:46). Running parallel to this great increase in knowledge has been a similar astonishing recovery of truth in Christianity. The only difference is, while the Information Age is fueled by new discoveries, this great spiritual renewal is fueled by rediscoveries of the truths that Jesus taught.

We must honor our spiritual fathers and mothers as much as our natural fathers and mothers for our days to be lengthened and for things to go well with us (see Deuteronomy 5:16). Many great revivals and movements have died prematurely because they failed to honor those who went before them. This was the only commandment the Lord gave with a promise of both longevity and success. We must never fail to attribute our progress to the faith and courage of those who have gone before us. Heritage is important, which is why the Lord instructed every generation of Israelites to celebrate feasts of remembrance. Yes, study Azusa Street for understanding, but also to honor our spiritual fathers and mothers, so our own hearts may be stirred to have encounters with the Lord. Study with the intent of seeing God move again.

God is moving. We are now well into "the atomic age of the Spirit," meaning the pace of spiritual change has already exceeded our ability to understand it, much less implement it. However, the timing of the release of rediscovered truth combined with the conditions of this present world make it clear that the Spirit is in control, though we can no longer fully understand the natural or spiritual realm. Still, to understand the essence of these movements is essential for anyone called to lead in these times or to become responsive to what the Spirit is doing.

Many churches and denominations birthed out of this movement have stopped moving. In many places, we see only remnants of past glories with little to no continuing fire. However, worldwide, multitudes of Pentecostal-Charismatic Christians are ablaze with the presence and activity of God. In fact, in countries where the greatest advances of the gospel are now taking place, Pentecostal-Charismatics are invariably found.

Like every other move of God, the Pentecostal Movement had a spectacular beginning, followed by upheaval from within and persecution from without. Many mistakes were made, which threatened to sidetrack the entire movement. Most of these were resolved in ways that gave greater stability to the movement and enabled its advancement. The lessons learned from these mistakes can help advance any church or movement. However, before we become too concerned with avoiding the traps of revival, we need to start one!

SEEK THE LORD, NOT REVIVAL

The most important step to any journey is the first, so understanding how true moves of God begin is crucial. Yes, learn from their mistakes, but be far more concerned with what they did right. A few hours of studying history can save us years of misguidance.

Most of all, we must recognize Jesus as the seed of the church. Whether studying Scripture or history, He is the One for whom we look. After Michelangelo finished his great sculpture of King David, he was asked how he did it. He said he had a picture of King David in his heart and simply carved out everything that was not him. That is what all "master builders" of the church must do: have a clear picture of Jesus and remove everything else. Since our goal is to honor the past and prepare for these times, we must learn the basic principles illuminated in the Azusa Revival, like plowing before planting seeds. This is necessary to fully benefit from this remarkable story.

We seek the Lord, not revival. Those who find Him ignite revivals. Revivals are the fruit of lives who seek, love, live, and abide in Him. Being consumed with managing a revival rather than continually pursuing Him is one reason revivals wane and die. One tragic error of those who experience revivals is the foolish pursuit of trying to keep people excited. Like Peter Lord said, "The main thing is to keep the main thing the main thing," and the main thing is to pursue God. Perhaps William Seymour was one of the most desperate seekers of God to walk the earth since Enoch. Such will always find God and be used to spread His wonder throughout the earth.

The greatest move of God since Jesus walked the earth is yet to come. The great harvest will be the result of the gospel of the kingdom being preached throughout the earth. The Azusa Street Revival was a foretaste of this.

It is difficult to look at a seed and see the great tree it will become. You can count the seeds in an apple, but who can count the apples in a seed? As great as the Azusa Street Revival was, it was not the end of the age, so the harvest has not yet come. As great a marvel as it was, there is much more to come!

LOOK FOR THE STABLE

In biblical times, stables were most offensive. The floors were composed of decades of compacted dung and other filth. The stench was so great they were placed as far away from any other dwelling as possible. By modern standards, they would not even be fit for animals. That the Lord of glory would choose such a place to make His entry into this world is a profound revelation and message to mankind. We would do well not to miss this point. He has not stopped using such places to make His appearances. He chose Wales, the least principality of the British Isles. Then He chose a tiny stable on Azusa Street to change the face of modern Christianity.

Human reasoning would never lead us to a stable to find God. The only way is by revelation or being led by the Spirit. That which is born of God is repulsive to the pride and presumptions of men. The Lord has never birthed a true revival out of the great theological centers or bastions of influence. "God resists the proud, but gives grace to the humble" (James 4:6). The humbler we are, the more grace we receive.

The gospel is foolishness to the natural man and always will be. It will never attract those who live by human wisdom, pride, or political influence—only those who love the Truth more than anything else. The birth, life, and death of Jesus put the ax to the root of the tree of human wisdom and pride (the Knowledge of Good and Evil). This is the most powerful message creation has heard and the most profound testimony of the character and nature of God. When we embellish the gospel to appeal to carnal men, we destroy its power and begin to drift from the path of life. Paul preached nothing but Christ and Him crucified. All other messages lead to false conversions.

To see what the Lord is doing today, we must go to places that require the death of our flesh and reputations. We must have the heart of Simeon and Anna to see the salvation of the world. Yes, look for the fruit, but look for the seed that will become the fruit. God is usually found among the poor, wretched, and despised:

> But God has chosen the foolish things of the world to put to shame the wise, and God has chosen the weak things of the world to put to shame the things which are mighty; and the base things of the world and the things which are despised God has chosen, and the things which are not, to bring to nothing

the things that are, that no flesh should glory in His presence (**1** Corinthians 1:27-29).

In Wales, a band of youth brought heaven to earth with such power it quickly became front page news around the world. These were the "elders" who opened the gates for this revival, then sat in those gates as judges.

> Assuredly, I say to you, unless you are converted and become as little children, you will by no means enter the kingdom of heaven. Therefore whoever humbles himself as this little child is the greatest in the kingdom of heaven. Whoever receives one little child like this in My name receives Me. But whoever causes one of these little ones who believe in Me to sin, it would be better for him if a millstone were hung around his neck, and he were drowned in the depth of the sea (Matthew 18:3-6).

The great men of God at that time came and humbled themselves to sit at the feet of youth who led this revival. They were great in the kingdom. Others came with spiritual pride thinking these youth needed their guidance. One of them became a stumbling block to the entire revival. Never go to a revival thinking it needs you; go with an open heart to learn. Just as Uzzah died for thinking he could steady the ark of God (see 2 Samuel 6:6), we are foolish to think we can steady the glory of God. God may use us to help, but we are foolish to touch His glory without His clear guidance.

DIVINE LINKS

No two revivals are alike, yet nearly all have divine links or connections. To be part of the next nearly always requires rediscovery of the previous. Just hearing or reading revival stories stirs us to seek the Lord in new and fresh ways. The fire at Azusa was so intense that when letters or articles from it were read in other parts of the world the fire spread. Some of the stories were so electric one cannot help but be jolted by them. More than a century later, this is still true.

One principle found near the heart of every true revival is humility, which our calling demands. It is more likely that all of us were called for our foolishness than our great wisdom. Thus, we lean heavily on His grace and wisdom instead of presuming to be "God's people of faith and power." We are living in these times for this purpose, and the Lord has gifted each of us, but all those gifts operate by His grace, as it is written, "God opposes the proud but gives grace to the humble" (James 4:6 ESV). So no matter how gifted we are, we need grace, and we continue to receive that grace so long as we remain humble.

Still, the church is to be the light of the world. We are not called to be thermometers but thermostats. We are not here to interpret world events but to set their course. This is not arrogance; this is our appointment—to be humble yet powerful. The Lord has also appointed persecution as a fire to keep us true and humble. The Azusa Revival was viciously and continuously attacked by negative articles in the media, yet even these helped spread the word and drew many to the revival.

PROPHETIC PARALLELS

Many prophetic parallels can be found between Azusa and today. In both times, we have experienced a great secularization and moral meltdown of society, and in both, revival can help turn the tide. We must know history to know where we fit into God's plan. The Bible is two-thirds history and one-third prophecy, and most prophecy has been fulfilled, so most of biblical prophecy is now history. This is the most accurate map for showing where we have been, where we are now, and where we are going. The Azusa Street Revival was a major signpost on this map.

Understanding how the foundations were laid for this revival will help us understand the foundations the Lord is laying today to prepare His church for the coming harvest. In the last decades, the world has experienced the greatest harvest of souls in history, mostly in Africa, Latin America, and Asia. Consequently, more people have come to salvation since 1988 than between Pentecost and 1988. This is partly because more people now live on earth than in all human history combined, but also because of a great harvest of souls. However, as I warned in my book *The Harvest*, this first wave was only to bring laborers for the second wave, which will be much greater. There is a coming worldwide move of God that will bring between one and two billion new believers into the faith. This move will be different from any other but also like the Azusa Street Revival which, again, is why we must study it. Jesus did not heal any two people the same way.

Like all revivals, there were many aspects of the Azusa Revival to emulate and some to avoid, but we must also understand the bridge between the Welsh and Azusa Revivals. Everything the Lord intended to do in Wales, after a misfortunate turn of events, God did in Los Angeles and began the modern Pentecostal Movement. When the Welsh leaders made that turn, the revival quickly died and immediately re-erupted in Los Angeles. When Wales missed its opportunity, revival broke out elsewhere. This pattern continues to this day.

So the seedbed of true revival is first to have one, then to seek the grace of God with humility to keep it going. But even if we get sidetracked, it is still better to start one than not to have one. As John Wesley once prayed, "Oh, Lord, send us the old revival, without the defects; but if this cannot be, send it with all its defects. We must have revival."

THE BAPTISM OF FIRE

Many Christian leaders, even at Azusa, have long maintained that more is coming. Many have prophetically described what happened at Azusa as a releasing of the baptism in the Holy Spirit. Many have further described what is coming as a releasing of the baptism in the Holy Spirit *and* fire (see Luke 3:16).

First Corinthians 13 tell us, "we know in part and we prophesy in part," so to see the whole picture we must put our parts together. This is the genius and glory of the church that will one day compel us to come together in a unity that is so great that the Lord can trust us with such unprecedented power and authority. Still, to describe what it means to be baptized with the Holy Spirit *and* fire cannot be answered in a single statement without tragically reducing its meaning. A new Pentecost is coming that is not new, but a recovery of some aspects of the baptism in the Holy Spirit yet to be recovered.

This belief has been at the foundation of possibly every move of God since Pentecost. To believe we have all there is or that the present church is all we are called to be is pride, delusion, or both. Some of these major missing factors include holiness, integrity, morality, and the fear of the Lord, which is the beginning of wisdom (see Psalm 111:10)—all things the great Pentecostal leaders told us came with the baptism of fire. The baptism with fire will both purify and embolden us.

In Acts 4:31, the disciples who had lost their courage were filled again and "spoke the word of God with boldness" and without fear of consequences. This remained a hallmark of the first-century church, but where is this courage today? Today, there is a new stirring of the Spirit and a new critical mass forming that will bring a release of the baptism with the Holy Spirit like a nuclear reaction. A new Pentecost is coming, and it is right to ask for more. The Bible was not written just so we can believe what happened in it was true, but so we can believe for the same to happen in our lives today and to honor what happened in the past. Azusa was a seed, but now is the time for the harvest, and you may be the one who strikes the match that releases that fire!

The humbler you are, the better candidate you are for revival. When the Holy Spirit comes, all flesh and presumption flee. This was the hallmark of Azusa Street. Knowledge and eloquence bowed a knee to love and pure devotion, just as the apostles before the Sanhedrin in Acts created no small stir.

There's a difference between preaching from knowledge and preaching from a well of living water that flows from God's throne. This was a central lesson of Azusa. When God wants to move, He doesn't look for someone wise enough, He looks for someone humble enough to follow Him. That the Lord chooses people as His habitation is one of the greatest marvels of creation. God also chooses people to do His work and often chooses individuals to ignite new moves of the Spirit. We see this throughout Scripture and history. There were also others who were prepared to keep those fires burning and lay the foundations for those gains.

Few in history have been able to find the delicate balance between being used by God and trying to use God, or as one Christian teacher put it, seeking one's own recognition at the expense of God's glory. Seymour's hunger to see God move led him to keep men's hands off the revival, and so long as he maintained this devotion, the revival fires continued to burn. From beginning to end, the revival could not be attributed to human charisma or promotion. When it did, the revival ended.

True moves of God are not fueled by money, organization, or advertising. True revivals come when the presence of God (the pillar of fire) moves. To try and organize, promote, or sell a move of God is profane. Instead, when the Spirit wants to move in some creative way, He looks for humble people, those without all the answers, who invariably stimulate a holy desperation and dependency on God. They are the ones who are responsive to the Lord when He wants to do a new thing. In times of dynamic outpourings of the Spirit, like at Azusa Street, the Lord can only use people who are completely yielded to Him to do something new. As Jesus explained to Nicodemus: "The wind blows where it wishes, and you hear the sound of it, but cannot tell where it comes from and where it goes. So is everyone who is born of the Spirit" (John 3:8).

Those who have tried to duplicate the Azusa Street Revival have often become pitiful caricatures of the original. There is not a single example in church history of a church (wineskin) being built before a revival (new wine) was given. Those who have tried to build the wineskin first were unable to receive the new wine. One common quality in those mightily used by the Spirit throughout history has been hearing the Spirit move, then moving the way He wanted.

I have studied church history for nearly fifty years now and much of that has been devoted to revivals, but the Azusa Street Revival is, by far, among the most interesting and compelling. My goal, and I know Jeff's goal, has been, not only to share insights from history, but also to help prepare those who will make history. Though I have tried to study every true move of God in history, my greatest interest remains in the one to come. The final move of God and greatest of all will be a combination and culmination of all revivals. You could be among the main characters in that one!

NOTES

1. Larry E. Martin, *The Life and Ministry of William J. Seymour and a history of the Azusa Street Revival: The Complete Azusa Street Library* Vol. 1 (Pensacola: Christian Life Books, 2006), 123 (hereafter *LMWS*).

2. Frank Bartleman, *Azusa Street* (New Kensington, PA: Whitaker House, 1982), 25 (hereafter *AS*).

3. Cecil M. Robeck Jr., *The Azusa Street Mission and Revival: The Birth of the Global Pentecostal Movement* (Nashville: Thomas Nelson, 2006), 59 (hereafter *ASMR*).

4. *AS*, 16.

5. Ibid., 35.

6. *ASMR*, 60.

7. *AS*, 9.

8. *LMWS*, 125.

9. Frank Bartleman, *Azusa Street* (Plainfield, NJ: Logos, 1980), 33; Roberts Liardon, *God's Generals: Why They Succeeded and Why Some Failed* (New Kensington, PA: Whitaker, 1996), 144 (hereafter *GG*).

10. *AS*, 15.

11. Wayne E. Warner, "The Miracle of Azusa," *Pentecostal Evangel*, vol. 22 (Sept. 1996), 11; Vinson Synan, *The Century of the Holy Spirit: 100 Years of Pentecostal and Charismatic Renewal* (Nashville: Thomas Nelson, 2001), 45 (hereafter *CHS*).

12. S. Henry McGowan's testimony in Clara Davis, *Azusa Street Till Now* (Tulsa: Harrison House, 1989), 16; *LMWS*, 128.

13. Psalm 34:18.

14. "Pentecost With Signs Following," *The Apostolic Faith* (December 1906): Larry E. Martin, *Saved & Sanctified: The Complete Azusa Street Library* Vol. 3 (Pensacola: Christian Life Books, 2005), 21, 23 (hereafter SS).

15. *AS*, 38.

16. Rachel A. Sizelove, "Pentecost Has Come!" Fred T. Corum and Hazel E. Bakewell, *The Sparkling Fountain: Larry E. Martin, The True Believers: The Complete Azusa Street Library* Vol. 2 (Pensacola: Christian Life Books, 1998), 76 (hereafter *TB*).

17. Rev. Lawrence Catley, recorded by Russell Chandler, "Pasadena Cleric Recalls Mission," *Los Angeles Times* (January 11, 1976); Larry E. Martin, *The Chosen Vessels: The Complete Azusa Street Library* Vol. 4 (Pensacola: Christian Life Books, 2010), 133 (hereafter *CV*).

18. Tommy Welchel, Narrator, Dr. J. Edward Morris & Cindy McCowan, *Azusa Street: They Told Me Their Stories* (LaVergne, TN: Dare 2 Dream Books, 2010), 107 (hereafter *TMTS*).

19. Etta Auringer Huff, "A Scriptural Pentecost," The Herald of Light (July 14, 1906); SS, 104.

20. Kelso R. Glover, "God is in Pentecost!" excerpt of sermon preached at Angelus Temple (1946); CV, 169.

21. William J. Seymour, transcription of May 1, 1907 service at Azusa Street Mission, *The Apostolic Faith* (May 1907); Ibid., 27.

22. Frank Bartleman, "Letter from Los Angeles," Way of Faith in Carrie Judd Montgomery, *Triumphs of Faith* (December 1906); Ibid., 137.

23. A.H. Post, "Testimony of a Minister," *The Apostolic Faith* (January 1907); TB, 70.

24. A.G. Osterberg, "I Was There," *Full Gospel Business Men's Voice* (May 1966); Ibid., 96.

25. *AS*, 10.

26. Ibid., 123.

27. A.G. Osterberg, "Tears—The Secret of the Azusa Street Revival," *The Voice of Healing* (July 1954); SS, 58.

28. Ibid., 58–59.

29. Ibid., 63.

30. U.S. Census, St. Mary Parish, Louisiana (1860); *LMWS*, 33.

31. Alexander A. Boddy, "At Los Angeles California," *Confidence* (Sunderland, UK: October 1912); *TB*, 112.

32. Peyton McCrary, *Abraham Lincoln and Reconstruction* (Princeton: Princeton University Press, 1978), 199; *LMWS*, 37.

33. "Pentecost Brings Healing," (2009) Healing and Revival Press, healingandrevival.com/BioWSeymour.htm (accessed February 10, 2013).

34. Jennie C. Rutty, "The Gift of Tongues," *The Gospel Trumpet* (September 18, 1902), 3; *LMWS*, 90.

35. Emma Cotton, "The Inside Story of the Azusa Street Outpouring," *Message of the Apostolic Faith* (April 1939); *SS*, 40–41.

36. Mrs. Charles Parham, *The Life of Charles F. Parham* (Baxter Springs, KS: Apostolic Faith Bible College, 1930), 48; Great Commission Bible College: gcbcedu.us/TheLifeOfCharlesFParham470pages.pdf (accessed February 8, 2013).

37. Ibid.

38. Ibid., 52.

39. Ibid., 52–53.

40. Ibid., 53.

41. Ibid., 54.

42. Dorries, "Edward Irving and the Standing Sign," Gary B. McGee, ed., *Initial Evidence: Historical and Biblical Perspectives on the Pentecostal Doctrine of Spirit Baptism* (Eugene, Oregon: Wipf & Stock, 1991), 49; Eddie L. Hyatt, *2000 Years of Charismatic Christianity* (Lake Mary, FL: Charisma, 2002), 141 (hereafter CC); Douglas Jacobsen, ed., *A Reader in Pentecostal Theology: Voices from the First Generation* (Bloomington: Indiana University, 2006), 31.

43. J. Roswell Flower, "Birth of the Pentecostal Movement," *Pentecostal Evangel* (November 26, 1950), 3; *CC*, 141.

44. Ibid., 137.

45. Parham, *Life of Parham*, 137.

46. Howard Goss, The Winds of God, 73: "A negro Baptist preacher from Houston was selected—a Brother Seymour, who had often attended the morning session of the school"; Rev. Pauline Parham, lecture given in 1989, "William Seymour humbly asked Bro. Parham if he could sit outside and take in the lessons, but Bro. Parham gave him a place in the class-room with the other students to learn the truths about the Pentecostal message," *The Apostolic Faith Report*, May, 1921: "One negro man by the name of Seymour, became a regular attendant, taking his seat in the classes: and it was here that he gained the full knowledge of the Full Gospel message," Research Center, Section 2, Apostolic Archives International: www.apostolicarchives.com/ ps3.html (accessed February 11, 2013); Eddie L. Hyatt, "Across the Lines: Charles Parham's Contribution to the Inter-Racial Character of Early Pentecostalism" from the Fall 2004 issue of the *Pneuma Review*, Pauline Parham, "Dad Parham, being from Kansas, was not used to such laws and customs and he welcomed Seymour into the classroom. The account I heard from those present was that he was welcomed into the class along with everyone else," Pneuma Foundation, www.pneumafoundation.org/article .jsp?article=EHyatt-AcrossTheLines.xml (accessed February 11, 2013).

47. Goss, *The Winds of God*, 65: *LMWS*, 92.

48. *ASMR*, 50.

49. W.F. Carothers, "History of Movement," *The Apostolic Faith* (Houston, Texas: October 1908); *LMWS*, 94.

50. James S. Tinney, *In The Tradition of William J. Seymour* (Spirit Press, 1978), 15; quoted from "Father of Modern-Day Pentecostalism," in *Journal of the Interdenominational Theological Center* (Fall 1976); GG, 145.

51. *ASMR*, 52.

52. *CV*, 92.

53. Charlotta A. Bass, *Forty Years: Memoirs from the Pages of a Newspaper* (Los Angeles, n.p., 1960), 2; *LMWS*, 102.

54. Ralph Bunche, narrator, John and Laree Caughey, *Los Angeles: Biography of a City* (Berkeley: University of California Press, 1976), 284; Ibid., 106.

55. *ASMR*, 53.

56. *The Los Angeles Express* (July/August 1906): *LMWS*, 111.

57. *ASMR*, 59–60.

58. John G. Lake, "Origin of the Apostolic Faith Movement," *The Pentecostal Outlook* (September 1932); *CV*, 32.

59. John G. Lake, *Spiritual Hunger—The God-Men* (Dallas: Christ for the Nations, 1980), 60; *CC*, 144.

60. "Pentecost with Signs Following," *The Apostolic Faith* (December 1906), 1; *LMWS*, 140.

61. Cotton, "The Inside Story...": *SS*, 41.

62. *ASMR*, 64.

63. Roberts Liardon, *The Azusa Street Revival: When the Fire Fell* (Shippensburg, PA: Destiny Image, 2006), 93 (hereafter *ASR*).

64. Ibid., 184.

65. Jennie Evans Moore, "Music from Heaven," *The Apostolic Faith* (May 1907), 3; *LMWS*, 143.

66. Cotton, "The Inside Story..."; *SS*, 44–45.

67. *TMTS*, 27–29; *The Apostolic Faith* (September 1906) Amos Morgan, "The Azusa Street Mission Time Line," Chap. 1 "About April 1, 1906," Azusa Books: www.azusabooks.com/time.shtml#1 (accessed 13 February 2013).

68. *ASR*, 185.

69. Ibid.

70. *ASMR*, 68.

71. Ibid., 146; see John 4:14 (*The Passion Translation*).

72. Moore, "Music from Heaven"; *TB*, 57.

73. Ibid., 58.

74. Lake, "Origin of the Apostolic..."; *CV*, 33.

75. Acts 4:31; Charles William Shumway, "A Critical Study of 'The Gift of Tongues,'" (A.B. dissertation, University of Southern California, 1914), 175; *LMWS*, 148.

76. *Pentecostal Evangel*, vol. 6, no. 4 (1946) 6; Walter J. Hollenweger, *The Pentecostals* (London: SCM, 1972), 23; *CHS*, 49.

77. *TMTS*, 27.

78. Douglas J. Nelson, "For Such a Time as This: The Story of Bishop William J. Seymour and the Azusa Street Revival" (PhD diss., University of Birmingham, UK, 1981), 191–192; Stanley M. Burgess, ed., *Christian Peoples of the Spirit* (New York Univ.: NY, 2011), 237.

79. Lake, "Origin of the Apostolic…"; *CV*, 33.

80. *TMTS*, 32.

81. Osterberg, "I Was There"; *TB*, 101.

82. *ASMR*, 73.

83. Unknown Author, "The Azusa Mission," *Way of Faith* (October 11, 1906); *TB*, 32.

84. Clara Lum, "Miss Clara Lum Writes Wonders," *The Missionary World* (August 1906), 2; *LMWS*, 159.

85. Lake, "Origin of the Apostolic…"; *TB*, 25.

86. *AS*, 40.

87. Ibid.

88. "Gracious Pentecostal Showers Continue to Fall," *The Apostolic Faith* (November 1906); *TB*, 34.

89. Ibid.; Addie M. Cook, "Apostolic Work," *Word and Work* (April 1907); *CV*, 58.

90. Leonard Lovett, "Black Origins of the Pentecostal Movement"; Vinson Synan, *Aspects of Pentecostal-Charismatic Origins* (Plainfield, NJ: Logos, 1975), 132; *LMWS*, 166.

91. Osterberg, "I Was There"; *TB*, 103.

92. *Los Angeles Daily Times* (April 18, 1906), 1.

93. *AS*, 44.

94. Acts 4:31; 16:26.

95. *ASMR*, 76.

96. Ibid., 81.

97. Rachel Sizelove, "A Sparkling Fountain for the Whole Earth," *Word and Work* (June 1934), 11; *LMWS*, 168.

98. *AS*, 47,50.

99. Ibid., 47.

100. *ASMR*, 136.

101. Osterberg, "I Was There"; *TB*, 104.

102. Stanley M. Horton, "A Typical Day at Azusa Street," *Assemblies of God Heritage* Vol. 2 No. 3 Fall 1982, 3, 6, Flower Pentecostal Heritage Center, http://ifphc.org/pdf/Heritage/1982_03.pdf (accessed 16 February 2013).

103. *AS*, 46.

104. Ibid., 56.

105. Ibid., 57–58.

106. Sizelove, "Pentecost Has Come!"; *TB*, 79–81.

107. A.C. Valdez, Sr., *Fire on Azusa Street* (Costa Mesa: Gift Publications, 1980); *SS*, 49.

108. *ASMR*, 159.

109. "Pentecost Has Come," *The Apostolic Faith* (September 1906); *TB*, 29.

110. A.W. Orwig, "My First Visit to the Azusa Street Pentecostal Mission," *The Weekly Evangel* (1916); *TB*, 60.

111. *AS*, 58.

112. Ernest S. Williams, "Memories of Azusa Street Mission," *The Pentecostal Evangel* (24 April 1966), 7; *LMWS*, 211.

113. *GG*, 128; *ASR*, 81–82.

114. "Gracious Pentecostal Showers"; *TB*, 35.

115. *ASMR*, 178.

116. Glenn A. Cook, "The Azusa Street Meeting: Some Highlights of the Outpouring" (n.p., n.d.); *TB*, 54.

117. William H. Durham, "A Chicago Evangelist's Pentecost," *The Apostolic Faith* (Feb–Mar 1907); Ibid., 41.

118. Ibid., 42–43.

119. John 18:6; Acts 9:4; Rev. 1:17.

120. Mrs. W.H. McGowan, "Another Echo from Azusa," (n.p., n.d.): *TB*, 87.

121. Glover, "God is in Pentecost!"; *CV*, 169–170.

122. Phillips, Evan Roberts, 303; Wesley Duewel, *Revival Fire* (Grand Rapids, MI: Zondervan, 1995), 196–197 (hereafter *RF*).

123. Ibid., 299–302; *RF*, 196.

124. Evans, *Welsh Revival*, 141; *RF*, 201.

125. Ibid., 171–173; *RF*, 202.

126. Burton, "My Personal Pentecost," *World Pentecost*, I (1973), 19; Ramon Hunston, "The Welsh Revival 1904–05," Awstin, *The Religious Revival in Wales, 1904* (Cardiff, Wales, 1905), 10–11; Evans, *Welsh Revival*; Michael P. Hamilton, ed. *The Charismatic Movement* (Grand Rapids, MI: Eerdmans, 1975), 96.

127. Lake, "Origin of the Apostolic…"; *CV*, 33.

128. Osterberg, "I Was There," 18; *LMWS*, 177.

129. Author unknown, "Pentecost Has Come"; *TB*, 26.

130. Ibid., 103.

131. "Women with Men Embrace," *The Los Angeles Daily Times* (September 3, 1906), 11; *LMWS*, 177.

132. Frank Bartleman, *How Pentecost Came to Los Angeles* (1925), 54, Christian Classics Ethereal Library: www.ccel.org/ccel/bartleman/los.i.html (accessed February 17, 2013).

133. William Manley, "True Pentecostal Power with Signs Following," *The Household of God* (September 1906); *CV*, 80.

134. Cook, "The Azusa Street Meeting"; *TB*, 54–56.

135. Bartleman, "Letter from Los Angeles"; *CV*, 140–142.

136. Ibid., 143–144.

137. Orwig, "My First Visit…"; *TB*, 66.

138. Post, "Testimony of a Minister"; Ibid., 72.

139. Bartleman, "Letter from Los Angeles"; *CV*, 142.

140. Ibid., 151.

141. Acts 2:8–11.

142. Valdez, *Fire on Azusa Street*; *SS*, 51.

143. "Some people drove 500 miles by wagon to Los Angeles to seek the Pentecost," *The Apostolic Faith* (December 1906), 3; *LMWS*, 198.

144. Cook, "Apostolic Work"; *CV*, 59.

145. "Gracious Pentecostal Showers"; *TB*, 33–34.

146. *TMTS*, 100.

147. Fred Andersen, "A Letter to Richard Crayne," *Pentecostal Handbook* (n.p., 1989), 195; *LMWS*, 198–199.

148. Valdez, *Fire on Azusa Street*; *SS*, 49.

149. Ibid., 52.

150. Andersen, "A Letter to Richard Crayne"; Ibid., 118.

151. Ibid., 53.

152. "Tongues of Fire—Gift of Languages and Holiness Union," *Daily Oregon Statesman* (Salem: October 4, 1906), 6; *LMWS*, 199.

153. Ibid.

154. *AS*, 50.

155. Frank Bartleman, Apostolic Light (1906); *AS*, 96.

156. 1 Samuel 19:18–24.

157. Del Tarr, "Hold It Gently," *The Pentecostal Evangel* (November 8, 1998), 20; *LMWS*, 188.

158. *AS*, 58–59.

159. Vinson Synan and Charles R. Fox Jr., *William J. Seymour: Pioneer of the Azusa Street Revival* (Alachua, FL: Bridge-Logos, 2012), 186 (hereafter *WJS*).

160. *AS*, 45–46.

161. "Before the fire," *The Apostolic Faith* (November 1906), 1; *LMWS*, 259.

162. *AS*, 43–44

163. Cook, "Apostolic Work"; *CV*, 58.

164. *ASMR*, 127.

165. *ASR*, 80.

166. Author unknown, "Pentecost Has Come"; *TB*, 28.

167. Ibid., 27–28.

168. North Chicago News, September 26, 1906; Blumhofer, "Christian Catholic Apostolic Church"; Cecil M. Robeck Jr., ed., *Charismatic Experiences in History* (Peabody, MA: Hendrickson, 1985), 136 (hereafter *CE*).

169. *Waukegan Daily Gazette*, October 15, 1906; Blumhofer, "Christian Catholic Apostolic Church"; *CE*, 136.

170. *Toronto Evening Telegram*, January 19, 1907; Blumhofer, "Christian Catholic Apostolic Church"; *CE*, 136.

171. Gordon P. Gardiner, *Out of Zion Into All the World* (Shippensburg, PA: Destiny Image, 1990), 3; *CC*, 154.

172. Blumhofer, "Christian Catholic Apostolic Church"; *CE*, 126.

173. Parham, *Life of Parham*, 160–163.

174. Ibid., 163–170.

175. Charles William Shumway, "A Critical Study of 'The Gift of Tongues'" (A.B. dissertation, University of Southern California, 1914), 178; *LMWS*, 269.

176. Parham, *Life of Parham*, 163–170.

177. Ibid.

178. Cook, "The Azusa Street Meeting"; *TB*, 52.

179. 1 Corinthians 1:12; "Speaking with Tongues," *The Church Herald and Holiness Banner* (15 December 1906), 1; *LMWS*, 274.

180. *The Apostolic Faith* 1 (June–Sept 1907), 1; Blumhofer, "Christian Catholic Apostolic Church"; *CE*, 138–39.

181. Blumhofer, "Christian Catholic Apostolic Church"; *CE*, 140.

182. Gordon P. Gardiner, "The Apostle of Divine Healing," *Bread of Life* 6 (March, 1957), 15; Blumhofer, "Christian Catholic Apostolic Church"; *CE*, 138–139.

183. Parham, *Life of Parham*, 164–202.

184. Cook, "The Azusa Street Meeting"; *TB*, 52.

185. Parham, *Life of Parham*, 164–202.

186. Charles F. Parham, "Free Love," *The Apostolic Faith* (Baxter Springs: n.p., n.d.), 118; *LMWS*, 269.

187. Jerry Jensen and Jonathan Ellsworth Perkins' interview with A.G. Osterberg (May 1966); Ibid., 270.

188. *The Apostolic* Faith (December 1906): Cecil M. Robeck Jr. and Amos Yong, ed., *The Cambridge Companion to Pentecostalism* (Cambridge University Press, 2014), 29.

189. *ASMR*, 187.

190. Donald Gee, *The Pentecostal Movement* (London: Elim Publishing Co., Ltd., 1949), 19; *LMWS*, 259.

191. *ASMR*, 130.

192. *ASMR*, 9.

193. Valdez, *Fire on Azusa Street*; *SS*, 53.

194. Manley, "True Pentecostal Power"; *CV*, 83.

195. *SS*, 54.

196. *The Apostolic Faith*, Vol 1, No. 3: *ASR*, 135.

197. Huff, "A Scriptural Pentecost"; *SS*, 104.

198. "California Trivia Tuesday: How Did Azusa Get Its Name?" (February 25, 2014) CaliforniaCityNews.org, www.californiacitynews.org/2014/06/california-trivia-tuesday-how-did-azusa-get-its-name.html (accessed December 30, 2022). *The Jack Benny Show* aired in America in the 1950s to early 1960s.

199. J.G. Speicher, "As Dr. Speicher Sees It," *Zion City News* (June 28, 1907), 1, 2; *LMWS*, 178.

200. Ibid.; Manley, "True Pentecostal Power"; *CV*, 81.

201. *CV*, 82.

202. Orwig, "My First Visit…"; *TB*, 60–63.

203. J. Narver Gortner, "An Incident of the Early Days," *The Pentecostal Evangel* (April 28, 1934); *SS*, 82.

204. Ibid., 82–83.

205. A.G. Garr's testimony quoted by William A. Ward, "Filled With God" (n.p., n.d.); Ibid., 90.

206. George B. Studd, "My Convictions as to the Pentecostal Movement" (Bedford, England: n.p., n.d.); *TB*, 122.

207. Ibid.

208. Ibid., 124

209. Ibid., 125–126.

210. Seeley D. Kinne, "From Whence Is It?" *The Household of God* (March 1910); *CV*, 39–40.

211. George B. Studd, "America," *Victory!* (April 1909); Ibid., 153–154.

212. Acts 10:38.

213. A.S. Worrell, "Wonderful Times Coming," *The Household of God* (May 1907); *CV*, 155.

214. *TMTS*, 99.

215. Valdez, *Fire on Azusa Street*; *SS*, 49,52.

216. Josephine M. Washburn, *History and Reminiscences of the Holiness Church Work in Southern California and Arizona* (South Pasadena: Record Press, 1912), 383–389; Alma White, *Demons and Tongues* (Zerapath, NJ: 1949), 71–73, Frank J. Ewart, *The Phenomenon of Pentecost* (Hazelwood: Word Aflame Press, 1975), 45; Vinson Synan, *The Holiness-Pentecostal Tradition: Charismatic Movements in the Twentieth Century* (Grand Rapids, MI: Eerdmans, 1971), 101 (hereafter *HPT*).

217. Ibid.

218. B.F. Lawrence, *The Apostolic Faith Restored* (St. Louis: Gospel Publishing House, 1916), 78; *LMWS*, 194–195.

219. Florence Crawford, "The Witness of the Power of God," *Apostolic Faith Mission* (Portland, Oregon: n.d.); *TB*, 139; Florence Crawford, "The Light of Life Brought Triumph," *Apostolic Faith Mission* (Portland, Oregon, 1936); *SS*, 96.

220. Washburn, *History and Reminiscences*, 383–390; *LMWS*, 195.

221. Ibid.

222. Thomas R. Nickel, *Azusa Street Outpouring: As Told to Me By Those Who Were There* (Hanford, California: Great Commission International, 1956), 15–18; Ibid., 253.

223. "In Jail for Jesus' Sake," *The Apostolic Faith* (November 1906), 4; Ibid., 254.

224. Frank J. Ewart, *The Phenomenon of Pentecost* (Hazelwood: Word Aflame Press, 1975), 70; Ibid., 198.

225. *ASMR*, 208.

226. *AS*, 73.

227. Dan L. Thrapp, "Pentecostal Sects to Convene Here," *The Los Angeles Times* (September 9, 1956), III, 11; *LMWS*, 285.

228. Author unknown, "Pentecost Has Come"; *TB*, 25.

229. *ASMR*, 95–96.

230. Ibid., 98.

231. *AS*, 86–87.

232. McGowan; Davis, *Azusa Street Till Now*; *SS*, 139.

233. *ASMR*, 53.

234. Sarah Haggard Payne, "The Fulfillment of a Life Dream," *The Weekly Evangel* (January 13, 1917), 4; *LMWS*, 180.

235. *ASMR*, 137.

236. Catley; Chandler, "Pasadena Cleric..."; *TB*, 135.

237. *ASMR*, 153.

238. Ibid., 150–151.

239. Orwig, "My First Visit..."; *TB*, 62.

240. Durham, "A Chicago Evangelist's Pentecost"; Ibid., 41.

241. John G. Lake, *Adventures in God* (Tulsa: Harrison House, 1981), 189; *ASR*, 106.

242. Williams, "Memories of Azusa"; *TB*, 49.

243. Cook, "The Azusa Street Meeting"; Ibid., 55.

244. Ibid., 53–54.

245. *ASMR*, 149.

246. Ibid., 152.

247. *AS*, 53–55.

248. Frank Bartleman, "Letter from Los Angeles"; *CV*, 144–145.

249. Manley, "True Pentecostal Power"; Ibid., 82.

250. Cook, "Apostolic Work"; Ibid., 59.

251. *TMTS*, 54–55, 58.

252. Jerry Jensen and Jonathan Ellsworth Perkins' interview with A.G. Osterberg (May 1966); *LMWS*, 180.

253. *ASMR*, 144.

254. Ibid., 143.

255. *AS*, 41.

256. Ibid., 86.

257. William H. Durham, "Personal Testimony of Brother Durham," *Pentecostal Testimony* (Vol. 3 No. 2 n.d.), 4; *LMWS*, 180.

258. John Sherrill, *They Speak with Other Tongues* (Minneapolis: Chosen, 2018), 59.

259. Catley; Chandler, "Pasadena Cleric..."; *TB*, 134.

260. McGowan; Davis, *Azusa Street Till Now*; *SS*, 139.

261. Osterberg, "Tears..."; Ibid., 57.

262. *TMTS*, 36.

263. *AS*, 95.

264. *TMTS*, 49.

265. Ibid., 91.

266. Ibid., 21.

267. Ibid., 66.

268. 1 Kings 8:10–11, 2 Chronicles 5:13–14.

269. *TMTS*, 58.

270. Ibid., 101.

271. Bartleman, Azusa Street, 60; *LMWS*, 180.

272. Bartleman, Azusa Street, 6; *ASR*, 101.

273. *TMTS*, 50.

274. Ibid., 37.

275. "At Azusa Mission," *The Apostolic Faith* (May 1907), 2; *LMWS*, 190.

276. William Seymour, "The Precious Atonement," *The Apostolic Faith* (September 1906); *WJS*, 175–176.

277. Cotton, "The Inside Story..."; *SS*, 45.

278. A.G. Osterberg, "From the Personal Writings of A.G. Osterberg," typescript, 3; *LMWS*, 191.

279. Ibid.

280. Ibid.

281. Society for Pentecostal Studies interview with Lawrence Catley, 1974; Ibid., 193.

282. Azusa Street 1906, "Azusa Street Revival Eyewitness Accounts—Pentecostal History," June 26, 2020, YouTube, www.youtube.com/watch?v=qFC6vou4Ahg (accessed September 5, 2022).

283. "Tongues of Fire—Gift of Languages and Holiness Union," *Daily Oregon Stateman* (Salem: 4 October 1906), 6; *LMWS*, 193.

284. Fred T. Corum and Hazel E. Blakewell, *The Sparkling Fountain* (Windsor, OH: Corum & Assoc., Inc., 1983), 39; Ibid., 192–193.

285. Acts 19:11–12; Ibid., 200; Fred Corum, "Azusa's First Camp-Meeting," *Word and Work* (January 1936); *SS*, 72.

286. Max Wood Moorhead, "A Short History of the Pentecostal Movement," *Cloud of Witnesses to Pentecost in India* (Bombay, India n.p.: November 1908); *CV*, 134.

287. Lum, "Miss Clara Lum Writes Wonders," 2; *LMWS*, 178.

288. *TMTS*, 96.

289. Ibid., 105.

290. Ibid., 75.

291. *AS*, 64.

292. *TMTS*, 32–33.

293. Ibid., 63.

294. Ibid., 74.

295. Ibid., 70–73.

296. Ibid., 43–47.

297. Ibid., 85.

298. Ibid., 65–66.

299. Ibid., 87–89.

300. Ibid., 91–93.

301. Ibid., 109–111.

302. Ibid., 104.

303. Ibid., 116–117.

304. Ibid., 55–56.

305. Ibid., 59–60.

306. Ibid., 125.

307. Ibid., 77.

308. Ibid., 78.

309. Ibid., 35.

310. Ibid., 48.

311. Osterberg, "Tears…"; *SS*, 59–60.

312. Ibid., 61.

313. Valdez, *Fire on Azusa Street*; Ibid., 49–50.

314. "A Night at the Azusa Street Mission," *The Apostolic Faith* (May 1907); *CV*, 23.

315. Gortner, "An Incident…"; *SS*, 81.

316. *TMTS*, 36.

317. Raymond Robert Crawford, *The Light of Life Brought Triumph: A Brief Sketch of the Life and Labors of Florence L. (Mother) Crawford 1872–1936* (1936; repr., Portland: Apostolic Faith Publishing House, 1955), 9–10; *WJS*, 101–102.

318. *TMTS*, 47.

319. Vinson Synan, "William Seymour," *Christian History* (Issue 65), 17–19.

320. John G. Lake, *Adventures in God* (Tulsa: Harrison House, 1981), 18–19.

321. Lake, *Spiritual Hunger—The God-Men*, 14; *CC* 145.

322. *ASMR*, 91.

323. A.C. Valdez, Sr., *Fire on Azusa Street* (Costa Mesa: Gift Publications, 1980); SS, 49.

324. *ASMR*, 91.

325. Cook, "The Azusa Street"; *TB*, 53.

326. Ephesians 4:11–12.

327. "The Apostolic Faith Movement," *The Apostolic Faith* (September 1906); *WJS*, 173.

328. *ASMR*, 13.

329. Ibid., 13–14.

330. *The Apostolic Faith* (September 1906); *ASR*, 103–104.

331. Cook, "The Azusa Street Meeting"; *TB*, 56.

332. *AS*, 13.

333. Frank Bartleman, *Azusa Street*; *ASR*, 99.

334. John 14:11.

335. Author unknown, "The Azusa Mission," *Way of Faith* (October 11, 1906); *TB*, 32.

336. Dan L. Thrapp, "Pentecostal Sects to Convene Here," *The Los Angeles Times* (September 9, 1956), III, 11; *LMWS*, 185.

337. Manley, "True Pentecostal Power"; Ibid., 185–186.

338. *ASMR*, 115.

339. William J. Seymour, "Salvation According to the True Tabernacle," *The Apostolic Faith* (September 1907), 3; *WJS*, 68–69.

340. William J. Seymour, "Behold the Bridegroom Cometh," *The Apostolic Faith* (January 1907); Ibid., 191.

341. William J. Seymour, "The Holy Ghost is Power," *The Apostolic Faith* (May 1908); Ibid., 241–43.

342. *The Apostolic Faith* (September 1906).

343. W.J. Seymour, *The Doctrines and Discipline of the Azusa Street Apostolic Faith Mission* (Los Angeles: 1915); *WJS*, 272.

344. "William J. Seymour's Doctrines and Discipline," Article K, River of Revival Ministries, azusastreet.org/WilliamJSeymourDiscipline.htm (accessed February 18, 2013).

345. *ASMR*, 125.

346. Lawrence, *Apostolic Faith*, 86; Chandler, *Los Angeles Times*, 5; Nelson, "For Such a Time as This," 235; *LMWS*, 189.

347. Lum, "Miss Clara Lum Writes Wonders," 2; *LMWS*, 189–190.

348. *ASMR*, 163.

349. *AS*, 79–80.

350. W.J. Seymour, "Counterfeits," *The Apostolic Faith* (December 1906); *ASR*, 114.

351. William J. Seymour, "To the Baptized Saints," *The Apostolic Faith* (Jun–Sep 1907), 2; *WJS*, 73.

352. *The Apostolic Faith* (June 1907).

353. *AS*, 51–53.

354. W.J. Seymour, *Doctrines and Discipline*, preface; *WJS* 265.

355. W.J. Seymour, "The Baptism with the Holy Ghost," *The Apostolic Faith* (Feb–Mar 1907); Ibid., 206.

356. William J. Seymour, "Character and Work of the Holy Ghost," *The Apostolic Faith* (May 1908), 2; William J. Seymour, "Praying for the Holy Ghost," *The Apostolic Faith* (October 1906), 3; Ibid., 79, 96.

357. William J. Seymour, Untitled article, *The Apostolic Faith* (Oct–Jan 1908), 4; Ibid., 82.

358. Robeck, "Seymour and 'the Bible Evidence,'" in McGee, *Initial Evidence*, 88; Ibid., 83.

359. Ibid., 85.

360. William J. Seymour, "The Baptism of the Holy Ghost," *The Apostolic Faith* (May 1908), 3; William J. Seymour, "Jesus, our Projector and Great

Shepherd," *The Apostolic Faith* (December 1906), 1; Ibid., 88–89.

361. William J. Seymour, "To the Baptized Saints," *The Apostolic Faith* (Jun–Sep 1907), 2; Ibid., 94.

362. William J. Seymour, Untitled article, *The Apostolic Faith* (September 1906), 2; Ibid., 95.

363. William J. Seymour, Untitled article, *The Apostolic Faith* (May 1908), 4; Ibid., 97.

364. W.J. Seymour, "The Holy Spirit Bishop of the Church," *The Apostolic Faith* (September 1907); Ibid., 208.

365. Ibid., 209–210.

366. Ibid., 210–211.

367. Ibid., 211.

368. Lake, *Adventures in God*, 18–19.

369. Sizelove, "Pentecost Has Come!"; *TB*, 80.

370. *ASMR*, 124.

371. Moorhead, "A Short History..."; *CV*, 135.

372. "Everywhere Preaching the Word," *The Apostolic Faith* (September 1907), 1; "From Azusa Mission," *The Apostolic Faith* (January 1908), 1; *LMWS*, 276–277.

373. *ASMR*, 284.

374. Ibid.

375. Osterberg, "Personal Writings," 3; Jensen and Perkins interview; *LMWS*, 275.

376. *ASR*, 134.

377. *ASMR*, 290.

378. Ibid., 297.

379. *AS*, 89.

380. Ibid., 113.

381. *ASMR*, 177.

382. Azusa Street 1906, "Azusa Street Revival Eyewitness Accounts—Pentecostal History" June 26, 2020, YouTube, www.youtube.com/watch?v=qFC6vou4Ahg (accessed September 5, 2022).

383. *TMTS*, 36.

384. Osterberg, "Tears"; *SS*, 58.

385. Seymour, "Apostolic Address," *Doctrines and Discipline*; *WJS*, 272.

386. Proverbs 6:19; 1 Corinthians 3:3; Titus 3:10–11.

387. *AS*, 95.

388. Ibid., 97.

389. Bartleman, *Azusa Street*, 143–146; *LMWS*, 283.

390. Anderson, "A Letter to Richard Crayne"; *SS*, 117.

391. "Camp Meeting: Apostolic Faith," *Time* (19 August 1935), 34–35; *WJS*, 112–113.

392. *ASMR*, 126–127.

393. *ASR*, 164.

394. William J. Seymour, "Bible Teaching on Marriage and Divorce," *The Apostolic Faith* (January 1907), 3; *WJS*, 113.

395. *ASMR*, 310.

396. Ibid., 286.

397. "A Historical Account of the Apostolic Faith: A Trinitarian-Fundamental Evangelistic Association" (Portland, Oregon: Apostolic Faith, 1965), 70; *LMWS*, 278.

398. *ASR*, 168–169.

399. *ASMR*, 302.

400. J.C. Vanzandt, *Speaking in Tongues* (Portland, Oregon: Vanzandt, 1926), 37; *LMWS*, 280.

401. *ASMR*, 304.

402. James Tinney interview with E. S. Williams (November 8, 1978); *LMWS*, 281.

403. Ibid.

404. *ASMR*, 311.

405. Alma White, *Demons and Tongues: A Work of Christian Demonology* (1910), 119–121; *LMWS*, 283.

406. *AS*, 115.

407. *ASMR*, 312.

408. *AS*, 115.

409. A.W. Frodham, "A Pentecostal Journey in Canada, British Columbia, and the Western States," *Confidence* (June 1911), 139; *LMWS*, 285.

410. Frodsham, "A Pentecostal Journey"; *TB*, 144.

411. Ruth Fisher Steelberg Carter, "I Remember," (1961); *CV*, 163–164.

412. Durham, "A Chicago Evangelist's Pentecost"; *TB*, 40.

413. Ibid., 43.

414. Ibid., 44.

415. *AS*, 150.

416. Ibid., 150–152; William H. Durham, "Personal Testimony of Pastor," *Pentecostal Testimony* (July 1912), 1–16; *WJS*, 128.

417. William H. Durham, "The Great Revival at Azusa Street—How it Began and How it Ended" *Pentecostal Testimony* (n.d., Vol 1 No 8), 4; *LMWS*, 288.

418. Ibid., 287.

419. Ibid., 289.

420. *WJS*, 137.

421. Boddy, *Confidence*, 222; Ibid., 139.

422. Nelson, "For Such a Time as This," 258; Ibid., 140.

423. Bartleman, *Azusa Street*, 145; *WJS*, 145.

424. William J. Seymour, *Doctrines and Discipline*, 12; *WJS*, 142.

425. *ASMR*, 319.

426. *ASR*, 191.

427. Nelson, "For Such a Time as This," 41; *LMWS*, 327.

428. Daniel Mark Epstein, *Sister Aimee: The Life of Aimee Semple McPherson* (New York: Harcourt Brace, 1993), 152; Ibid.

429. John Matthews, *Speaking in Tongues* (n.p., 1925), 14; "Brother Seymour Called Home," *The Pentecostal Herald* (October 1, 1922), 1; "Home-going of Rev. W.J. Seymour," *The Bridegroom's Messenger* (Nov–Dec 1922), 3; Nelson, 270; W.J. Seymour, Standard Certificate of Death; Ibid., 329–330.

430. "Brother Seymour Called Home," 1; Ibid., 330.

431. *WJS*, 167.

432. Nils Bloch-Hoell, *The Pentecostal Movement*, (Oslo: Universitetforlaget, 1964), 54; *LMWS*, 331.

433. *Assemblies of God Heritage*, Vol. 25, No. 4, Winter 2005–06, "The Azusa Street Revival: Celebrating 100 Years," Flower Pentecostal Heritage Center, ifphc.org/pdf/Heritage/2005_04.pdf (accessed February 19, 2013).

434. Cotton, "The Inside Story..."; *SS*, 45.

435. Cecil M. Robeck Jr., "Azusa Street Revival," Stanley M. Burgess, ed. and Eduard M. Van Der Maas, ed., *The New International Dictionary of Pentecostal and Charismatic Movements* (Grand Rapids, MI: Zondervan, 2002), 349.

436. Zechariah 6:4; *ASMR*, 314.

437. *AS*, 100.

438. Ibid., 121.

439. Osterberg, "I Was There"; *TB*, 108.

440. Ashley Sample, "William Joseph Seymour: The Father of Pentecostalism, Azusa Street: The Impact," April 17, 2001, HIS 338 Student Website Page Georgetown College, spider.georgetowncollege.edu/htallant/courses/his338/students/asample/WJSASIMP.htm (accessed February 20, 2013).

441. Sydney E. Ahlstrom, spoken in a 1972 lecture: Vinson Synan, "The Origins

of the Pentecostal Movement," April 17, 2006, Holy Spirit Research Center, Oral Roberts University, www.oru.edu/library/special_collections/holy_spirit_research_center/pentecostal_history.php (accessed February 22, 2013).

442. Sydney E. Ahlstrom, *A Religious History of the American People* (New Haven, CT: Yale University, 1972); *The Azusa Street Revival*, www .theazusastreetrevival.com/home.html (accessed February 22, 2013); Vinson Synan, "Pentecostalism: William Seymour" (January 1, 2000) *Christianity Today/Christian History & Biography* www.ctlibrary.com/ch/2000/issue65/3.17.html (accessed February 22, 2013).

443. Wesley, *Journal of John Wesley: Christian Classics Ethereal Library*, www.ccel .org/ccel/wesley/journal.vi.iii.v.html (accessed February 5, 2013); *LMWS*, 315.

444. Cecil M. Robeck, *The Colorline Was Washed Away in the Blood: A Pentecostal Dream for Racial Harmony* (Costa Mesa: Christian Education Press, 1995), 12; *LMWS*, 197–198.

445. *TMTS*, 102, 106.

446. Carl Brumback, *Suddenly…from Heaven* (Springfield, Missouri: Gospel Publishing, 1961), 64–87; Bartleman, *How Pentecost Came to Los Angeles*, 54–60; *HPT*, 103.

447. Sizelove, "Pentecost Has Come!"; *TB*, 84.

448. "In the Last Days," *The Apostolic Faith* (Jun–Sep 1907), 1; *LMWS*, 311.

449. Speicher, "As Dr. Speicher Sees It"; *CV*, 49–50.

450. Speicher, "Is It the Latter Rain?"; Ibid., 55.

451. Cook, "Apostolic Work"; Ibid., 59.

452. Bartleman, "Letter from Los Angeles"; Ibid., 137.

453. John G. Lake; Kenneth Copeland, *John G. Lake: His Life, His Sermons, His Boldness of Faith* (Tulsa: Harrison House, 2013), 88; *LMWS*, 313.

454. Nelson, "For Such a Time as This," 269; Ibid., 314.

455. Mark Martin, "Whole Communities Touched by Fire of the Holy Spirit: Native American Tribes Experience Christian Revival," February 2, 2022,

CBN News, www1.cbn.com/cbnnews/us/2022/february/whole
-communities-touched-by-fire-of-the-holy-spirit-native-american-tribes
-experience-christian-revival (accessed February 4, 2022).

456. *ASMR*, 218.

457. Vinson Synan, *The Old Time Power: A History of the Pentecostal Holiness Church* (Franklin Springs, Georgia: Advocate Press, 1973), 97; Ibid.; *LMWS*, 220–221.

458. Thurman Carey, Dunn, North Carolina, December 30, 1906; *HPT*, 107.

459. Florence Goff, *Tests and triumphs: being a sketch of the life of Rev. J.A. Hodges, coupled with some of the Lord's dealings with H.H. Goff and wife, evangelists of the Cape Fear Conference of the Free-Will Baptist Church* (Falcon, N.C: n.p. c. 1924), 51; *HPT*, 115.

460. *HPT*, 113.

461. Homer A. Tomlinson, *Diary of A.J. Tomlinson, vol. 1 1901–1923* (Church of God World Headquarters, 1949), 27–29; *HPT*, 124.

462. I.C. Clemmons, "Charles Harrison Mason," Stanley M. Burgess and Gary B. McGee, ed., *Dictionary of Pentecostal and Charismatic Movements* (Grand Rapids: Zondervan, 1988), 585; *LMWS*, 214.

463. E.W. Mason, *The Man...Charles Harrison Mason: Sermons of His Early Ministry (1915–1929) and a Biographical Sketch of His Life* (n.p., n.d.), 14; Ibid., 216.

464. Ibid., 15–19; Ibid.

465. "The Founder & Church History," The Church of God in Christ, www.cogic.org/our-foundation/the-founder-church-history (accessed March 15, 2013).

466. "Negro Bluk Kissed," *Indianapolis Morning Star* (June 1907), 3; *LMWS*, 305.

467. *ASMR*, 224.

468. "Bluk Crowd Runs Over," *Indianapolis Morning Star* (June 10, 1907), 12; *LMWS*, 308.

469. "Statistics on the Assemblies of God (USA) 2014 Reports", Assemblies of God, ag.org/top/About/statistics/index (accessed April 7, 2016).

470. Fred J. Foster, *Think It Not Strange: A History of the Oneness Movement* (St. Louis: Pentecostal, 1965), 51–52; *HPT*, 156.

471. In 380, Emperor Theodosius decreed that anyone who did not follow Nicene Trinitarian Christianity had been judged "demented and insane." *Codex Theodosianus* XVI 1.2; Bruce L. Shelley, *Church History in Plain Language, Third Edition* (Nashville: Thomas Nelson, 2008), 96–97.

472. Eric Patterson; Edmund Rybarczyk, *The Future of Pentecostalism in the United States* (New York: Lexington Books, 2007), 124; "Oneness Pentecostalism," Wikipedia, en.wikipedia.org/wiki/Oneness_Pentecostalism (accessed March 15, 2013).

473. Lawrence, *The Apostolic Faith Restored*, 80; *LMWS*, 227.

474. McGowan; Davis, *Azusa Street Till Now*; *SS*, 139.

475. "A Night at the Azusa Street Mission"; *CV*, 25.

476. *The Apostolic Faith* 1, No. 1 (September, 1906), 2.

477. *The Apostolic Faith*, (January 1907), 1; *HPT*, 130; *The Apostolic Faith*, (Feb–Mar, 1907).

478. "Pentecost Both Sides the Ocean," *The Apostolic Faith* (Feb–Mar 1907), 1; *LMWS*, 233.

479. William J. Seymour, "In Money Matters," *The Apostolic Faith* (November 1906); *WJS*, 185.

480. *HPT*, 129.

481. *ASMR*, 240; Ward, "Filled with God"; *SS*, 91–92.

482. *ASMR*, 245.

483. Ibid., 248.

484. Thomas Ball Barratt, *In the Days of the Latter Rain* (Oslo, Norway, 1909); T.B. Barratt, *When the Fire Fell: An Outline of My Life* (Oslo, Norway, 1927), 99–126; *HPT*, 130–131.

485. T.B. Barratt, Oslo, 1907; *HPT*, 129.

486. Alexander A. Boddy, "A Meeting at the Azusa Street Mission, Los Angeles," *Confidence* (November 1912); *TB*, 115.

487. Gordon Lindsay, ed., *John G. Lake: Apostle to Africa* (Dallas: Christ for the Nations, 1979), 25; *GG*, 179.

488. *ASMR*, 280.

489. *ASR*, 204.

490. Office Bearers of the Apostolic Faith Mission of Africa (accessed September 2, 2010); "Apostolic Faith Mission of South Africa," Wikipedia, en.wikipedia .org/wiki/Apostolic_Faith_Mission_of_South_Africa (accessed March 7, 2013); Rita M. Byrnes, ed., *South Africa: A Country Study*, Washington: GPO for the Library of Congress, 1996, "Zion Christian Church," countrystudies.us/south-africa/54.htm (accessed March 7, 2013).

JEFF OLIVER

JEFF OLIVER is Associate Pastor for MorningStar Fellowship Church in Fort Mill, South Carolina. Jeff authored the *Pentecost to the Present* trilogy on the Holy Spirit's work in history and is founder and president of Global Wakening, www .globalwakening.com a ministry that is inspiring and equipping a new generation with a supernatural worldview. Jeff and his wife, Faith, enjoy spending time with their Corgi and Pyrenees-Lab mix.

RICK JOYNER

RICK JOYNER has authored more than 70 books, including *The Christian Duty to Resist Tyranny, The Final Quest Trilogy, Overcoming Evil in the Last Days, The Second American Revolution/Civil War,* and *Marxism's Strategy for Destroying America.* He is the founder of MorningStar Ministries, a multi-faceted mission organization known around the world.

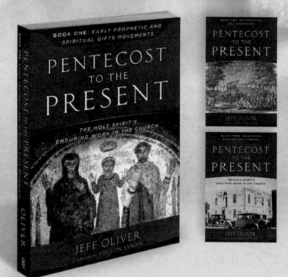